THANK YOU, AMERICA

Biography, Autobiography, Memoirs Series

THANK YOU, AMERICA

by

Charlotte Shedd

ARIADNE PRESS
Riverside, California

Library of Congress Cataloging-in-Publication Data

Shedd, Charlotte
    Thank you, America / Charlotte Shedd.
        p. cm. -- (Biography, autobiography, memoirs series)
    ISBN 1-57241-056-6
    1. Shedd, Charlotte. 2. Women journalists -- United States --
Biography. 3. Austrian Americans -- Biography. I. Title. II. Series:
Studies in Austrian literature, culture, and thought. Biography,
autobiography, memoirs series.
PN4874.S455A3 1997
830.9'9436--dc21
                               97-34913
                                   CIP

Cover Design:
Diane Neff

Published by Ariadne Press
270 Goins Court
Riverside, CA 92507

This book is dedicated to my beloved daughter
Christobel Eleanor Shedd Selecky
and
in grateful memory to her godmother
Eleanor Roosevelt

Acknowledgments

My special appreciation goes to Dorry Ross, an instructor at the University of Delaware Writers Center who invested great care, endless hours and enthusiasm to edit my memoirs to a printable volume.

My gratitude goes in equal measure to Diane Neff of the Communication Design Group in Wilmington, Delaware for designing the dustjacket of my book according to my ideas and did so splendidly.

To all those who urged me to publish my memories goes a heartfelt "thank you."

Contents

Christobel's christening in Arden, Delaware, 1955

Prologue

1

A few minutes before midnight. I stood at the rail of the ship in Rotterdam's harbor. This New Year's Eve was very different from that noisy one a year ago. Then it had been time to celebrate: champagne corks popping, funny hats bobbing, dancing couples kissing, pastel spirals of paper streaming through the air and draping on the Japanese lanterns, the band playing and then ... gongs striking twelve ... Prosit! Happy New Year!

That was how I had celebrated New Year's Eve just one year earlier in Vienna, the city where I was born and grew up. There was nothing of that now, midnight December 31, 1938, as I stood on the lonely deck of the Holland-America Line steamship Volendam. There was only darkness and the regular "blop, blop" of the water which lay in a thin black strip between the hull of the ship and the dock. That narrow strip of water, far below me and blacker than the dark bulk of the ship, held my eyes as though I were mesmerized. It was the border between Europe and the unknown: between my familiar past – Lotte Kraus, one of the two girls of the well-known Kraus family in the town of Klosterneuburg, Nieder-Österreich – and my uncertain future. As long as that strip of water grew no wider, I felt that I could get off the ship and go back, that I had not cut my ties irrevocably.

The last stragglers coming aboard at that late hour looked haggard and exhausted. They made no sound as they glanced past me – a girl of twenty-five, slender to the point of being almost too thin, of medium height, with brown hair falling to her shoulders – standing in the dim light by the railing. Snow was beginning to cover my hair with freezing flakes, so I pulled my woolen cap deeper around my face. The cold – or was it the leaving – shook my entire body, but I stayed on deck, waiting for the moment when the ship would leave the dock ... leave Europe ... leave home. I was glad no one stood with me at the railing for I could not have explained the confused emotions overwhelming me. I was saying goodbye to my past.

There had been wonderful days of fun and laughter; secret rendezvous and long walks in the Vienna woods on sun-drenched

Sundays as well as on warm, moonlit nights; glamorous evenings of waltzing on polished parquet floors under magnificent chandeliers, surrendering to the melodies of Johann Strauss in the ballrooms of the Imperial Hofburg during the long Viennese ball season; and glorious days of skiing and nights of singing and drinking *Glühwein*, a hot spiced wine, far into the night. So many splendid memories until the Nazi terror began casting its long, brown shadow over Austria and forecasting, for those who had the courage to admit it, the total conquest of our land and later all of Europe.

There were none of the usual celebrations that accompany a transoceanic departure. There were only a few muffled shouts between the men on the dock as the Dutch longshoremen slipped the hawsers from the mooring. I glanced downward; the inky strip of water, so narrow only a moment earlier, widened rapidly and the dock faded into the night. I was alone. Goodbye to my family a thousand miles away. Goodbye to my friends. I had escaped; many would not.

As the ship moved into the night, I felt a choking sense of guilt and shame for having deserted my family in Nazi-occupied Austria.

2

Freedom was murdered in my homeland at exactly 7:15 p.m. on March 11, 1938. We were sitting around the dinner table listening to music on the radio. The music stopped in mid-melody. After a few moments the announcer, in a curiously strained voice, said, "Ladies and gentlemen, Chancellor Schuschnigg will direct a few words to you." Another pause. Then the low voice of Schuschnigg, hoarse with emotion, "My dear Austrian compatriots, It has been reported to me that troops of the Third Reich are crossing the borders into Austria. In order to avoid bloodshed, I have given orders not to resist. God bless our Austria."

We sat as if turned to stone. My father was deathly pale. The catastrophe he had predicted had now become reality. As soon as the Chancellor had ceased speaking, another announcer enthusiastically informed the listeners that units of the Security Police (Gestapo) had taken control of the state-owned network. Instead of Viennese music, we were now treated to Nazi songs. Then, in jubilant tones, the announcer told of the "victory parade" that surged through Vienna's streets shouting "Sieg Heil! Sieg Heil!" and "Juda verrecke im eigenen Drecke" – Jews drop dead in your own excrement.

We had never heard anything like it, but at that moment we realized we were outlaws in our homeland. The people I had known all my life became strangers who passed me on the street and did not stop to talk as they had done in times past. I found myself looking at their lapels rather than into their faces. But it was not as important to look for the party button in the lapel of your friends as it was to see who among your enemies now wore the new mark of power and privilege. For it was from your enemies that sudden danger now threatened.

What enemies can you have in a community in which you have lived all your life? It was enough to have reprimanded a workman for negligent service, to have returned a bad piece of meat to the butcher, to have chastised the housemaid for breaking your best piece of china.

Fear . . . cold ever present fear entered our daily lives.

****

The *Machtübernahme* as it was called, "the taking of power" by the Nazis meant that the Nuremberg Race Laws were put into effect. Very few people knew anything about the far-reaching importance of those laws for the individual in the countries in which they were applied. Nothing about them was known in America, as I had a chance to find out later when I emigrated to the USA.

But in Vienna they were of critical importance to my family because my parents' marriage was a *Mischehe*, a mixed marriage. My father came from a Jewish background, my mother was an "Aryan." My sister and I, therefore, were classified as *Mischlinge* Grade One. Everything depended on the number of Jewish grandparents and whether ours was a Christian household. Since my father became a Christian before 1923 (the year the Nazi party was founded), and my sister and I were raised in the Christian faith, we had, according to the Nuremberg Race Laws, certain rights and privileges before the law that Jews did not have. We could own property. But I could not continue to pursue a stage career because to do so I would have to possess the *Arier Nachweis*, proof that I was a pure Aryan, which I was not. My sister, a teacher, was able to teach, but only in private schools and only to students who were as she was, a *Mischling*. That is why she was able to remain in Vienna, while I was not – all theatrical doors were closed to me. My profession was singing and acting. That was all I knew, so I had no choice but to leave my homeland in search of freedom.

3

I was born on January 13, 1913, and my sister Trude was born two years later on July 10, 1915. Home was a villa, which my father – a wealthy man with a Ph.D. in law and a secure future working for the Department of Finance – had bought as a wedding gift for my mother in Klosterneuburg, on the outskirts of Vienna. My mother, at 26, was twelve years younger than my father. She had no money, was not "society" (her father was a postal clerk with a drinking problem) and was not particularly pretty, but she was smart – very smart – and unlike other women made no attempt to pursue him.

Home, number Three Alleegasse, was a three-story brick home, stuccoed as are all brick structures in Austria. Under the gabled roof the swallows nested every year. The house was new when my parents moved in, and at that time the first timid fingers of ivy had begun to climb up its front walls. (During the years my family lived there, the ivy worked its way up the entire front of the house, practically obscuring its shape and making it difficult for my mother to open the windows.)

The house stood behind an iron picket fence with a double iron gate which was always locked. The lock had only two keys, which were supposed to be hung on a nail next to the front door. Everyone, including every member of our family, had to ring the bell at the gate and then wait for someone to come from the house to unlock it. The trouble was that much of the time the keys mysteriously disappeared. The result was that quite often we could neither enter nor leave our house without taking the gate apart. Everyone in the family became an expert at this . The practice of being asked to hang the keys on the nail, and incidentally forgetting to do so, persistently continued. Somehow it never occurred to my parents to give everyone in the family a key of his own. That simply was not the custom, and innovations were distrusted.

The house was not built with a thought for convenience or comfort. We had no central heating. The hallways and stairs were icy in the winter. The water pipes froze and burst regularly, inundating the lower floors. Yet no steps were taken to remedy the condition permanently. The inconvenience was accepted stoically as "unavoidable." There were only cold water faucets throughout the house, so water had to be heated in big pots on the wood-burning stove. Washing dishes was a major operation and was often postponed, leading to an accumulation of soiled dishes stored discreetly under the kitchen table.

But we walked on beautifully polished parquet floors covered with precious oriental rugs. Every room was furnished with elaborate furniture, and fine paintings embellished the walls. From the ceilings hung crystal chandeliers and on side tables stood charming Meissen and Augarten figurines. It was, in short, a home that spoke of taste and a preference for the finer things in life. In its total disregard for the requirements of daily living, it was an uncomfortable house. But my parents loved it as it was and resisted any improvements.

****

Many of the comforts of our lives disappeared as World War I ended. My father had invested most of his money in now-worthless government bonds. It wasn't just letting the servants go, it was not enough food and not enough clothing and not enough wood for the stoves. Food became the single most important thing in our lives; this was a time when no one ever discarded a crust of bread or the core of an apple. No one rejected a partially spoiled piece of fruit; one savored every last scrap of anything edible. Life was a constant striving to make connections to get an extra ration of milk, of worrying over being the last in line and arriving too late to get a small piece of meat. There was a daily search for sources that might supply us with a few potatoes, some dried peas (complete with worms), acorns that, when roasted and ground, produced *Ersatz Kaffee*. Such pursuits took every ounce of our attention and time.

These near-famine conditions were particularly critical in my case because I had suffered a bad bout of pneumonia and needed good food and care to be healthy enough to start first grade. It was decided therefore that I should spend one year in Karlsbad with my father's sister, Lotte, the childless wife of a physician, my godmother and the first of the many women who "saved" my life. Karlsbad, in newly created Czechoslovakia, with its hot mineral-rich geysers and sulphur springs, attracted thousands of people seeking a "cure" for intestinal and rheumatic ailments. Thus, within a very short time food and everything else necessary for a pleasant, healthful, recreational life was soon to be found in the three famous Bohemian health spas: Karlsbad, Marienbad, and Franzenbad.

I can still remember that certain smell which enveloped me when my father and I got off the train in Karlsbad. It was a mixture of pine from the surrounding hills and something that lingered in the air and came, I supposed, from the mineral and sulphur content of the soil and water. I also remember the tall figure of my Aunt Lotte, slender and very elegant. Even I, young as I was, noticed that everything she wore was coordinated and obviously very expensive. Hat and gloves, pocket-book and shoes, everything matched. She was very beautiful, and I liked her immediately. Thus began what was probably the greatest and most decisive influence of my youth, perhaps even my life.

Years later, she described her impression of me. "I went to the railroad station," she said, "and there you were with your father. A tiny, little, thin girl, long disheveled hair, huge eyes that looked at me very observantly and curiously, but not at all frightened as I worried you would be. You were dressed in a boy's coat, much too large for you, and of course, buttoned on the wrong side. A sailor's hat, badly worn shoes and gloves. Quite a pathetic sight, really. And I thought the first thing I'll do with her is buy her a brand new outfit from head to toe. Next, I'll see that she gains at least ten kilos."

At House Billroth (every house in Karlsbad had a name rather than a number), I met Uncle Heinrich, Lotte's husband. Tall, blond and handsome, his clear blue eyes welcomed me as much as his words did. The home was spacious and richly furnished, but strangely there was no place to take a bath. For baths we had to go across the street to the public bathhouse with its many bathrooms attended by white-clad ladies, who scrubbed the white enameled tubs with long-handled brushes and let the naturally hot mineral water stream into the tub, stirring it with a thermometer as it flowed from the faucet.

For our arrival Ida, the cook, had prepared a lovely meal of veal and mushrooms, potatoes and vegetables, and there was milk for me, and white bread and a rich torte for dessert. I had more to eat on that one day than I had during a whole week in famine-stricken Austria.

My father stayed a few days to see if I would be able to mold myself into the new environment. On the morning of his departure, he fully expected me to want to go back to Vienna with him. Instead,

I was happily ensconced on Tante Lotte's bed, surrounded by dolls and toys, completely assimilated. I think he was a little hurt that I so easily separated myself from him and from my family. But I had found my niche and with a kiss and embrace, I let him go home alone.

I loved life in Karlsbad. It was the relaxed, luxurious life of a *Kurort*, a place where people of means went for the "cure" and to regain lost health. It was an international meeting place of prominent and famous people and the perfect place for people watching: American movie producers and stars, Indian maharajahs in their white turbans and narrow trousers, kings and queens (and sometimes kings without their queens, but with their mistresses – incognito, and while everyone knew, everyone acted as if they didn't.) There were American millionaire widows with European gigolos, easily identified because they were the only older women to wear pastel-colored clothes and beautifully coiffed, snow-white hair.

The day followed a regular schedule beginning at nine in the morning with a stop at the bakery and coffee shop, then lunch at home, a nap, then to a concert-café, where in the shaded garden, an orchestra played lilting operetta tunes that I adored. Sometimes I rolled the printed program into a conductor's baton, stood on my chair and conducted the music to the evident entertainment of the guests. In the late afternoon all of Karlsbad met on the *Alte Wiese* the most elegant shopping street with its sidewalk cafes and lovely shops.

Because Tante Lotte included me in everything, I learned how to greet strangers, curtsy, and behave in an adult world. Second only to her love for me was her recognition of my exceptional love for the theater, the stage, and everything related to the performing arts.

It is not surprising that my year in Karlsbad set me apart from my family. *Die Lotte ist anders als wir*, they kept saying about me, "Lotte is different from us." And I was. It was perhaps inevitable that my departure from Europe, as the Nazi menace came upon us, should be from Karlsbad, that the last good days I had in war-threatened Europe should be with my Aunt Lotte, who, irrationally, resisted being saved herself.

Nor is it so surprising that Karlsbad became a magic place, a light on the horizon whenever things became difficult. Nearly every summer thereafter, as soon as school was over, I followed the call to

Karlsbad and Tante Lotte. Each summer I learned by heart complete librettos and scores of the many operettas I attended there. My parents (as proud parents are wont to do) often called on me to display my "talents" and entertain their guests with songs and dances. I even enlisted my little sister to play "straight man," a role she hated. My parents smiled and Papa called me his "little opera singer." They thought that this pre- occupation with singing would fade away as I grew up.

****

I spent the first five years of elementary school at the Stiftsschule, housed in the Monastery and Cathedral of Klosterneuburg. Although the school was a public, not a parochial, school, we were fully oriented toward a Catholic education because all public schools taught religion as an obligatory subject and held the students to the observation of all Catholic holidays and rituals. The non-Catholics – Jews and "Evangelicals" as Protestants were called – represented only about one percent of the student population; they received their own religious instruction in separate classrooms.

On Sundays we assembled at the school at nine in the morning to attend mass with our teacher in the richly decorated cathedral with its intricately carved images of saints created by medieval and baroque artists. It was unthinkable not to attend and required a medical certificate to authenticate an illness. Each Sunday we sang the Schubert mass in all its simple heart-warming beauty, so reminiscent of Austrian folk tunes. It was almost inescapable that the atmosphere of art and music, perhaps only subconsciously, should become part of every one of us. It certainly became part of me.

****

There comes a moment in a girl's life when she begins to change emotionally from child to woman. That moment came when I was fourteen and met the Lieutenant. He smiled as he passed me on the street, put his fingers to the visor of his cap in a salute, and bowed slightly. I smiled back and felt the blood rushing to my face. I made it a point to pass the same spot, at the same time, the next day. He came. This time he stopped to talk, and I violated the iron rule for "nice" girls: Never talk to a man to whom one was not properly introduced and never, never on the street.

But I did stop, and we talked, and he walked me home. Not quite home, we stopped at the corner, where my mother was not apt to see me. The Lieutenant, his name was Leonhardt, asked if he could see me again.

"Yes, tomorrow."

"Could we, perhaps, take a little walk along the Danube?"

"Yes," I said, "we could."

We met every day. The sun shone warmly and the air was filled with the perfume of April. Is it any wonder that one day he took me into his arms and kissed me? It was my first kiss, just like a scene in a movie. I was floating on a soft silver cloud. He was much older than I and must have discovered that I had never kissed anyone before. It must have raised doubts in his mind as to the appropriateness of our friendship.

When I got home that day, the experience was too much for me to keep to myself. I told my sister about kissing and explained how it is done properly. My sister went straight to my mother.

"Lotte has kissed a Lieutenant."

The heavens fell on me! First I was given a sound thrashing, then I was placed under house arrest. Next, my father, my kind sweet father, tried to explain the terrible dangers that lie in kisses – kisses awaken all sorts of irresistible desires that lead to inevitable doom.

You will become erotic," he said.

"What's that?" I asked.

"Never mind," he stuttered. "It's something you are too young for."

Then, my mother went to the military commandant of the local garrison where my Lieutenant was stationed and told him of the "incident." She demanded that the culprit be banned for trying to seduce a minor. (He was sent away, poor thing!) Worst of all, I was sentenced to a convent boarding school called Zum Armen Kinde Jesu.

It was a huge, gray building, with an enormous heavy portal that was always locked. My dormitory room, where I slept with four other girls, had a bed, a night table and a chair for each girl. We shared one closet. One unshielded bulb of low wattage, designed to prevent reading in bed, hung from the ceiling.

When I saw the room, I felt as if I were physically choking and began to cry.

"Stop crying," the nun said unperturbed, "you'll get over it."

I doubted that, and I was right.

The regimen was strict. Up at 5:30. No breakfast until after mass which was held at 6:00 in the ice cold, dark and forbidding chapel. After mass we had breakfast consisting of water cocoa and bread with jam. Then school. There was no chance for fun and laughter. Everything was regimented, including our clothes: navy blue skirt, blouse, coat, a round hat that made my head look like a mushroom, black stockings and shoes, and black gloves. Every step was supervised, every spoonful of food was observed, every word we spoke was overheard and often criticized. When we were taken out for walks, we had to walk "two by two," a nun in front and a nun at the end of the line, and we were not permitted to talk to anyone. I felt as if I were being slowly strangled. No doubt my intense desire for independence stems from those claustrophobic days at convent school.

Fortunately for me, Sister Karina – pale, tall, spare with aristocratic hands – became my friend and another of the women who "saved" me. With her there, school was almost bearable. She found out that I sometimes sneaked off to the auditorium with one or two other students and entertained them presenting one-woman shows of singing and dancing. She recognized that I had talent, that I was different than the other girls. One night I told her I hated the convent and felt that prison could be no worse.

She answered me, "Discipline is one of the most important things in life; we need it to progress in whatever we are doing, and it will do you good to learn to submit to discipline, for later in your life you cannot do without it. "She gently stroked my face and bid me goodnight. How often her words came back to me when I was on my own.

Mercifully, toward the end of the year I developed a severe case of pleurisy and was sent home. I was ill for several months and felt tremendous satisfaction in telling my mother it was her fault because she "stuck me into that convent, where I was so sick that I almost died."

The following fall, I was sent back to my regular school.

4

I was always an optimist. I had the truly Viennese temperament which expresses itself so well with the tongue-in-cheek proverb, "the situation is critical, but it isn't serious." No matter how many times I was put down, the next minute I was up again, smiling hopefully trusting that everything would be all right. And this trait was a lifesaver when graduation from Gymnasium, high school, was imminent.

My father brought up the subject of my future and the question of which profession I might choose. "Even if you get married, have children, and are taken care of by your husband," he said, "a girl should have a profession to fall back upon because one never knows what may happen later in life."

He fully expected me to follow family tradition and enter the University for an academic career, as my sister did two years later. Determined and brilliant, Trude graduated summa cum laude with a Ph.D. as a botanist-chemist. But I had made up my mind. No university for me; instead . . . the stage.

My father was stunned; his face grew red and his hands shook. Then came what in the Viennese idiom is known as *ein Krach*, an outburst. My poor father was hurt, disappointed, and utterly opposed to my plans. My mother sat by and said nothing – for once. She was a theater aficionado herself, loved to go to the opera, and attended all the plays performed in the many theaters of Vienna, ten months out of twelve. Perhaps she secretly wished to have done it herself, instead of having to settle for being a housewife.

But to Papa "the stage" was something reminiscent of Sodom and Gomorrah. He visualized all actors living a life of sin and moral decay. Also, he had no illusions about the difficulties of the dog-eat-dog competition for prominence and success in the world of make-believe. During the days that followed, Papa enlisted the help of all sorts of people active in theater management to warn me of the hardships I would have to face. I was admonished that talent had very little to do with success, but that it was *Verbindungen* – connections – that made a star. I was reminded that for every actor who is employed there are thousands who end up starving in garrets. And, of course, everyone knew that all roads to theatrical stardom were "via the couch" of the director and/or producer.

"Why," lamented Papa, "can't you choose a normal profession? Teacher, secretary, or better even physician, lawyer, scientist, or perhaps, diplomat." But I remained adamant: the theater or nothing.

After weeks of silence, alternating with periods of constant argument, Papa relented . . . slightly. "I will give my consent only if you can make the grade in the Opera. I shall arrange an audition for you at the *Staatsakademie*."

The State Academy for Music and Performing Arts was the hallowed temple for the study of classical music of all types. Students from all over the world attended its classes to study with a faculty that included some of the most famous quality names of opera and concert stage. Vocal, as well as instrumental, instruction together with theory, composition, conducting and stage design were taught. It was, in my father's eyes the only acceptable institution to give me the proper preparation for a singing career.

But what Papa did not realize was that the Academy provided a university-level education, and in order to qualify, one had to have prior professional music instruction, which I did not have. My only experience, so far, was singing in school productions and amateur recitals before benevolent friends and relatives. I had never before auditioned professionally for anyone – thus I had no idea how to prepare myself.

There was no difficulty in obtaining an appointment for the audition. Papa's "connections" opened the necessary doors. We arrived at the Academy, located in the famous Konzerthaus, where the Vienna Philharmonic Orchestra and the Vienna Symphony Orchestra played for what was then and still remains the most discerning audience in the world. Countless times I had waited in line for hours to buy standing room tickets, and then stood to hear the glorious music for another two hours. How often I had imagined how it would feel to be standing on that stage myself.

As Papa and I entered the school section of the building, I suddenly realized the critical importance of the audition and experienced, for the first time, a paralyzing case of stage fright. My stomach and throat constricted; my terror was so great that I felt each hair on my head was standing straight up. My father knew nothing of this as he introduced himself and me to the Kammersängerin, an imposing woman with iron-gray hair piled on top of her head, who was to conduct the audition.

The Frau Kammersängerin sat down at the piano, ran her ringed fingers forcefully over the keyboard and asked, "What will you sing for me?"

I wanted to disappear into the nearest mousehole as I said, "From *Countess Maritza*?"

"Operetta?" She was clearly horrified. "I am sorry but I cannot accompany that." And she began to play scales. "Sing after me: do, re, mi, fa." Her voice was majestic and beautiful. My voice, in comparison, sounded like a canary.

She closed the piano and stood up. "You have a very sweet voice. Small and worth training, but not for opera, not for this school. I could send you to my assistant, Harriet Hauser, who would train you for operettas or that new thing they have now, musical comedies. Try the New Vienna Conservatory. They might be better suited to your type of talent." She nodded to me condescendingly, then inclined her head toward Papa. We were dismissed.

As we left the building, he said, "So! That is that. You just don't have it. Now you will give up your hopeless notions because, obviously, she was only being polite." To show his compassion at my supposed defeat he continued, "If you want to take private singing lessons with that Harriet Hauser, I will even pay for them. And I will, of course, pay for the University, for you will study there."

The next day, unbeknownst to anyone, I took the bus to Vienna, then the street car to the Conservatory. The Conservatory, unlike the Academy, was not state funded. Also, unlike the Academy, it did not concentrate solely on classical music, but also taught operetta, acting, dance, film technique, microphone technique, and preparation for careers in radio. Frequently students from the Conservatory were recruited as "extras" for work in Vienna's film studio "Rosenhügel." This was exactly what I was looking for.

This audition was very different. I sang for Herr von Perfall, who taught the operetta classes, in the hall between classes. "If you want to be on the stage," he said, "you must be ready to perform at the drop of a hat."

I began to sing the first thing that came to mind, "Play Gypsy" the tenor solo from the Kalman operetta *Countess Maritza*. After a few moments, he started to move my arms and posture with me, to demonstrate the movements that should accompany the song. "Excellent," he said as I finished. "When do you want to begin?"

That was when I explained my problem. "Herr von Perfall, my father doesn't want me to do this. He won't pay for it, and I have no money of my own. Is there a chance for a scholarship?" To my delight and amazement, Herr von Perfall convinced the director of the Conservatory, Professor Reitler, to give me a scholarship. Slowly it began to sink in. I had done it. All by myself, without connections!

It was a miracle that I caught the right streetcar home I was so excited. All that was left was to break the news, very carefully, to my father – a very formidable task. But then, I hit upon the solution to my problem. I would enroll at the University also. That way I would please my parents, and they could tell their friends that their daughter studied at the University, and at the same time I could begin my quest for a stage career by attending the Conservatory.

When I told them I was enrolling in the University to study the history of music and English, they were delighted. But when I told them I had also enrolled in the Herr von Perfall's operetta class at the New Vienna Conservatory they were horrified. While operettas were fine entertainment, they most emphatically did not want their daughter performing in them.

****

A few days later I had my first lesson with Harriet Hauser, the singing teacher. She was a tall and voluptuous woman of about thirty-five, with a wonderfully feminine and kind face. "Come in, come in," she said. "You are the girl who doesn't have an opera voice, and they sent you to me to see what I can do with you." She laughed, and so did I.

Harriet, the daughter of a Viennese father and American mother, had studied voice at the Vienna State Academy for Music and had chosen teaching instead of a stage career. In a short time she acquired a reputation as one of the best voice teachers in Vienna. Most of her pupils were State Opera singers whom she prepared for new roles, but she also coached artists with "small voices" like mine.

I sang "Das Heidenröslein," that enchantingly beautiful tune by

Franz Schubert. She told me I had a charming voice, but for the next three months I was not going to sing anything but scales. And that is all I did.

I was very fortunate to have landed in Harriet's studio for the initial phase of my vocal studies, because many singers have been ruined by ambitious or careless teachers who rush their pupils into a volume or range that is unsuitable. Harriet explained that my voice was a mezzo-soprano, and she led me step by step with careful vocalizing to the expansion of my voice volume, stressing that the voice does not originate in the throat but rather in the diaphragm. She taught me to "hold" the air and slowly let it "escape" through the throat, using the vocal cords as "strings" to form tone, vibration, and flexibility.

In those first months of intensive training with Harriet, I was not allowed to sing in my operetta class. I was restricted to acting in scenes with only spoken dialogue. Von Perfall believed that one could do "the light stuff" only after mastering "the heavy stuff," so we studied Shakespeare, Shaw, Goethe, Schiller, and Lessing. At the same time I was taking lessons in tap dancing, modern dancing, and precision Rockette-style chorus-line dancing. It was a tough schedule for me to manage because university lectures had to be dovetailed with courses at the Conservatory, and voice lessons got priority because one cannot sing properly when overtired.

During that first year, I became acquainted with the disillusioning work of a movie extra. A call would go out for extras. Hundreds of desperate, unemployed actors as well as starry-eyed students of the theater schools and workshops would compete for relatively few openings as roving gypsies, milling mobs, fierce warriors, Germanic knights, or elegant guests at balls. Selection seemed to depend on how well one knew the director or his secretary.

My experience as an extra showed me that perhaps my father was right, and there was, after all, another side to the glittering world of stage and screen. For the first time I became aware of the good fortune which permitted me to live in a comfortable secure home with my family, while trying to build a career.

5

Every spring, talent scouts representing the German-language theaters from Germany, Switzerland, Czechoslovakia, and the capitals of the Austrian provinces descended upon Vienna to recruit actors. Like all young theatrical aspirants, I believed the world has been waiting for me. As a graduate of the operetta class of Franz von Perfall and as a student of Harriet Hauser, I had visualized myself being snapped up by those talent scouts within the first few rounds of auditions.

Reality was a bit different. Many times I walked onto a darkened stage, lit only by a single, naked bulb. I handed my music to the pianist on stage.

"What do you have?" came a voice from the darkened auditorium.

I announced my number. I sang. I was interrupted.

"What else do you have?"

I announced a second number. I sang. I was interrupted.

"Thank you. We will let you know."

They never did.

Instead of moping around and being forced into a non-theatrical job by my I-told-you-so parents, I decided to audition for more study in the highly prestigious, internationally respected school of drama, "The Reinhardt Seminar." The school had been founded in 1929 in Berlin by Max Reinhardt, who had helped make Berlin the theatrical center of Europe. In 1933 he had to flee Nazi Germany because he was a Jew, so he returned to his native Austria, bringing his school with him. The Reinhardt method demanded complete naturalness and behavior on the stage, in contrast to the pathos which had been the style. A Reinhardt actor was asked to visualize a "fourth wall on the stage," to act not toward the audience but toward the other actors, and to keep the voice at a normal level.

I auditioned with the famous speech from Bernard Shaw's *St. Joan* and a song from an operetta. I was accepted and given a scholarship. The deciding vote was cast by Otto Preminger, who was later to become an outstanding American producer. While he was one of the most difficult teachers to please, he was also one of the best teachers.

The best part about being a Reinhardt pupil was the prospect of participating in the Salzburg Summer Festivals. In one production I was allowed to play a *Tischdame*, a lady at the table of Everyman, in the medieval morality play *Jederman*. I called out, "Bells? Has anyone heard bells?" I also played the woman who found the mortally wounded Valentin in *Faust*. In that play I cried, "Help, help."

It was an enormously stimulating, exhilarating summer, observing Reinhardt as he directed these plays. I often forgot to eat and slept only when exhaustion did not permit another waking moment.

Salzburg became for me, as it does for millions of music lovers, a pilgrimage to the altar of the performing arts. From the last week of July to the end of August, Salzburg offered an avalanche of daily symphony concerts, operas, Mozart serenades, chamber concerts, and solo recitals by the world's greatest artists. To be part of this illustrious conglomerate of artists was more valuable than money. My pay was nominal. All I wanted was to call myself a member of the Salzburg Festival. Who could blame me! The fringe benefits included free tickets to rehearsals of the Vienna Philharmonic under Arturo Toscanini, tickets to concerts conducted by Bruno Walter, tickets to Mozart's *Don Giovanni* with Ezio Pinza as the Don.

I found here that same international ebb and flow of social life which I had come to love so much in Karlsbad. But while the crowds came to Karlsbad to seek health in quiet waters, they came to Salzburg to submerge themselves in waves of music.

****

The glamor and gaiety of the Salzburg Festival Season of 1937 could not quite conceal what was happening in neighboring Germany, where, since Hitler's rise to power in 1933, a reign of terror had begun to affect those who, for religious or political reasons, displeased the ruling Nazi party. The border of Germany's Bavaria is only a few miles from Salzburg, and there was heavy clandestine traffic, mostly at night. Among the happy, international patrons of the arts could be seen the worried, haggard faces of those who were exiles from their homeland, Germany.

Many well known personalities of the German theater, art, and literary world fled to Austria because they were Jewish, or had opposed Hitler, or had simply criticized his doctrines. They came hoping to find new contacts that would make it possible for them to emigrate to other countries, preferably America. The appearance of these unhappy wanderers, in marked contrast to that of the Austrians, made it quite evident that the artistic world of Austria did not wish to face reality. Neither did I.

No one even mentioned the words "concentration camps" or the persecution of the Jews, Catholics, or any other Nazi victims. But we knew, without mentioning it, that the bully boys, who hung around street corners arrogantly blocking the way of strolling pedestrians, were underground members of the illegal Austrian Nazi party. We recognized them by their unofficial uniforms – white knitted knee stockings. Even though swastikas were chalked on sidewalks and scrawled on the windows of Jewish shops, and even though we read about clashes between loyal Austrian citizens groups and members of the illegal Nazi party, we played ostrich and thought, "It will go away."

A few people were more realistic. The brothers Raymond and Noel Bring, well-to-do attorneys were among them. Raymond, twenty years older than I, courted me. We often sat at a marble-topped table in the Café Bazaar until it closed at 2 a.m., discussing the concerts and operas we had seen. After many long conversations he confided in me that he and his brother were planning to emigrate shortly to America, where a sister already lived.

Through his law practice he had met several German exiles and had learned about their tragic circumstances. As a Jew and outspoken critic of the Austrian Nazis, and as a lawyer who had worked against the Nazis in the courts, Raymond knew that he and his brother would be on the Nazi blacklist. He planned to give up his beloved law practice and buy a hotel in Miami Beach, where he could start a new life in a country safe from totalitarianism. I listened and pondered his words.

****

When the Festival season was over and I was back in Vienna, I received a letter from Raymond asking me to meet him. When we met at the Hotel Bristol, he was emotional and depressed. He had sold everything and was in Vienna to say goodbye to his friends – and maybe to me.

"Come with me to America," he said. "Perhaps when you get to know me better, we might find a future for both of us, together, there."

I was deeply moved. I tried to find the right words to tell him why I could not accept his offer. Much as the thought of seeing America intrigued me, much as Raymond's cultured charm and intelligence impressed me, I loved my life in Austria and was certain that soon I would be a success in the theater.

"If I were to leave Vienna now," I said," I would always feel that I had missed my chance. Perhaps if things turn out other than I expect, I might someday ask you to make good on your offer."

He said he understood. "I will go first. You will follow someday."

He took a card from his wallet. "Here is my address in Miami Beach. If you should decide to come to America, let me know, and I will help."

The card was to play a decisive role in my life.

****

The day after Raymond left for America I auditioned for a spot as a singer/actress at the popular literary cabaret, "Literatur am Naschmarkt," so called because the small theater was near Vienna's sprawling produce market, the "Naschmarkt." I was hired by the director, Franz Engel, and became part of an ensemble of young actors, musicians, and authors presenting the usual fare of political-satirical sketches and blackouts for sophisticated intellectual audiences. (It is noteworthy that the entire ensemble emigrated to America independently of each other, and that in 1940 we all met in New York and united to present a Broadway revue called appropriately "Reunion in New York," an Americanized version of the type of review we had played in Vienna.)

Next door to the "Literatur" was the most famous of Vienna's operetta theaters, the Theater an der Wien, on whose stage a stunning, red-haired actress from Sweden, Zarah Leander, performed nightly as the star of *Axel at the Door of Heaven* written by the popular Viennese composer, Ralph Benatzky. I was fascinated by the story, loved the music, and dreamed of only one thing – to play the role of Gloria, just as Zarah did. After sneaking over to see "Axel" at least twenty-five times, I knew the role by heart. During several of my visits I talked to the stage director of the show and confided my dreams of playing Gloria. One day, as I was putting on make-up in my dressing room, the stage director of "Axel" knocked at the door with a wonderful proposition.

The actress who was to play Gloria at the Stadt Theater in Eger, Czechoslovakia had fallen ill, and a replacement was needed in three days. Would I go? Of course I would go.

"But," he added, "there's one more thing. You must also play the lead in *Auf der Grünen Wiese* (In the Green Meadow), another operetta. "Can you do that?"

"Sure, I can," I instantly and confidently replied, even though I had neither seen nor heard the play. Nothing in the world could have made me pass up such an opportunity.

My mind raced: I didn't have a star's wardrobe. I didn't know the words or the music to *Auf der Grünen Wiese*. My hair was the wrong color.

First, I called a friend whose closets were always bulging with elegant clothes. I came away with silver foxes, negligees, evening gowns, sophisticated suits, and boxes full of costume jewelry. Next I stormed Harriet's studio. We studied for hours and hours until I knew the *Gruenen Wiese* score fairly well. Then I raced to the hairdresser and had my hair dyed so that it matched Zarah's red hair.

When my father saw me, he almost collapsed. "You look like a cheap streetwalker," he roared. "Don't come in the house looking like this! I am ashamed that anyone might see you."

"My hair will be dyed back to normal, Vati," I promised, and that calmed him somewhat.

*****

The theater in Eger was sold out. Since I was billed as a star, I knew I must act accordingly and not let anyone know this was my first major role. In other words, I had to give a very professional, wholly sophisticated performance not only on the stage, but also in real life.

The role of Gloria didn't worry me; I had seen it so many times

I knew all the locations, movements, and cues from start to finish. The other operetta was a nightmare. I studied the lines and forgot them. I tried to remember the music, but it evaporated.

Suddenly it was opening night. I wanted to scream, "I'm not ready!" But then the curtain went up. Instantly I was a different person, confident and assured. The words came from my subconscious and the music flowed from my lips. My body moved as if directed by some unknown power. The curtain came down after the first act to roaring applause. I had done it! I had pulled it off!

While my success in far-off Eger remained unpublicized in the sophisticated world of Vienna, it had given me valuable self-confidence and professional experience. So, when I approached Radio Wien, known as RAVAG, the only radio station serving the two million citizens of Vienna, I had considerable self-assurance. In those days RAVAG was government owned and subsidized and non-commercial. Artists were hired for specific programs – not on a contract basis. Pay was very low and competition was very high.

But I found myself singing and acting into that coveted microphone enough times to discover that it was, indeed, my favorite form of communicating with an audience. It was even more satisfying than performing on a theater or concert stage, though I won more theatrical roles as I became better known through my radio work.

Theater, concerts, radio, and motion pictures – it all seemed to fall into place in that year of 1937. I did not know that it was the last good and hopeful year left to me, or to most people, in Vienna.

6

One day I arrived at the studios of Radio Vienna to do a broadcast only to be told that the songs I had chosen – selections from works by Kalman and Oscar Straus – could not be used because the composers were Jewish. In addition, I couldn't sing *Two Hearts in 3/4 Time* by Robert Stolz because he had a Jewish wife. That same stupidity spread to every phase of our culture, art, government, education and economy. Everywhere our roots of decency and innate humanitarian instincts were being ruthlessly destroyed and supplanted by crudity, ignorance, and unbearable cruelty. I felt myself changing from a cheerful, lighthearted into a serious, high-strung person, impatient with the ridiculous rules and regulations.

I began to plead with my family to get out while it was still possible. But my parents and my sister never considered flight for a moment; in fact, they would hardly discuss the subject. I argued that the rapidly growing restrictions were making people afraid of their own shadows.

"At least let me go," I begged. "One of us must get out to save the others." However, they were adamant. This was their homeland, their house, they were lifelong citizens, and they had faith that everything would be all right.

These arguments became a daily occurrence, getting louder and angrier as time passed.

****

Early in 1938, I decided that I must present my family with a *fait accompli*, so I secretly began making arrangements to emigrate to the United States.

I knew nothing about life in America except what I had seen in the movies. I did not know what I could do once I got there, but I was confident and ready to try anything. So, in March I wrote Raymond Bring, reminding him of his promise and requesting that he send me an affidavit of support. I anxiously waited for his reply. Finally in May came a reply. "Unfortunately," he wrote, "all of my financial resources have been exhausted with affidavits for my relatives in Poland and Czechoslovakia. But some friends will send you a certificate of employment which will at least get you here on a temporary visa. And later," he assured me, "you could leave for Canada or Cuba and wait there for an immigration visa. I will send your papers to the American Consul, and they will notify you."

My parents knew nothing of this, and I intended to tell them nothing until I had everything in place. But one day as we were eating lunch, the phone rang and my mother answered it. "It's the American Consulate; they want to see you in person tomorrow." I had to tell them I was going to America. My parents went pale. My sister registered no emotion; just a direct gaze that I could not interpret. Then we resumed our meal in silence.

After a few minutes, my father looked up and said, "To America? Why? Who is waiting for you in America? The President?"

Who could have foreseen that, one year later, by the strangest turns and twists of fate later I would write them on stationery whose gold embossed letterhead would read: The White House, Washington, D.C. The letter began, "I am here as the house guest of the President and Mrs. Roosevelt . . . you see, he was waiting for me!"

****

Now began the long and dangerous procedure of securing the *Ausreisebewilligung*, the exit permit for my passport. As is the case in every dictatorship, citizens were not free to come and go as they pleased. I had a passport, but it needed to be renewed and extended. Under the circumstances, this was a problem because it had been announced that – as part of Hitler's plan to erase the Austrian identity – Austrian passports would lose their validity on December 31, 1938 and that new German passports, testifying to one's new German citizenship, would be issued instead.

I had to deal with the Gestapo, which involved an element of danger since it called attention to my family. Fortunately I was able to establish my credentials by submitting the necessary papers: birth certificate, baptismal certificate, and my parents' marriage license. I knew they would ask why I wanted to leave Hitler's paradise to emigrate to *verjudete* (Jewish) America. It could mean harassment and possibly detention. So, I told the authorities that I planned to visit relatives in Czechoslovakia, as I had done so often before.

The hardest part was waiting for the affidavit from Raymond. I began to doubt that he really meant to help me. Feeling I had to get out of Vienna,I decided to visit Tante Lotte in Karlsbad and wait there for my papers. Prague was only a hour's train ride from Karlsbad, and my papers, if they arrived, could be sent to the American Consulate in Prague.

Then came the moment to leave. Strange how the mind, perhaps willfully, eradicates difficult moments. I cannot remember saying goodbye to my sister. I don't know where she was when I left. I know that I held my mother in my arms a long, long time, any differences washed away by our tears. I stood at the gate and looked at our home – not sure that I would ever see it again – and stroked our dog, a St. Bernard.

Finally my father said, "Come on now, Lotterl. You'll miss your train." We walked to the tram for Vienna, where I would change for Karlsbad.

As I got on the train I held my father's hand and looked at his kind and gentle face. I leaned my head on his shoulder and thought, "How can I leave him in this terrible hell. I love him so much. Please God, protect him and mother and Trude. Please God, let me help them when they need it."

Vati stood outside the window, trying not to cry. Then the train began to move and his figure became smaller and smaller. I saw him pull out his handkerchief and hold it to his eyes as his shoulders shook convulsively. Damn Hitler! Damn the Nazis.

The train rolled toward the Czech border.

****

Ten minutes after leaving the station, the train passed through my hometown, Klosterneuburg. When I was a child, I often stood at the foot of our street and waved at the train on its daily run to Karlsbad. Sometimes a passenger would wave back.
Now, in 1938, as the train passed the street, I saw the flutter of a white cloth and knew it was my mother. I rolled down my window and waved to her, certain that her face was as wet with tears as mine.

As the train moved through town after town, the Nazi flag, Hitler's swastika, flashed from every rooftop, every flagpole, every window. The government had ordered that private homes as well as public buildings be decorated with the symbol of the Third Reich. But even if it had not been so ordered, I knew that many of the flags were there because the people wanted them there.

Sitting on that train, I remembered my first visit, as a sick child of six, to Karlsbad. I remembered many carefree trips after that. But this time I was not the carefree, happy-go-lucky vacationer. I was one of the thousands on the move; one of the vanguard of hundreds of thousands to follow in the years to come.

My journey was a total gamble. I had a wealthy relative, Uncle Siegfried in Czechoslovakia whom my father had helped many years earlier. Would he help me? Would Raymond Bring send the Affidavit of Support? How could I manage to get to America with the very limited funds I was allowed to take out of Austria?

At the border crossing in Gmünd, a Gestapo agent studied my passport. "This passport is no longer valid," he said. "Why do you travel on an Austrian passport? You are German now. Austria has ceased to exist."

I replied, feigning calm, "I was told the new passports won't be ready until January and to be content to use this one for now. Besides, I will be returning in September."

Then something happened in the next compartment. There was a commotion. He returned my passport and ran into the next compartment. Someone was being dragged off the train screaming and weeping. I looked at the couple opposite me. Our eyes met. It could have been one of us.

The train moved a few yards and the Czech passport officers appeared. We were free! I got off the train to stretch my legs. I was suddenly very hungry, so I bought knockwurst and beer and a newspaper. The newspaper headlines drained away my elation. Hitler was threatening to "liberate" the German minority in Czechoslovakia. And Britain – in spite of its treaty obligations – was as reluctant to commit itself as it had been to help what Lord Baldwin called "that speck on the map," Austria.

That summer when I tried to warn people in Karlsbad, I found, to my dismay, that very few people shared my concern. Business as usual was the recipe for daily living. The population deluded itself by saying, "The French, the English, the Russians won't allow Hitler to march in. After all we have treaties."

****

Eighteen years had passed since the day when I arrived in Karlsbad to find my way back to health under the tender loving care of Aunt Lotte and Uncle Heinrich Munk. This visit would be the last time I would take up residence in the comfortable, richly furnished second floor apartment Tante Lotte moved into after the death of her husband. He had left her securely settled financially. His will had stipulated that his money would be invested in a house which would bring in an income, while at the same time providing her with an appropriate place to live.

The international crowd appeared as usual in lovely Karlsbad in the summer of 1938. People played bridge, attended the theater, sauntered along the promenades, gossiped at tea dances, and played golf. The forcible occupation and the ensuing horrors of neighboring Austria were happening on another planet. The only individuals I found to be very much aware and conspiratorially united were the members of the Sudeten German People's Party who met on street corners and raised their arms in the Hitler salute.

Then what I dreaded happened. Konrad Henlein, the leader of the Sudeten German People's Party, instigated riots against the government, giving Hitler the excuse to send his troops to "liberate" his "German blood-brothers." This action convinced Tante Lotte to do what I had been unable to make her do before: sell her house – at a huge loss – and take an apartment in Prague, which was in pure Czech territory.

Prague was dear to me, not only for its baroque and rococo beauty and cultural history, but also because all the male members of my family had studied at Prague University. In the fall of 1938, the city was full of despair. The streets were choked with refugees from areas handed over to the Nazis by Britain's Chamberlain and France's Daladier – whose respective countries had previously guaranteed Czechoslovakia's independence. The refugees, many of whom had escaped with only the clothes they wore, had lost everything. They had discovered the fragility of friendship. Neighbors who coveted someone's property suddenly remembered critical remarks directed at Hitler. The property owner was denounced and arrested, and the neighbor was rewarded with the victim's house and belongings.

It was easy to recognize these refugees by the furtive glances they threw over their shoulders, by the sudden lowering of their voices when someone approached, by their marked apologetic attitude when in the company of people who "belonged" in Prague.

****

Being typically Viennese, I was optimistic by nature, but the enormity of my precarious situation began to dim my optimism. I could do nothing to escape if Hitler decided to take over Prague. My affidavit papers had not arrived, and without them I could not get the coveted American visa for my passport – a passport that would be worthless on January 1, 1939, only a few weeks away. I had no money, and I couldn't ask Tante Lotte for any because she had already lost most of her possessions and was herself in a precarious position. The American Consulate was inundated with requests for immigration visas. Here, as in Vienna, guards at the gates turned the keys in the locks against the long lines of forlornly waiting people, admitting only those blessed few who had the proper "connections."

Refugees seeking to escape landlocked Czechoslovakia found that other countries – most conspicuously Switzerland, France, and Hungary – were not willing to take them in. Notably humanitarian were the Scandinavian countries and Italy, which although saddled with a fascist government, turned a blind eye to the refugees.

I combed the coffeehouse circuit looking for Uncle Siegfried hoping he could pay my passage to America. When I found him, he not only offered to cover all my expenses in getting to America, but also handed me a big bundle of money.

"Better you have it than Hitler," he said. "Spend it. Buy yourself a new wardrobe. Who knows what the future holds for all of us. At least you know for certain that you can get out."

But did I? I had the money but not the papers. Even so, the money in my pocket gave me inner security and my optimism began to return. To celebrate I bought a bathing suit the very next day! A two-piece, white Jantzen bathing suit, very revealing for those days.

The saleslady was slightly taken aback at my buying a bathing suit in the late fall.

"I need it for Miami Beach," I explained. "I am planning to be there shortly."

When I got home, there was an envelope with my name on it and an American stamp in the corner. Raymond wrote that he had found a sponsor, Senator Claude Pepper had endorsed the sponsor, and the papers should be at the American consulate. Moreover, I should prepare for an immediate departure.

Clutching the letter in one hand and the bathing suit in the other, I sat down at the table and cried hot, happy tears. I knew it was going to be all right. I had the papers, and the money. All that was needed was to speed up the slow machinery at the American Consulate.

I needed to tell Uncle Siegfried about the wonderful news. I found him in his favorite coffee house talking to a stranger – a stocky Czech, about fifty, poorly dressed yet with an air of authority.

"This is Consul X," my uncle said. "He was the Czech Consul in Turkey. He knows a lot of people and will help you with the American consulate."

I explained that he needed to locate my papers and get the American Consul to process them quickly because I had to leave Europe by December 31. I also needed passage on a ship to America and a plane ticket from Prague to a port city and finally, because I could not take any money with me, I needed transportation from New York to Miami.

"That will be three thousand KC (Czechoslovakian Crowns) for me, and, of course, the cost of the journey is extra."

Uncle Siegfried didn't bat an eye. "Fifteen hundred now, and fifteen hundred when she boards the plane," he responded.

"I will call you when I am ready," he said as he pocketed the money and left.

My uncle and I looked at each other. The Consul was a stranger. Would he carry out the assignment or would the money and my future be lost?

On November 9 – later called Kristallnacht for all the windows that were broken – what peace of mind I had was shattered when the Nazis went on a rampage against the Jews that equaled any pogrom in history. A young German Jew was reported to have killed a minor

German official in Paris, and that was all the excuse the Nazis needed. In every German and Austrian town, rampaging mobs burned synagogues, looted stores, and beat, tortured and killed citizens.

I was terrified for my parents. Miraculously my phone call got through and I heard my mother's tired voice. Because we knew that our conversation would be monitored, we used previously arranged coded phrases.

When I asked my mother how she was, she replied, "Very well, thank you. We have had a very lively social life, many visitors, and because they are such nice people, we gave them lots of our winter apples and pears."

I asked, " Mother can you loan me some money? I need a few things I can't get here."

"Unfortunately, I can't do that. We have no money, not a penny left." So now I knew the Nazi thieves had looted my parents house and stolen their money.

I determined to get some money to them, but it had to be secretly. Moreover, I had no guarantee that once I handed over the money to the emissary, he would deliver it. My other worry was that I might be dealing with a Gestapo agent who would use this opportunity to arrest my family. The man who agreed to act as messenger did not inspire trust. But he delivered every penny of the money.

A few days later I received a letter from my mother who described in coded language how she followed the intruders from room to room, as they tore open beds, pulled clothing from closets, and threw books from bookshelves. My mother did not know fear. In all the years that followed she battled the Gestapo and the Party thugs by the simple tactic of reminding them of "the Führer's high principles" and telling them how "ashamed the Fuhrer would be to see them insult an Aryan woman with a pure blood line going back to the thirteenth century." They didn't know how to handle such arguments and always let her go.

When they left, my mother went to the trap door that led to the underground rootcellar and told my father to come up. She was now the strong one in the family. Often survival depended on behavior based on strength – the Nazi bullies were basically cowards and lived by the fear they were able to instill.

Every day I walked the streets of Prague, ending up at the coffee house where I was to meet the man who had promised to help me. For all I knew, he could have pocketed the money and flown. On December 14, the Consul called to tell me that we were now going to apply in person at the Embassy for my United States Immigration Visa.

The American Embassy was more than just a building to all who waited for admission: it was the gateway to freedom. It was a strange feeling to enter the building, because it was American territory and no harm could befall me there. In that building I first heard American speech – the slightly slurred sounds and relaxed pronunciation so different from the clipped precise English I had learned to speak in school.

We were motioned by the guards to proceed along those marble-floored hallways. I was a little embarrassed by the loud clicking sound my high heels made. When we reached a door with a name card on it that my companion recognized, he said, "You go in alone. I'll follow later."

"Come in," said a male voice, and I entered a large room. I was motioned to sit down in an armchair facing a slightly built, pipe-smoking man.

He studied me and the papers.

"Not much of an affidavit," he said.

My heart sank.

"What is it then?" I asked.

"Well," he said. It's really a job. A job as a governess to a little girl in Miami Beach. Do you know anyone in Miami Beach?"

"Yes," I said and pulled out Raymond's photograph.

"Aha," he smiled. "Getting married?"

"Perhaps."

"Where did you learn to speak English so well?"

"In school, Gymnasium."

"Who is President of the United States?"

"President Roosevelt."

"It's people like you we want," he said. "You'll be all right. It's not an affidavit really, but you'll make it. Good luck."

With the questioning over, the American rose, came around the desk and said, "Now, let's have your passport for the visa." I hadn't thought of that. To be without one's passport was terrifying.

"Don't worry," he said. "You'll get it back in time."

"But you don't understand. I have to leave Europe on December 31, in seventeen days."

There was knock on the door, and my Consul entered. He took my passport, handed it over to the American, and told me to wait outside. A few minutes later, he emerged looking pleased.

"Everything is fine," he said. "I'll take care of the tickets. Now you go home and relax. Mission accomplished."

For two days I stayed inside my room because I didn't dare going outside without my passport, my only identification. On the third day the doorbell rang and there was the Consul with my passport.

Now with the certainty of escape came the renewed realization that I was really leaving everything and everyone I knew and loved. I went to the coffee house where I could place long-distance calls. After an hour's wait, it was my turn. I told my mother I had the visa.

Two days later she arrived in Prague. We just stood and held each other. We didn't want to let go. I felt so guilty about abandoning her and the rest of the family. She explained that one of the reasons she came was to give me some financial help. She had no money, but she did give me jewelry – a brooch made from her and Father's engagement rings, and the diamond necklace Tante Lotte had given me as a Christening present. What a chance she took. Had the jewels been found on her, she would have been deported to a concentration camp.

I was shocked by my mother's appearance. In a few months she had aged years. She stayed for only two days and we never left each other's side. I learned more about her in those two days than I had in all the preceding years. I learned of her integrity and honorable character. I learned that she was hiding Jews in our underground coal cellar – a capital crime. I learned of her great pain and shame because both of her brothers had immediately joined the Nazi Party and become hateful and aggressive big shots.

My mother had changed in other ways as well. She had never been physically demonstrative, in fact just the opposite. But this had changed. We sat with arms around each other, her cheek leaning against mine, her hand stroking my hair.

"Lotterl," she whispered, "all alone you are going across the ocean. How will you manage? What will become of you? Will I ever see you again?"

When she left, I buried my head in the pillows, and my body shook with sobs.

****

Not for a moment did the thought enter my head that perhaps life might be holding some pretty grim difficulties and handicaps in this new and strange land, with a new language, customs, and lifestyle. Life had been pretty easy for me. What I had earned with my singing and acting, modest as it had been for a budding actress, had been enough to cover the frills: my father had always taken care of the necessities. It was going to be different in America. I was going to be entirely on my own. Yet the thought did not bother me. America beckoned as a haven of freedom and a wonderful adventure.

****

Before I left I tried to convince Tante Lotte that Prague was not a safe haven, that she should go to Switzerland, which would welcome her because of her financial resources. But she continued to believe that Hitler would honor his promise not to invade Prague.

On December 24 I was to fly to Amsterdam, Holland and then would spend one week in Rotterdam waiting for the liner Volendam to depart on December 31, at midnight. I had never flown before and was nervous. It was the only plane scheduled for Holland for the remainder of the year. Friends in Prague had relatives in Rotterdam – Georg Schneider and his wife and four children – who offered me their hospitality during my stay.

As I boarded the airplane, the dark, slightly stooped figure of my beloved Tante Lotte stood outside the terminal in the driving snow. I watched her through the plane's window; so lonely, so loyal and loving, waving goodbye, a handkerchief fluttering in her hand. Then she turned and walked away. I never saw her again. She died in a concentration camp.

7

I arrived in Amsterdam in a snowstorm with a small suitcase and a large hatbox containing several hats, which I thought indispensable for a lady's wardrobe. My trunk, an enormous and unwieldy thing, had been shipped directly to the S.S. Volendam.

Georg Schneider met me at the airport. As we drove to Rotterdam, he told me a bit about his family. Both he and his wife, although Catholic, were born to Jewish parents in Germany. They and their four children had moved to Holland in 1934 to get away from the Nazis, who regarded them as Jewish.

When we got to his house, I realized that the family had been waiting for my arrival before lighting the Christmas tree with the real candles customary in all European homes. We gathered around the tree and sang Dutch and German carols. It was a warm and friendly home, peaceful and happy, but my heart was torn because all I could think of was my family living under Nazi occupation. I worried about them. Would they have enough to eat? Would they be warm enough? Would they feel it was really Christmas Eve? Would they be safe?

My thoughts were interrupted by Mr. Schneider, "We have a Christmas present for you, a telephone call to your parents." I heard my mother's voice, "Ja, Lotterl, we are all right. Trude bought a small tree and we put candles on it and we even have carp and potato salad for dinner. Here is your papa." "Lotterl, my child," he said. "Don't worry. We're all right. Take care of yourself. Don't get sick. Write to us. We love you and miss you." His voice broke and then the connection was broken.

****

Two days later, as he was showing me around the city, I asked Mr. Schneider what he planned to do if Hitler moved into Holland. He shrugged his shoulders. "I don't think that is going to happen. Holland is a neutral country. The Nazis won't violate our neutrality. We have run once," he added, "and we will not run again."

Not too much time passed before Nazi bombers unleashed a savage attack on Rotterdam, reducing much of the city to rubble. I do not know if the Schneiders were among the victims of the bombing or if they were caught by the Nazis and sent to a concentration camp. Although I wrote several times and inquired about them, I never heard from them again.

On December 31 at 11 o'clock in the evening the Schneiders drove me to the pier where the Volendam was docked. Before boarding I handed the customs officer my passport. He looked at it, turned it over in his hand, examined the picture and the pages and finally said, "This passport is not valid."

"What?" I screamed.

"It's Austrian," he replied.

"What do you mean?" I jumped back at him. "This passport is valid until twelve o'clock midnight tonight and what's more it contains a valid American visa. You can't keep me from boarding this ship. Once we are at sea, I won't need a European passport. I don't intend to come back here, and if I ever do, it will be with an American passport. Now get out of my way!"

He was flabbergasted. He looked at me for an instant and then without a word handed me my passport.

I ascended the gangplank at 11:45. My journey to America had begun.

****

As I stood there at the ship's railing, alone in the falling snow I realized the enormity of my undertaking – to venture forth, totally alone; to start a new life on another continent, in a new, strange land, equipped only with what knowledge I had stored up in my brain, a profession which depended for success not as much upon talent as on luck; a modest knowledge of the English language; and a friend in Miami Beach whom I had not seen in two years and whose ability to assist me was uncertain. Above all, however, I was painfully aware of having twenty American dollars in my purse and that was all the money I possessed because it was forbidden to export money from Czechoslovakia.

In my steamer trunk and suitcase I had a complete and elegant new wardrobe which, thanks to my generous Uncle Siegfried, had been made to order in Prague. Several pairs of fine shoes and all the accessories to match the ensembles would hopefully divest me of the necessity of buying new clothes for several years. But the means to pay for food, rent, and everything else I would have to earn by myself from then on – and that suddenly weighed heavily on my mind.

****

The next morning I went in search of breakfast. A friendly steward pointed me toward an imposing stairway that led into the dining room. It was a marvelous background for a "grand entrance." In the center of the dining room was an enormous buffet crowned in its center by a gigantic fresh-fruit display. There were cold cuts and cheeses, plus fish and meat platters of mouth-watering attractiveness. Also, I saw glasses filled with red and yellow liquids which I could not identify.

"Juice." I was told. "Orange juice, grapefruit juice, and tomato juice."

"All this for breakfast," I thought, and was not prepared for the menu card which was handed me when the dining room steward placed me at a table for eight. I found that in addition to the selections on the buffet table, there were even more delicacies at my disposal. Bacon – fried crisp and brittle – I had never known bacon to be so good. In Europe, the bacon was fried only slightly and retained its fat and a stringy consistency. Toast was something I had read about in articles about America but had never tasted and I loved it. The greatest taste sensation was the juice. Tropical fruits were so rare when I had been at home in Vienna that no one would have dreamed of just squeezing out the juice – that would have seemed an awful waste.

This was the first time in my life I had an unlimited amount of food at my disposal, even when there were no food shortages, when there was a full table at my parents' home, even in Karlsbad when I spent the summers with my Tante Lotte. I had always been restricted to "the proper amount" at the dinner table. When my father took me to the Konditorei, or sweet shop, in Vienna, I was allowed to select one piece of cake, two at the most. I was used to restrictions, to "keeping within the limits," to carefully selecting only small amounts, and to controlling my desire that I always had the feeling someone would tap me on the shoulder and say, "That's enough."

And now suddenly I was able to eat and order as much as I wanted of anything I wanted. It took me a while to get used to it.

Every day I learned something new, such as the secret of eating grapefruit without squirting juice all over my face. When, on rare occasions, my mother served us grapefruit, she just cut it in half and left us to the task of somehow or other digging the flesh out of the fruit with a spoon. The secret of the grapefruit knife was unknown to us. On the ship the grapefruit came beautifully cut in sections and eating it was a breeze. How I wished I could tell my mother about it. American steaks, roast beef, and lamb had also been on the "unknown" list. And ice cream. We had had ice cream at home, but while it contained ice, it had no cream and I couldn't get enough of this new taste sensation.

The days went by, one by one. The passengers made friends, exchanged experiences, photographs, and addresses if they knew where they were going to be after arrival in America. We sat on deck if the weather permitted and were pampered by the stewards. In the evenings we congregated in the ship's salon to listen to an orchestra play popular tunes, to dance, and to reminisce. Then – I think it was the evening before we were scheduled to arrive in New York – the master of ceremonies arranged a talent night and I was asked to sing. I chose a song which had been written for me by a young composer who had hoped that I could make the song a hit on one of my radio shows. I had sung the song, and it did create immediate audience response. It told the story of a little boy named Peter who cries bitter tears because someone broke his favorite doll. The song's refrain went like this:

> No more crying, little Peter,
> Let me hold you and be still.
> You'll have many trying hours
> When your life seems all uphill;
> Then we cannot always be weeping
> We must do though we don't care
> Therefore, cheer up, little Peter,
> May your dreams be sweet and fair.

In the salon of the ship Volendam I sang with much feeling. The song expressed the fate which had befallen so many of us. So much had been broken and destroyed in our lives, yet we had to go on as if nothing had happened. In this lovely ship's salon, fresh flowers everywhere, good food, and luxurious comfort surrounding us, we carried on and laughed and sang and made conversation. But deep down inside our hearts, most of us were deeply aware that we were tossed out to the periphery by life's cruel carousel – spinning, spinning, and spewed out this way and that, and few of us knew how and where we would end up.

On the last day of the voyage, a seagull alighted on the railing not far from where I stood, straining to see land. A seagull from America! All day the passengers lined the railings, some in happy anticipation of seeing their loved ones after a long absence from home – some, as I, with a growing nervousness and apprehension.

Out of the mist a shoreline appeared, dotted with houses, lawns, trees, and wide stretches of vacant land. The excitement among the passengers swelled to a universal gasp and exclamations in many tongues.

"There she is, look over there! Just like I saw her in the movies: the Statue of Liberty." Tears began to flow and passengers embraced each other at the sight of the symbol of freedom. Many stood quite still, their eyes riveted on the statue, thinking perhaps, as I did, of those unfortunate ones who did not have a chance to escape the horrors that all of us were convinced were about to descend upon Europe.

The ship docked in Hoboken. We were told to come into the dining room for customs Inspection. At a long table several men were sitting ready to inspect our passports. I could not help but remember my two last encounters with passport control, one at the Czech border and the other one at the dock in Rotterdam. I wondered: would this one be as nerve-wracking? I waited in line until my name was called. I stepped forward and handed my passport to the blue-clad officer. He looked at the visa, turned his gaze at me again and said: "Charlotte Kraus?"

"Yes, I replied.

"Where are you going?"

"Miami."

"Oh," he said, "very nice place this time of year. Is anyone waiting for you?"

"Yes."

"How much money do you have?" he asked.

"Twenty dollars."

"You mean that's all?"

"Yes."

"How are you going to Miami on that kind of money?"

"I have the ticket, and I have friends."

"Ah," then after a short pause: "Welcome to America." I could have kissed him. It was such a wonderful feeling to be treated like a human being by a government official. It set the tone for my judgment of America. If I later encountered things that shocked me, well – that's another story. But when I arrived I was greeted with friendliness that made me feel welcome.

"You may debark," I heard the official say. Then he added, "Good luck."

8

It was cold. The sun could not warm the icy air, and I was glad that I wore a warm coat, boots, gloves, and a hat that covered my ears. My luggage was delivered to the dock area where huge letters on the wall denoted the alphabetical location that coincided with the first letter of my last name. I went to "K." There I found Raymond Bring's sister and niece waiting for me. They seemed slightly flustered at having been assigned the task of getting me to Pennsylvania Station where I was to board a train with the romantic name "Orange Blossom Special." They were also disturbed at the amount of money a taxi drive from Hoboken, New Jersey, to Pennsylvania Station would cost.

I had my first look at the Wonder City from that taxi window. I was surprised to see that the streets were littered and that the people on the streets were poorly dressed and looked exactly like people anywhere, but the houses of red brick were of a style I had not seen in Europe. But then we crossed a river, which I later learned was the Hudson, and the architecture changed; the buildings were made of concrete and steel. The people also changed. The closer we got to Pennsylvania Station, the more prosperous the people on the crowded streets seemed to look. I longed to see skyscrapers and Broadway but only caught a fleeting glimpse of both as the taxi moved through the heavy traffic.

The ride took a long time, but the women didn't say much. They didn't ask me anything and I felt slightly uncomfortable. When we arrived at the railroad station, I paid the for the taxi. It was three dollars, I had seventeen dollars left.

I was hungry.

"Where might I have a bite to eat?" I asked.

"At the Savarin Coffee Shop," one of the women replied.

We went to the coffee shop and sat at the counter. The ladies suggested that I order a sandwich (twenty cents) and a cup of coffee (five cents). I could see that they were worried that they might have to pay for it. They themselves refused to eat anything because they planned to eat at home. They sat while I ate. It was just like two guards watching a prisoner, and I had the feeling that they wanted to get rid of me as soon as possible.

When it was time to get on the train, everything was confusing – the huge station, the milling crowds, the voice of the train announcer coming over the loudspeaker. It all seemed ten times bigger than anything in Europe. For the first time I felt uncertain and frightened.

I had a Pullman reservation. The ladies exchanged glances. They couldn't understand how someone with an expensive Pullman sleeper reservation could only have seventeen dollars cash. My porter arrived with my luggage, and I wondered why he seemed slightly familiar to me. Ah. yes, of course – the movies. Most American movies I had seen had porters in them. I gave him a ten cent tip. The two ladies waved good-bye. I could almost hear their sighs of relief.

I settled back and began to think of Raymond. What would he look like? Had he changed? Had I changed? I remembered the tender moments we had shared. I felt warm and relaxed at the thought of having him waiting for me. Perhaps it would be as if we had never been separated, perhaps even a love which did not have time to develop fully would now unfold and bring me happiness. I looked at his photograph and longed to see him. But first I had to get to Miami.

Throughout my life many women have been kind and helpful. The lady sitting opposite me on the train to Miami was one of those women. So I had a friend who interpreted and helped me. She accompanied me to the dining car, and assisted me in choosing the proper food at inexpensive prices.

While I had no trouble understanding my new found American travel companion who spoke slowly and distinctly, I simply could not understand the waiter in the dining car. At breakfast, I asked for a "cooked" egg and he shook his head. He said something which I tried desperately to interpret until my friend said, "Do you mean boiled in water?"

"Yes, yes, boiled four minutes in water."

When the waiter had gone, I asked in a whisper, "Does he speak English?"

"Yes, he does, but he speaks with a Southern accent."

I could see that there would be some linguistic difficulties ahead of me.

The sleeping car with its upper and lower berths and swaying curtains were very familiar to me, just as the porter had been. The movies again. How many American films had I seen in which those berths played an important part? Countless Sunday afternoons I had watched Harold Lloyd, Buster Keaton, and other American film stars get into comical trouble. I remembered the hilarious scenes of confusion when innocent maidens behind the curtains of the sleeper berths suddenly found themselves face to face with the horn-rimmed, straw-hatted Harold Lloyd, who had escaped from lions; what innocent fun we had way back in those days when Hollywood knew how to make people laugh without four-letter words.

****

I arrived in Miami in the early afternoon. The sky was blue, the sun shone on the tropical palm trees, and I was dressed as one dresses in New York City on January 11. Confidently I bid my travel companion goodbye, fully expecting to find Raymond waiting for me. There I stood on the station platform with my suitcase, hat box, and huge steamer trunk. Slowly all the passengers dispersed, and I still stood there, all alone.

I was afraid to call Raymond because one of the most difficult things to master in any foreign country is the telephone. When you see a person's face and mouth you can understand a language with which you are not thoroughly familiar. However, when that voice comes out of an impersonal box and reaches only your ear, a foreign language becomes a terror. Furthermore, I was afraid to leave my pile of luggage. Even worse, I didn't even know what kind of money to use for the telephone call. With all the confidence and courage I had been able to muster up until now, this was one of the moments when my self-composure left me and tears came. "This is a fine situation," I chided myself, "he has forgotten you are coming. Maybe he is ignoring your arrival. You stupid thing, how could you ever rely on a promise? God only knows what is going to happen now."

Then the station master came up to me. I easily identified him because he was the same red cap that was worn by station masters in Austria.

"Anything wrong?" he asked, "Can I help you?"

"I am waiting for Mr. Raymond Bring, he owns the Hotel El Mirasol," I replied. The station master asked if I had five cents to make a phone call. I opened my purse, and he showed me which coin to use.

"I will watch your luggage," he said, "but don't worry, nobody is going to take it."

I went to the phone and dialed the number which he had found in the phone book for me.

"I would like to speak to Mr. Bring," I said.

The voice on the other end said, "He is not here; he went to the station to pick someone up."

I wondered if that meant "fetch."

"What shall I do," I asked.

"Stay there and wait," was the reply.

At that moment, he arrived. "Ah, there you are. I went to the wrong station," he said, and he gave me a quick kiss. He seemed slightly embarrassed.

"Have I changed?" I wondered to myself. "Perhaps I look funny to him in my winter clothes and perhaps, he remembers me looking differently."

He spoke to me in German. "We will go to my hotel where you will be my guest for the next week while you get acclimated. After that, a job is waiting for you as a governess to a little girl from Chicago. Her parents are very rich hat manufacturers. Radoff is their name."

"Do you speak English?" he asked.

"Yes, I do."

I looked at him out of the corner of my eye. He was brown from the sun and looked as elegant as he did when I had met him in Salzburg. We rode in his car which was driven by the hotel chauffeur. I felt the heat of the day. I also felt a certain coolness in Raymond. I realized that he was concerned lest I expected to be taken care of financially. He very quickly told me that this was the beginning of the high season in Miami Beach, that every hotel room had been reserved, that this was the time when every hotel and business in Florida had to make all the money they could expect to make, and that the most he could do for me would be to let me stay in a hotel room for a few days.

He was a very different Raymond Bring from the one I had known in Salzburg. Clearly he had bitten off more than he could chew, this lawyer turned hotel-keeper. I felt a bit embarrassed by his defensive attitude, yet at the same time I was grateful for his help, not only in escaping from Europe but also for transplanting me to one of the most beautiful and luxurious places in America.

Once we got to the hotel, he showed me to my room. After he left, I rang for the maid. When she appeared I asked if I could iron my dresses.

"What yo say?"

"Iron, I want to iron."

"Ah cain't unnestan."

I laid out a dress on the table and made the motions of ironing.

"Oh, ai knows now – yous wanna press yo clothes."

"I wonder what language this is," I thought as she reappeared with an iron and an ironing board.

A little later, I decided to take a bath. In the bathroom, I was confronted with a puzzling piece of equipment – a curtain hanging on a rod over the tub. "I wonder what that's for?" I thought, "Maybe someone, will come into the bathroom while I am taking a shower and that curtain is to hide me." I pulled it over to conceal myself. Then I began to shower. Streams of water descended on the floor, a flood began to spread toward the door and I had to use the towels to wipe up the miniature lake. Funny people, these Americans.

After I got dressed for the dinner to which Raymond said he would escort me, I waited for the telephone to ring. When it did, I asked him to come up because I needed to ask him a crucial question. I think he was a little worried. I took him into the bathroom and asked, "What is this curtain for?" "Oh my goodness," he said with relief. "That curtain goes inside the tub to keep the water from running on the floor."

We went to a little restaurant where we met Raymond's brother, Noel. It was crowded, hot, sticky, and smelled of fried fish, decidedly not elegant.

"It's cheap," Raymond said, as if he read my thoughts, "but we are not doing so well and have to save money."

He handed me the menu and described the dishes listed. Breaded veal cutlet, he explained, was the closest thing to wiener schnitzel. I ordered it. But first there was a surprise: fruit cocktail made of canned fruit. I politely put it aside for dessert since I was not used to eating fruit as a first course. Then came the real shocker: veal cutlet smothered in tomato sauce. That was culinary high treason. Carefully, I scraped off every last vestige of the sauce. Everyone was drinking coffee with their meal, another custom foreign to me. "Southern cooking," Raymond explained. "You'll get used to it."

A country's cuisine is part of its culture and what you have eaten in your mother's kitchen, what you have been served in your own country's restaurants, the recipes you have learned to prepare when you learned how to cook, become part of your own personality and your own traditions. It is very difficult for immigrants to get used to an entirely different set of taste combinations. This accounts for stores selling foreign foods, restaurants serving foreign foods, and cookbooks specializing in foreign cuisines.

Back in the late 1930s, I often encountered Americans who deeply resented my longing for the foods of my native land. I was often reminded that being now in America, I should forget Austria and everything connected with it and become "an American." People who couldn't converse in any language but their own wherever they might travel, reminded me that I should not only learn to speak "American" but should also, as soon as possible, "lose my accent." Whenever I ate a typically American dish many eyes would focus on me to observe how I liked it. If I showed the slightest hesitancy, my companions could not conceal their annoyance with me.

That first evening some friends of Raymond's wanted to meet the newcomer from Europe, so we met with them somewhere in a hotel garden where they ordered rum and Coca-Cola for me. Everyone watched as I took the first sip. It tasted horrible to me, and I could barely swallow it. Politely, I let the drink sit there for the remainder of the evening without touching it.

"Come on, drink up," I was urged, "it'll make you feel happy."

Clearly, I was regarded as something of an oddball for not "drinking up." When I requested lemonade, I obviously embarrassed Raymond.

****

With my arrival in Miami Beach, I realized that the style of living I had been used to all my life was nothing like that which now lay before me. There was a wealth and luxury very different from that in Karlsbad. Everything was on a bigger scale, louder and more colorful. Large hotels, wide boulevards, big automobiles, miles and miles of beach swarming with bathers, and the palm trees with electric lights concealed in their gracefully swaying crowns indicated that everyone seemed to have a lot of money and to be spending it freely.

I had one week to be a lady of leisure, then my job would put me in the working class. Raymond continued to keep at a safe distance from me. He was polite and mildly interested in my reactions to my new life, but I knew he was determined to show me that if there had been any more than a friendly interest on his part in Vienna before his departure, it had been of a fleeting nature. My pride was hurt, but I realized that time had passed and we both had changed. He was very anxious to be "accepted" as an American; his English had improved dramatically and he associated exclusively with Americans. My presence reminded him of a past he would have much rather forgotten. Like so many intellectual immigrant bachelors, he was looking for the "big chance" – a rich American woman who could give him the financial security which would take him years to achieve were he to work for it in a profession.

****

After one week, it was time to begin my job as a governess. I met my employers, Mr. and Mrs. Radoff, and their six-year-old daughter Janet on Monday morning. Their apartment, one of about twenty in Noel Bring's El Mirasol Apartment Hotel, had a living-dining room, one bathroom, and two bedrooms, one for the parents and one for the child.

Mr. Radoff had immigrated from Russia with his parents when he was a small child. Although the Radoffs were Jewish, they seemed to know very little about Hitler's persecution of the Jews in Germany and Austria, and when I began to tell them about it, they cut me off quickly saying: "There is nothing we can do about it."

It amazed me that a surprising number of Jewish winter residents of Miami Beach believed or wanted to believe that the horror stories coming out of Europe were exaggerated, and because it evidently made them feel uncomfortable, they avoided the subject. Many times I was asked, "Did you see it with your own eyes?" or "How can you prove that this it true?" Knowing what I knew, I felt alternatingly furious and frustrated. "If they don't believe – who would?" I thought.

The Radoffs seemed perturbed and somewhat flustered at the kind of "help" they had engaged and didn't quite know how to treat me. They gave me no privacy. I slept in a corner of attic space where they had a folding cot for me. My clothes were hung up on nails protruding from the rafters.

Mrs. Radoff asked me if I could speak English well enough to answer the telephone. While I had no difficulties conversing in English face to face, speaking on the telephone was another matter. But I told her I thought I could. Then I was asked if I could cook. "Yes," I replied.

"All right, we will have lamb chops for dinner," Mrs. Radoff said.

Mrs. Radoff went shopping and came home with twelve lamb chops. We were only four, so I asked if she expected guests. She didn't but told me to cook them all. She showed me how to set the table in the tiny dining area. She told me to set the table for three.

"You will eat in the kitchen."

There was no room for a chair in the miniature kitchen.

"You can stand up while you eat, they all do."

I wondered who "they" were. I was not, as yet, as toughened by the hard knocks of my new life as I would become later. The tears mixed quickly with the lamb chop juice that I poured over the platter which I carried to the table. They each ate two chops. Six came back to the kitchen. I ate one. That left five. I asked Mrs. Radoff for a container to keep them in the refrigerator for the next day.

"We don't eat leftovers," was her reply. So, the five beautiful lamb chops went into the garbage can while I wept some more for the hungry people who would have been so happy to have them, for the people in concentration camps, and for the sinful ignorance of my new employers.

My new job was not exactly that of governess, as I had been told. I was simply a maid of all work. There was laundry to be done by hand every day, there were dishes to be washed, beds to be made, floors to be wiped, the bathroom to be cleaned. In the afternoons I had to take Janet to the beach. She was a very vivacious child, into everything, and not easily controlled. She didn't mind me, perhaps with my modest vocabulary I was not able to tell her what to do and what not to do. She simply ignored me. She came home covered with mud from head to toe. I was held responsible.

One morning Mrs. Radoff told me to squeeze some orange juice. I didn't know how to use the squeezer.

"I thought I had someone to take the work off my hands, but if I have to show you everything, I may as well do it myself," complained my employer.

After that, I thought I'd be smart and squeeze the orange juice the night before. She came into the kitchen and saw me doing it.

"No, No, No! It has to be squeezed daily. My, you are dumb."

One evening when I came home from the beach with my small charge, Raymond, who had stayed away, was standing in the yard talking to a tall blonde.

"This is Hildegarde," he said, introducing us to each other, "and this is Lotte Kraus. She just arrived from Vienna and has a job now as governess." Hildegarde was to be yet another link in the chain of fine women who helped me.

Hildegarde, he explained, was a famous singer, a chansonette, who had sung in Paris and London and who spoke German. She eyed me curiously and asked me if I was happy to be in America."

"Yes, but I am a singer like you and I yearn to sing. Would you be happy having to wash dishes and scrub floors, when all you want is to sing?"

"Oh, Lotte!" she replied sympathetically. "I'll talk to my manager, Anna Sosenko, about this."

Hildegarde, her full name was Hildegarde von Sell, was at the threshold of her meteoric ascent to fame and fortune when I met her in Miami Beach. In France she would have been called a diseuse – a singer who relies on interpretation and delivery more than on the quality of voice and technique.

She was born in Milwaukee of German-Danish descent and because her first language was German, she had a slight accent which, so she later told me, had made it difficult for her to find work on the American stage. Therefore, she did what so many other artists had found it necessary to do: she left her native land and went to Europe.

In the nightclubs of Paris and London she was a sensation and had among her admirers the King of Sweden and Edward, Prince of

Wales. She was a superb pianist and accompanied herself on the piano while wearing long black gloves, which became her trademark. Her songs were written especially for her – by some well known composers and some by Anna, her shadow who never left her side. Sosenko wrote the song – "Darling, je vous aime beaucoup" – which catapulted Hildy, as she called her, to the top of her profession.

When I met them they had just returned from Europe and were about to establish their foothold in America with an engagement in an exclusive club in Miami Beach. They had rented an apartment in the very El Mirasol Apartment Hotel where I worked.

The two of them came up with quite a plan for me. Hildegarde called the radio station WKAT and the magic of her name was the "Sesame" which opened the doors and got me an audition.

She asked what I was going to sing. I ran to my suitcase where I had some of the sheet music I had brought with me from Vienna, then downstairs again swiftly, unobserved by my employer. Hildegarde took one look, "You have to have something more up to date, wait here." She disappeared into her apartment and reappeared in a minute with a piece of sheet music, Cole Porter's "Heart and Soul," and told me to learn it by the next day.

When I told Mrs. Radoff that I would like to have a couple of hours off the next afternoon, she was annoyed. But when she heard that Hildegarde was involved in the plan, she was all smiles. "Oh, why didn't you say so in the first place? Bring her up!"

Mrs. Radoff melted having the "incomparable Hildegarde" right in her living room. Hildegarde explained that I would have to go to an audition tomorrow at two. Mrs. Radoff's enthusiasm dwindled to zero.

"I am paying her ten dollars a week and she is off on private business," she lamented.

"Let her go just this once," Hildegarde said, "I am going with her to accompany her."

Mrs. Radoff gave in.

The next day Anna drove us to the radio station because Hildegarde had never learned to drive. In New York they had their own chauffeur. Once we arrived at the radio station, we had no time for rehearsal; instead we depended upon each other's professionalism and feeling for music.

Among professionals, music is the perfect international bond of communication. Even language takes a back seat to music. And Hildegarde was a true professional, a trooper who was able to rise to any musical emergency. Her willingness to accompany me on the piano not only then, but also on several other occasions during the Miami season, was a testimony to the compassion and kindness which she was always ready to give to other musicians in need.

The studio was open, the piano was ready, the microphone was waiting. I stepped up to it, I saw the technician in the control room: it was all very familiar and I was at home. "To sing again, to perform, show them what you can do, make them feel the emotion, even if they can't understand the words. To make them feel it . . . ," I thought, "This is where I belong."

I sang and Hildegarde played for me with absolutely perfect support. She anticipated exactly what I wanted, instinctively pausing when I wanted to pause. We made a perfect team.

The station manager came into the studio. "We cannot pay you anything," he said, "but we would like you to sing for us twice a week."

I could not understand. "Then, how can you ever have programs?" I asked perplexed.

"Sponsors," he said.

I had never heard of sponsors. He explained that sponsors buy radio time and talent. Strange country! But I didn't care, pay or no pay, all I wanted was to be able to sing again. It would make my Cinderella role more tolerable.

Hildegarde had to hurry off to her own rehearsal and I decided to take the bus back home. The bus was fully occupied in the front. Every seat taken, so I proceeded to the rear. The bus driver stopped the bus, "Lady, get back here, you're not supposed to be in the rear."

I was comfortably seated in the rear. "Why?" I asked.

"Lady!" he was very stern, "you come here to the front, the rear is for colored only."

Then I saw that white people were in the front and a few blacks in the rear of the bus. Like a bad dream, the past emerged before my eyes: "Jews are not allowed"; on park benches, "only for Aryans"; in shops, "We only serve Aryans, Jews not allowed in this shop"; in restaurants, "Juden nicht erwünscht," Jews not wanted. Then I remembered seeing signs in the public rest rooms: "White only,

Colored not allowed." These had been in the restaurants, hotels, and once, when Raymond had taken me to the movies, I saw "Whites downstairs, blacks upstairs."

"Where is the difference?" I wondered. "One excludes the Jews, the other excludes the people who have black skin." I had not had the time nor the awareness to notice before. "I would like to sit here," I said to the bus driver.

"I am going to throw you off the bus!," he said menacingly, "you get back here or you get off the bus."

Everyone turned to look at me. Slowly I got up and went to the front. I knew that tone of voice; I had heard it before. It is the voice of brutality, better not provoke it, better comply. But is this what I came here for? It was something I did not understand.

****

The first question upon meeting anyone was, "Are you Jewish?" This seemed to be of the utmost importance to all I came in contact with. It was a point of confusion and consternation to my employers, the Radoffs, that I, a Catholic, had found it necessary to escape from the Nazis. "Only Jews do that," was the usual comment, "How come you?" When I was asked that question I asked, "Why the interest?" The answer was usually a shrug.

The bus trip and its incident concerning the location of my seating brought a new focus to the paradox of a country which kept its borders open to immigration and at the same time nurtured or permitted prejudice toward minorities. It takes a foreigner many years of living in America to come to an understanding of the undercurrents and complexities of the "Melting Pot."

****

Having returned to the Radoff's kitchen, Cinderella thought of ways to break the news of the radio job to her employers. Would they let her go singing twice a week? Mrs. Radoff said she didn't see how I could combine two jobs; in fact, she thought I should quit being a maid.

"But I don't get paid at the radio station, I'd starve if I didn't work during the day."

"Take your choice," said Mrs. Radoff.

I called Raymond. "Sorry," he said, "I did my part in making it possible for you to come to America. I must rent rooms now. It's the high season and I must make money!"

Dejectedly, I went to the beach with little Janet. I could not restrain myself any longer, I buried my face in my arms and wept. I felt a slight tap on my shoulder. Looking up, I saw a young woman standing by my side. I remembered that I had met her during the first few days after my arrival. She had been introduced to me by the brothers Bring, who were unaware that they were once again connecting me with another helpful and generous woman. But my first few days had been so full of new impressions that I had completely forgotten her.

"What's wrong?"

"Oh, everything is wrong," I sobbed.

"Tell me."

I told her everything.

She introduced herself again, "My name is Marian."

"Mine is Lotte Kraus."

"Yes, I know."

Marian was in Miami Beach with her parents. She was profoundly bored because she didn't know anyone and had no chance to meet young people. Her parents were wealthy (it seemed to me there were only wealthy people living in Miami Beach). They lived in a suite in one of the luxury hotels along the beach front.

"I think I can help you," she said; it was curious to watch her face when she talked because it was completely motionless. Only her mouth moved, her eyes, nose, cheeks, forehead seemed to be made of wax. I wondered what was wrong with her. Then I discovered the reason: she had layer upon layer of make-up on her face, her eyelashes were thick with mascara, her eyes rimmed in black, her eyebrows shaved and penciled in dark and heavy, her cheeks had a rosy sheen, and her lips were ruby red. She had long finger nails, ruby red, too. She was fully dressed in long pants and a blouse with a scarf tied around her neck. Not one piece of flesh was showing.

"I hate the sun," she said. "My parents pay forty dollars a day for their suite." The Alamac Hotel knows they are important. I will tell the manager to let you sing tonight." I had Janet with me. "Don't worry," said Marian, "I know several baby sitters. They will watch Janet, you come with me."

Without so much as a moment's hesitation she marched me into the hotel and to the manager's office. She told him the story of this displaced Viennese singer and what a sensation it would be for him to have her sing in his floor show. Marian would call the newspapers and tell them about my first appearance in America. It would do wonders for the reputation of his hotel. I listened, amazed at the glib flow of words from the lips of a woman who knew me only slightly. This would be impossible in Austria.

This was my first lesson in how to sell a product, and here the product was me. It worked. He said he was fully booked, but this was an unusual opportunity and I should be at the hotel at nine o'clock that evening.

Marian didn't seem surprised. "Sophisticated psychology," she said, "remember you must always use psychology. Figure out what the other person will react to favorably and then give it to them."

I had never used psychology.

She expanded on the topic. "For instance," she said, "You must use psychology when you deal with men," she instructed. "You are too direct. Everything you think shows immediately on your face, this is no good. Keep your face closed up, think about the effect you want to achieve, then act accordingly, but never, never be impulsive."

No money had been discussed with the hotel. Marian said that would come later. When we retrieved Janet, I asked Marian to come along because I didn't know how to ask my employers to let me go out at night. She used her psychology again. First, she introduced herself and told Mrs. Radoff that her parents were staying in an expensive suite at the hotel. Then, she told her that I had a chance to sing at the hotel and that Mrs. Radoff would certainly become known as a great patron of the arts and a benefactor of this young exile from Nazi Germany. Mrs. Radoff made a sour face.

Marian then offered to stay with Janet because she felt it was so important for me to sing before an American audience that night. Mrs. Radoff couldn't accept that offer and said she would stay home herself and wait for me to come back as soon as the singing was over. At that point, Marian said she was sure her parents would be delighted to meet Mrs. Radoff and Mr. Radoff and wouldn't they stop by their suite tomorrow for a drink. Marian said she would come for me at 8:30 in her car because I must be dressed to the hilt for the occasion. She smiled sweetly to Mrs. Radoff and left. I went into the kitchen to cook dinner. There was an ominous silence in the apartment. When Mr. Radoff came in a few minutes later, Mrs. Radoff asked him to come with her to the bedroom. They reappeared silently, never spoke one word to me. When I had cleared away the dishes and washed them, they said, "You can get dressed now."

I went to my attic and fished my evening gown out of my suitcase. I asked if I could use the iron. I ironed my gown and coat and asked to use the bathroom for a few minutes to take a bath and put on make up. When I reappeared, I was dressed as I had been when I played the role of Gloria in the operetta in Czechoslovakia. I wore a long powder blue taffeta gown with wide skirt and low neckline and pink taffeta coat. My hair was down and fell in soft curls to my shoulders. I had put on make-up and wore the glittering costume necklace and earrings I used to wear on stage. Cinderella emerged from the ashes of the hearth to go to the ball.

Mrs. Radoff took one look at me and said: "I am sorry, but you are fired." I had expected her to be surprised, but I did not expect this.

"I hired a maid, not a princess," she said. "You are of no use to me. Tomorrow you pack your things and get out. I need someone to cook and clean and stay home. I don't need someone who obviously is not used to that kind of work. You'll have to go."

I didn't know what to do or say. I had no place to go. I had no money except my first week's pay of ten dollars. In this desperate frame of mind, I was to go to the hotel and sing. At that crucial moment Marian arrived. The Radoffs minced no words. "She's fired," they repeated. "Look at her; is this a maid?"

Once again, Marian used psychology. "Can we let that wait until tomorrow? She has to sing now. If she's upset she won't be able to sing."

"I couldn't care less," said Mrs. Radoff as we left the room.

The room where I was to sing was crowded, filled with smoke, chatter, and loud music. The pianist, who had been alerted by Marian, was waiting for my sheet music. Because we had no time to rehearse, I had misgivings about his ability to accompany me correctly. I chose the song Hildegarde had taught me to sing as well as a lovely song titled "Jubilate" and "Two Hearts in 3/4 Time."

"And now, ladies and gentlemen, we have a special treat for you. This afternoon a young lady whose parents live here in the hotel brought us a young woman who escaped Hitler's hordes when they invaded Austria. She gave up her singing career to come to America to find the freedom and opportunities she was denied in her homeland. Ladies and gentlemen, we want you to welcome a lovely, young Viennese – Lotte Kraus."

Lights, fanfare, applause, silence. The piano played the introduction; I sang. Everything unpleasant, discouraging and sad fell away from me. I sang and my voice called out to the audience to listen, to feel with me, to accept what I longed to give them. It is the most wonderful feeling for an artist to have the audience fall silent and attentive, to hold their hearts in the palm of your hand, to know that they are with you and are waiting for every tone, every word, every nuance you are able to give.

I didn't need to tell them what I sang, they knew. They also sensed that this was not just another performance, but that this was a test to prove to myself that I could hold an American audience, and one of the most difficult audiences at that – a nightclub audience. The applause was my reward. I could have sung many more songs, but I felt it better to go when I was riding the crest.

Marian was ecstatic. She had indeed notified the Miami press, and reporters were there. When she saw that I had very little experience in talking to the press, Marian acted as my press agent. The result was a fantastic – if untrue – story in the next day's *Miami Daily Herald*, informing the readership that a new star had been born last night, a young Austrian who had only recently crossed the Atlantic in the steerage of a ship as a stowaway!!

There was some truth in the article. I had been a maid of all work and was discovered crying on the beach. I marveled at the imagination of the Miami press. But stardom or not, my immediate concern was where I would sleep the next night. For when I returned to the Radoffs' apartment, I was told that I had to leave the next morning.

That was one instance where Marian's psychology failed. Well, not quite. Before she left that night, she said casually, "What about Hildegarde?"

The next morning. I called Hildegarde and told her everything. Without a moment's hesitation, she offered her own apartment as a temporary refuge. Hildegarde, who at one time had a tough time of it herself and who was deeply religious, felt it to be her Christian duty to help a fellow human being.

"As long as I am in Miami," she said "you can stay here." It was a promise. Well-intended as I knew it was, I knew I would soon have to search for a home, a place to belong. Would I ever find it?

The atmosphere of Miami Beach, with its wealth and luxury on the one hand and my own lack of income on the other, made me acutely aware of the chasm existing between those who were securely anchored in home and job, and someone like myself, who had nothing to hold onto – deserted by those I had relied upon. It's one thing to be somewhere as a guest, to be welcomed and entertained knowing when it's all over you will return to your home, to your roots, to you family. It is quite another thing for the immigrant who knows there is no turning back. This is it, brother, you had better get out there and fight! Fight for survival, fight for food, fight for a roof over your head, fight for acceptance, fight competition, fight language barriers, fight the ridicule which often comes your way because you are so different.

Hildegarde and Anna, from some mysterious depth of their souls, or perhaps from their own experiences in Paris, understood my pain when I sat in their living room that day I left the Radoffs.

Wonderful Hildegarde spent hours coaching me on American ways. "You have to learn some new American songs. Here, I will select some for you. Sit at the piano and study. If you want to sing in hotels and night clubs, you must have a repertoire the audience will understand. You can't give them classical songs by Schubert and Brahms, they don't want that. A few Viennese waltzes thrown in, all right, but only a few. Don't worry about food, we have enough, but you need to change your attitude."

Mondays, Wednesdays, and Fridays had been selected for my radio appearances. Hildegarde, incognito, accompanied me at the piano. After the first week of singing songs by Cole Porter and Jerome Kern, the radio station found a sponsor for me: Butler's Shoe

Store. I did not know what the acquisition of a sponsor entailed and was puzzled and slightly annoyed when, after I had finished with my first song, an announcer stepped to the microphone and began to expound the virtues of the latest styles in shoes. I wondered how he could do that. Anna Sosenko tried to explain to me that Butler's Shoe Store had bought my program.

"They will pay you ten dollars a week for those interruptions," Anna attempted to clarify. I shook my head. I was used being paid by the Government Radio Station in Vienna. Commercial radio was totally unknown to me.

Hildegarde's engagements in Miami Beach ended and with them ended her hospitality to me. Before she left, she talked to Walter Jacobs, owner of the Alamac Hotel where I had sung that first night. "Let her sing at your hotel and find her a place to sleep. She has no one else to help her. You'll do me a personal favor if you will look out for her."

Jacobs said that he would pay me five dollars a night if I would sing for three nights a week. Unfortunately, he could not offer me a room.

Hildegarde phoned Raymond. "Do you know what your friend, Lotte Kraus, is doing, or don't you care?" she asked point blank. "She has been staying with me, but now I have an engagement at the Savoy Plaza Hotel in New York, and I want to know that she will not sit on the street when I am gone."

Raymond had, of course, known that I was staying with Hildegarde. He knew everything. But he acted as if he didn't know. "She can stay here for a few nights," he said, meaning his hotel, "but I can't guarantee for how long, this is our big season, you know."

I had no choice. I moved into a room at the Bring hotel with my huge steamer trunk, my suitcase and my hat box. The third night at eleven forty-five, when I had already gone to bed, the house phone rang. "Your room is rented," said a voice on the phone. "You will please vacate the room immediately."

I was stunned, "Now, in the middle of the night?"

"Yes, now. I am sending up the bus boy for your luggage." There was nothing for me to do. I packed and went down to the lobby. Noel Bring was there looking arrogant and hostile.

"We have done what we could," he said abruptly. "From now on, you are on your own; please don't bother us again."

"May I leave my luggage here while I go looking for a place to sleep?" I asked.

"No." He called the bell boy who loaded the steamer trunk, the suitcase and my hatbox on a dolly.

"Where to?" asked the boy.

"To the Alamac Hotel." It was only a short distance. Walter Jacobs was still there. I told him my tale of woe. "America, America you are not what I had envisioned you to be; I have freedom, yes, but I am stranded in the middle of the night, in a strange city and I do not know where to find a place to sleep," I sobbed.

He was sorry, but the hotel was full.

Then he said he had an idea. He disappeared and came back saying that he had contacted a man who would find me a place to sleep. That man appeared in a few minutes.

Walter introduced us, "Ray Redman, this is Lotte Kraus from Vienna. Leave your luggage here and go with Ray. He has a room for you."

Mr. Redman, about thirty-five, with a face like a dried prune, black mustache, eyeglasses, ill-fitting suit and very dirty fingernails, motioned me to follow him. We drove in his beat up car to an old frame house on the outskirts of town.

Redman approached a door and opened it. "You can sleep in there," he said. "Tomorrow I'll find you something better."

There were four beds in a small dark room and no light except from a street lamp, and three of the beds were occupied. I was out of that room in a flash. I ran outside and saw Redman get into his car.

"Wait, wait!" I screamed. "I cannot sleep in this house! What do you take me for? I'd rather sleep on a bench on the beach."

Redman got out of the car. "What do you want me to do?"

In a few words I described to him, as best I could, my relationship to the two Bring brothers.

We drove back to town and to the Bring hotel.

"Wait here," Redman said.

In a few minutes he came out. "They'll take you in for one more night. I'll pick you up tomorrow morning at eight." He disappeared into the night. The night clerk at the reception desk handed me a key.

It was a miserable room; it must have been a room for emergency service personnel. But it had a bed and was clean. I wearily got my clothes off and was asleep in minutes.

When I awoke the next morning, I thought of home. "I wonder what my mother would say if she knew." I didn't even want to think of the anguish my father would have in his heart if he knew how fate was buffeting me about. They would never believe it; nobody in Europe believed that it could be very difficult for an immigrant to survive the first months or even years. Most people who have a hard time are too proud to admit the struggle. They brag and paint a rosy picture and write glowing letters. Because I am a very bad liar, I didn't know what to write. Bad liar.

At eight o'clock the next morning, Mr. Ray Redman – rumpled suit, disheveled hair, chain smoking and nervous – was waiting for me in the lobby.

I was hungry and hoped that Mr. Redman would know a cheap place to have coffee and perhaps a piece of toast. I did not know who this Mr. Redman was, nor his profession nor his assignment. I was soon to find out.

Mr. Redman took me straight to the luxurious Roney Plaza Hotel, "the" hotel in Miami Beach. In the lobby of the beautiful hotel, with its oriental rugs, potted palms, mirrors, gilded chairs, crystal chandeliers, and reception clerks who looked like displaced Russian dukes, I was introduced to Mr. Jouffret, the hotel manager, who welcomed me and told me that he hoped I would find my stay there pleasant. I was, to put it mildly, speechless. But one look at Mr. Redman convinced me to follow his lead and so I thanked Mr. Jouffret graciously, assuring him that indeed I was certain my stay would be delightful. Then we went up the elevator and, following a busboy who held the room key, we entered a beautifully furnished ocean front suite with a bedroom, living room and bath.

I turned to Mr. Redman, "Can you explain?"

He fell into one of the chairs, stretched out his legs and told me to order breakfast, then he would explain. At his insistence, I ordered orange juice, scrambled eggs, bacon, cereal, toast, coffee. Redman was, so he told me, a promoter. This did not register with me, nor did his explanation that he was a press representative and public relations person. However when he said he was a personal manager,

I understood. He did some "work" for Walter Jacobs, and he had hired Redman to get me started in show business.

The man made me uneasy. He spoke a jargon I barely understood, he was furtive in his movements, and while he did nothing to make me feel physically threatened, he had a domineering attitude, which I later came to understand, was the attitude of many personal press representatives who believe they own their clients. Redman regarded himself as not only my press representative but also as my personal manager. With his instinct for news value, he foresaw that the story of "Cinderella, who came from the hearth to sing at the best hotels in Miami Beach," was one which could bring him the headlines he yearned for. I had never been exposed to press promotion and did not have the slightest idea what Redman's plans were. He had brought me to this hotel, I was treated like a star. All he had wanted, so far, was food, and I was certain I could protect myself against any impropriety, should he become amorous.

"Now," said Redman, who had eaten everything in sight, "we will talk business." He reclined on the couch and hung one leg over the side. "Tonight, you sing in the floor show, at nine and at twelve."

"Who is going to play for me?"

"Do you have music for the orchestra?"

"No. only for piano."

"That's bad, but," he shrugged, "it will have to do. What are you going to sing?"

I named some songs from my repertoire.

"Never heard of them." said Redman. "Don't you have something people know?"

It was clear he neither knew nor appreciated any kind of music. What I failed to realize, however, was that this was an indication of the taste of the average American nightclub audience, a misjudgment on my part which was my nemesis for several years.

"Will you arrange for a rehearsal with the pianist?" I asked.

He reluctantly got up and went to the door, then changed his mind and picked up the phone. He called the manager and asked for the pianist. He talked so rapidly I couldn't understand a word he said. But he did tell me to go downstairs in about an hour to rehearse with the pianist in the orchestra. Then he made a private call to his wife who lived, with his child, in a trailer outside Miami Beach. The thought that he had a family reassured me.

The piano was in the hotel nightclub, a dark and empty room. The pianist was a talented, friendly man of about fifty, who was thrilled to accompany a genuine Viennese. We selected three songs and two waltzes.

"You'll probably have to sing an encore," he cautioned. "Better get one more song ready." We decided on a song which he said everybody knew: "Vienna, City of My Dreams."

After that, I went to my room to rest. Redman had disappeared and I was alone. I took my shoes off, climbed on the bed and lay back, not realizing that I had left the door unlocked. So much had happened in three weeks. The cool reception from Raymond, the job that didn't work out, the radio station, Hildegarde, the night at the Atlantis Hotel, Marian – what in the name of heaven had ever happened to Marian? I found out later that she had gone to Chicago to meet her fiancé. And now, here I was in the Roney Plaza Hotel. I wondered what else could happen to top all the excitement of the past three weeks. Much, much more.

It was noon. Redman came into the room without knocking. "Mr. Redman, I don't like you to come in without knocking." "Who the hell, who do you think you are? If it weren't for me, you'd be sleeping out in the street somewhere."

I couldn't believe my ears. I didn't know how to respond to such insolence. Taking advantage of my meekness, he added, "The least you can do is order lunch for two. I get only five dollars a day from Jacobs for this job. I can't afford to buy lunches, so that's your responsibility." With that, he picked up the phone and ordered a huge lunch. All of a sudden I was not hungry. He ate every bit of the lunch for two.

He was excited that Walter Winchell was in the hotel. "I'll see that he gets you tonight and puts you in his column." There it was again – the strange language.

"I'm sorry, but who is Winchell, and where is he going to get me, and what is a column?" He looked at me as if he thought I were not quite right in the head.

"God!" he said. "Winchell? Winchell is just about the most important columnist! If he mentions you in his column, you are made."

"Nick Kenny is here too," he said, "and Milton Berle's mother. I'll introduce you. If she likes you she might introduce you to Milton, he does everything his mother tells him to do."

****

Money was still a problem. I had saved money from my few broadcasts at the radio station. Not much, I think, somewhere in the neighborhood of fifty dollars. I washed my own hair to save on beauty care and now at least my room and board were free. They didn't pay me anything or if they did, I didn't know it. I was too meek and inexperienced to ask. Maybe Redman pocketed it. He said it was all for publicity and to get me a "name" and prestige. He also went to the radio station and told them that I had to get much more money, since I was singing at the Roney Plaza. They in turn told him they didn't need me that badly, so my contract was canceled.

That first night I was very nervous. A lot was expected of me, and I was determined to live up to it. I knew I should look as glamorous as possible. I selected a beautiful white crepe gown with a deep V-neck and bare back and matching long flowing cape. I wore long white gloves and glittering long rhinestone earrings. I weighed only 110 pounds. But my pounds were well distributed, so well indeed that I had often been asked by painters and sculptors in Vienna to model for them. I also had a very nice tan, and in my shoulder length hair danced the chestnut highlights I had inherited from my mother.

The spotlight drew a white circle in the middle of the dance floor. Into the spotlight stepped Mr. Jouffret to introduce me. He gave me a beautiful buildup as "the young Viennese who escaped from the Nazis to come to America in search of freedom." He repeated the story that had previously made its appearance in the Miami papers but now with a twist toward the Roney Plaza Hotel. Inside me something revolted against the commercial exploitation of so tragic a cause, but if this was the only way I could find to my real profession, I decided to acquiesce.

I stepped into the spotlight to thunderous applause from the dressed-up audience. Among the American songs I had learned to sing while in Vienna was "Stormy Weather." I also sang "Heart and Soul."

Then I turned to my specialty, the Viennese repertoire. There is one song which seems to be popular everywhere: "Vienna, City of My Dreams." I waited until the audience was very still and all eyes were fixed on me. Then I began very softly and with great feeling, "Wien Wien nur du allein, sollst stets die Stadt meiner Träume sein." All the sorrow of parting with this – the city of my birth – the homeland which I had to leave and which had so deeply disappointed me, I put into the words of the song. Written by a man named Sieczynski and said to be his only composition, it has the intangible qualities necessary to be an international favorite. The song tells of the longing anyone who has ever been in Vienna has for the city of love, wine, and music.

When I finished, there was an instant of absolute silence. Then the audience rose to its feet and cheered and applauded and many of them, tears in their eyes, came to me, put their arms around me and hugged me. It was important to know that my voice reached the audience and not just my "story."

Mr. Jouffret handed me a huge bouquet of red roses while Redman busied himself making appointments with Miami newspaper columnists for the next morning.

It was long past midnight when I finally reached my room. I had barely closed my door when I heard a knock. It was Redman.

"It's too late to go home. I'll sleep here on the couch tonight," he told me.

I figured out how to handle Mr. Redman. "If you are not out of this room instantly, I will have you removed by the bellboy," I threatened.

The stories that appeared almost daily in Miami's news-papers about the "Cinderella from Vienna" amazed me in their artful combination of truth and fiction. One wrote that I had been a stowaway in the steerage of a ship, but when I sang for the captain, he allowed me to continue my journey. Another described how "her dainty hands that had never done anything heavier than play the piano had been forced to scrub floors". When one story stated that I had worked at the El Mirasol Apartments without pay – only for room and board – Noel Bring had his attorney tell me that if I used the name of his hotel without permission, he would have me thrown out of Miami.

I have always been a stickler for the truth. The inflated and distorted stories, as far as I was able to understand them, greatly disturbed me. I told Redman I wanted them corrected.

"You monkey with the press," he said, "and you're as dead as a door nail. The publicity you are getting can't be bought for a million dollars."

I didn't know that. All I understood was that Noel Bring was threatening to sue me, and I had visions of being deported. I didn't know why I was being held responsible for any trouble the stories might have caused him. I only knew that he was making life dangerous once more.

The stories, however, had their positive side. Overnight I became famous. People recognized me on the beach and stopped and spoke to me. I had offers to sing in other night clubs for five dollars a night. Redman would not allow me to accept, insisting that I stay at the more prestigious hotels and forego any salary. It was, according to him, good publicity and a way of making a name for myself. No one cared where the money for my expenses was coming from. Redman regularly suggested that I borrow money.

"From whom?" I asked.

"The Brings have hotels," he said. "Go to them and ask for money."

But I was not willing ask for help where I had already been rejected. Thus I was forced to accept the course which Redman had set for me. From the Roney Plaza he booked me into the prestigious Miami Biltmore at Coral Gables. The audience listened to my Viennese songs and "applauded them wildly" according to the review Wanda MacDowell wrote in the *Miami Daily News*. She also announced my acceptance of an offer to perform at the South Florida Music Festival. There I met Jack Dempsey, the famous pugilist and his pretty young wife. They invited me to sing at a benefit for college students one afternoon on the roof of the Alcazar Hotel where I sang "Two Hearts in 3/4 Time," and the audience loved it. Through all the ovations, I was never sure if it was my story or my voice they were applauding. But all that really mattered was that they were applauding, wasn't it? Only I found that hard to accept then.

One day Redman told me he wasn't going to handle me any longer, unless I signed a contract with him.

I hesitated. "Not unless you guarantee me income producing jobs."

"Of course!" he replied, insulted that I would even suspect that he would fail to make me rich. "I have them all lined up. But first, we will go to my attorney to sign the contract."

I asked Walter Jacobs for advice.

"Look, I hired Redman to take the worry about you off my shoulders. He wants a contract? Sign the contract."

Redman's lawyer wrote the contract which was richly embellished with wherefore's, whereas's, party of the first part, party of the second part and other such learned phraseology which, needless to say, I did not understand at all. At that point, I was able to make myself understood, but my English was far from fluent.

The customs of this country were foreign to me. The food was unfamiliar and not always acceptable in its unaccustomed combinations of sweet and sour, hot and cold, spicy and flat. I had not yet learned to handle with care the fragile American temper where even the slightest criticism is concerned. I did not know how to respond when I was asked how I liked America.

When you are very young and your illusions are badly shaken, you are not likely to be very diplomatic, you are more likely to be harsh in your judgment and, in the process, antagonize a lot of people who mean well but just don't understand. Did I like America? I liked the freedom I had, even though it was a freedom to struggle against seemingly insurmountable difficulties. I liked the atmosphere and the climate of Miami Beach. The fact that I had been more or less abandoned by the man who had helped me to come to America and that I was now broke with no one to stand by to help did not inspire me to great enthusiasm. Everything was strange and unfamiliar, I felt I was picked up by people who did so to promote something for themselves and as soon as they had accomplished it, they let me fall back to the abyss. I believed that all the nice things people said to me such as "Be sure to let me know if I can be of help," were empty phrases because when I did ask someone for an introduction or recommendation, I found that they were "out," "busy," or "not able to do a thing."

That is why I decided sign a contract in spite of the fact that when Redman left the room for a minute, the lawyer warned me not to. Perhaps with a written commitment I would be able to rely on him to get me a paying job.

When I signed that contract appointing Mr. Ray Redman my exclusive manager and press representative, I violated one of the cardinal rules for living in the world of western civilization: Never sign a contract without first reading and understanding every single word! I had no idea of what I had signed. It was later explained to me that I had signed away my freedom of choice in my profession, had given him exclusive power to accept or reject engagements, was not allowed to go anywhere, do anything, or sign anything without his approval. But nowhere in the contract was he held to any obligation to provide a steady flow of paying engagements for me. He was, however, entitled to fifteen percent of my income, no matter where such income might come from. In other words, I had practically signed my life away.

He told me he had signed me up at eight Olympia Theaters from Miami to New York City for a concert tour. But when we arrived at the Olympia Theater in Miami (or what he said was the Olympia), it was out of business. His reaction to this was blithe dismissal. He told me I should go back to Walter Jacobs to see if he would find me a job singing in his nightclub.

I had never had dealings with Redman's sort, and I regretted having permitted myself to be persuaded into signing a contract with him. Fortunately, I didn't need to worry about a continued association with him because, due to numerous debts he had accrued all over town, he disappeared.

I returned to Walter Jacobs, who, after listening to my sad story, reluctantly gave me a job singing three nights a week in the Alamac Hotel for twenty dollars a week. He found me a room, for ten dollars a week, in a lovely little house in the outskirts of town. The room looked out upon the garden. In the morning birds sang to wake me. I was able to hang up all my clothes, put out my personal belongings. For the first time since my arrival, I began to feel relaxed and even a little bit at home.

By now the hullabaloo of publicity and press promotion had died down. I sang steadily and to the evident enjoyment of the patrons. At last I enjoyed walking up and down the ocean front, looking at the hotels, walking along the shopping street with their elegant stores, stopping at orange juice stands and buying a glass of freshly squeezed juice – oh, how I loved it! I noticed with pleasure the palm trees and the lights that shone in their crowns at night time. What a difference it makes to have a steady source of income and a purpose for living. I had peace of mind and decided to enjoy sunning myself on the beach.

I wore the white two-piece bathing suit I had bought in Prague the day I despaired at ever getting my American visa. I remembered telling the sales girl that I bought the bathing suit to wear in Florida and her remark, "I envy you." No one else on the beach was in a two-piece bathing suit, and I noticed that I was drawing the attention of some of the bathers.

Looking over the crowd on the beach, I observed the tall, handsome figure of an athletic looking man, blond, suntanned to a deep bronze, busy performing some sort of acrobatic act with a young couple. Holding the girl high up in the air, he twirled her around over his head and then deftly let her glide to the ground. The young man, who had watched, attempted to duplicate the routine. Who could they be? Just then the telephone in the lifeguard's cabana rang and a voice called out, "Paging Mr. Miller, Mr. Earl Miller." The bronzed Adonis hurried to answer the call.

The sun was so hot that I decided to go into the water. When I swam out to the shark net, Mr. Earl Miller also splashed into the water. In a moment he held on to the net next to me. We looked at each other and smiled.

"Are you the young Viennese lady I heard singing the other day at the Hotel?" he asked.

He complimented me on my performance. We talked about the water and the weather. When we had enough of the water, we swam back to the beach. Because this was the first time I had worn my new bathing suit, I was not prepared for what happened next: my wet bathing suit, being made of unlined wool, was transparent. Horrified, I slipped back into the water.

What to do? I had to confide my predicament to my new acquaintance. He thought it was hilarious and teased me, saying that the beach guard had already told him that there was a woman on the beach, a foreigner, who was wearing a "much too revealing" bathing suit and that he would tell her to cover up or leave. And now this! But after a few moments of letting me suffer, he brought his beach towel and, holding it protectively aloft, wrapped me in its concealing folds.

It took only a very short time for the new bathing suit to dry and return to its respectable consistency, but the incident contributed to an awareness that we liked and were curious about each other.

"Would you like to join me for a drink?" he asked.

We decided that we would also have dinner together after the drink. Earl introduced me to his two friends – Miss Cheyney, a dancer, and her partner. The three shared an apartment at the El Mirasol. It seemed that my destiny was inextricably interwoven with that hotel – first my ill-fated job there, then Hildegarde's hospitality to me in the same place, and now Earl Miller, who, my sixth sense told me, would also play an important part in my new life.

He was a strikingly handsome man. Wherever he appeared, women looked twice. I have always been very cautious in my approach to the very handsome men because many of them become spoiled by the attention they get from women. They are selfish, demanding, and arrogant, expect homage and submission from every woman they meet and are generally so impressed with their own importance that they develop into social bores. This was not the case with Earl Miller.

I had fallen head over heels in love with him, and I did not hide the fact that I enjoyed his company. We met every day on the beach. He seemed not to have any other steady companion except the two dancers with whom he shared his apartment and who, so he told me, had come down from New York City with him in his car. He was fascinated by my reports about the Nazis and Europe. He also was very interested in my family, my background, my education. In turn, he told me about his own life and experiences. At one time he had been traveling with a circus as an acrobat. He was at present, a policeman. Ahh, I thought, that accounts for his inquisitiveness.

Then I began to wonder. For a policeman he lived and behaved rather elaborately. He drove a brand new Cadillac convertible, took me to the finest restaurants for dining, and his manners and attitude seemed to indicate that there was definitely something very unusual about him. I decided I'd better be on my guard.

I was feeling relaxed, safe and comfortable in my niche as a singer in the hotel when one bright, blue-skied day, Walter called me to his office. "The season draws to a close," he said, "I am afraid you will have to find another job."

"What shall I do?" I asked.

"I'd suggest you go to New York," he said, "where the action is."

Go to New York? How? Once more the gates of uncertainty opened wide, behind them a yawning sea of impenetrable darkness.

About that time, Raymond fell seriously ill with bleeding ulcers. He wanted me to come and see him. I took a bus to the hospital and asked for his room. When I entered, I was shocked to see him lying in his bed, thin and pale, a mere shadow of the buoyant Raymond I had seen when I arrived in Miami. He cried when he saw me. It is strange that one sometimes goes along one's merry way, callously inflicting pain and disappointment on others until fate takes a hand and teaches its stern lesson.

I looked at him and felt nothing but pity. The anger, the bitterness, and the disappointment I had felt disappeared when I faced this unhappy, ill man. After all, I thought, he fulfilled his promise and brought me to America. Without his help, I would not be in beautiful Miami Beach. It would show ingratitude were I to forget this. Never mind what followed. There is a reason for everything, although we often don't recognize it until later. Therefore, when he asked me how I was getting along, I stroked his pale forehead and told him not to worry; I told him that I was thinking of going to New York soon.

"How are you going to do this? Do you have someone there to help you find a place to live?" he asked.

"No, I don't, but the Lord has helped me so far. He will, no doubt, continue to arrange things," I answered, smiling.

He had been ill for a long time, Raymond said apologetically, and that was why he paid no more attention to me. I wondered if this were really true. After more chatting, Raymond asked me to get his robe and slippers out of the closet because he wanted to get out of bed. As I stooped down to pick up his slippers from the closet floor, I saw a dangerous looking bug. I quickly pulled back my hand and jumped out of the closet.

"What is this?" I asked.

Raymond, getting out of his bed, took one look and yelled, "A scorpion! Quickly! Get someone to kill it!" Then to me, "You were very lucky. It could have killed you."

"You see," I told him, "the Lord IS watching over me." And I meant it.

Illness or not, by that time Raymond had evaporated from my emotional consciousness. I am not one to stay where I am not received with open arms, and his total neglect of my difficulties caused me to write him off as anything more than a casual friend. In retrospect, I realized that he was actually doing me a favor by letting me do my own fighting. Had he constantly protected me and smoothed the paths I had to take, I might not have learned to deal with the hardships all of us who immigrated at that time had to face and overcome.

Actually, everything that happened to me in Miami Beach contributed to the developments in my life and my career later on. But the recognition that the tribulations of certain periods in one's life are a down payment on future gains comes only much later when one has a chance to look back on the years and to discover the grand design.

A couple of days after visiting Raymond, he sent me a card which had been forwarded to him with the mail from his hotel. It was addressed to me "care of Dr. Raymond Bring." The writer, Dr. Robert Langer, was a friend of my father. He was a judge who fled Vienna disguised as a laborer and later made his way to America via Sweden.

My father had asked him to get in touch with me and help me if I should need it. Dr. Langer was now in New York and notified me that he could assist in finding me a place to live if I wanted to live there. It was another one of those lucky strokes of fate which emerge whenever the future seemed uncertain and the handicaps insurmountable. Now I knew I would not be alone In New York. But how was I to get there? I did not have the money for the train fare, and I was not about to borrow money.

I showed the letter to Earl Miller who, together with the acrobats, was about to drive back to New York. I hoped he would find an empty seat in his car for me but did not ask him for it. After huddling with the others, he invited me to me to come along with them. I looked forward to the long ride to the skyscraper city.

Florida had been a great experience for me. Unlike the swarms of foreigners and immigrants who descended upon New York throughout the years, the south of Florida saw only an occasional European immigrant. I was more of a novelty in Miami Beach than

I would have been in New York. I doubt whether I could have made as many friends, established as many connections, amassed as much publicity, learned as much about the style and character of Americans, and built as strong a foundation for future developments of my life and career if I had remained in New York right after my arrival.

The fact that I was forced to speak English from the very first day also helped me in the future. So many immigrants tend to stick closely to their ethnic friends and associate only during business and professional hours with English-speaking citizens. Thus they don't learn to speak English quickly and properly, a serious handicap in a country where English is the language of communication. I realized this from the very first and made mastery of English my top priority. It proved an invaluable advantage.

9

I had been fortunate to spend the winter months in a tropical resort. Pleasant as it had been to live in the monotony of the blue skies, the colorful vegetation, the warm weather began to be boring. I remembered the old European proverb, "Nichts ist schwerer zu ertragen als eine Reihe von schönen Tagen," – nothing is more difficult to bear than a steady diet of beautiful days. I longed for spring as I had known it, the slow awakening of nature from its icy sleep, the first young fresh green on the branches of birch and elm and willow.

On March 22, 1939, two and a half months after I arrived in Miami, we left for New York City. After we crossed into Georgia, I saw some very miserable shacks along the road, with refrigerators on broken down porches. The shacks did not seem to have any of the facilities I had expected everyone in the rich United States to have. On the steps of the porches I saw people sitting, just sitting, almost motionless, save for the children, clad in rags and barefoot, running about and playing. It was quite a contrast after the luxury in Miami Beach. I also noticed that all the people living in those shacks were black.

"Who are those people? Why do they live like that?" I asked Earl Miller.

"Negroes," the answer came, "they work on farms around here. They are all right, don't worry about them. That's the way they want to live." He didn't want to discuss the subject. Earl could be very final; he could put a hard edge into his voice when he was not comfortable discussing a subject. I didn't pursue the subject. But I wanted to know more. None of the magazine articles about America I had read mentioned anything about these conditions.

We rode along in Earl's beautiful 1939 Cadillac. He was very proud of it. On the second day as we were passing through a small town, a car suddenly shot out of a side street. When Earl slammed on the brakes, I was thrown against the windshield. The windshield cracked, looking like a spider web with a hole in the middle.

When he saw the cracked windshield, he exclaimed, "Oh my beautiful car!" I sat there holding my throbbing head. Earl, however, was concerned only with his car.

"My head hurts," I said.

"Let's see, is it bleeding? No! Ah well, some ice will do the trick."
He looked around and saw a nearby soda fountain. A few minutes
later he returned with a bag of ice for my forehead.

The incident gave me food for thought. I contemplated the
callousness of his remarks about the Negroes and the lack of concern
he showed for my injury. It says something about the man, I
thought. Therefore, I was not surprised when a subsequent incident
completed the picture.

In a roadside restaurant I asked the waitress for sweet butter.
Sweet butter was served exclusively in Europe. Earl was shocked.

He said in embarrassment. "Only Jews eat sweet butter."

I was aghast. Earl Miller was anti-Semitic. I challenged him.

"And what if Jews eat sweet butter. Is that something to be
ashamed of? Do you consider Jews inferior?"

"Yes," he said quite casually. "I think Hitler is right in many
respects. The Nordic race IS superior."

"Do you consider yourself Nordic?"

"Definitely."

I probed further. "If you met someone whose grandmother was
Jewish but all other members of the family were Aryan or Christian
what would you consider that person to be?"

The answer came without hesitation, "Jewish."

"You are more severe in racial prejudice than your idol Adolf
Hitler."

"He is not my idol. He has some very good ideas and I think we
should not fight him."

I couldn't very well get out of the car and walk to New York. I
was silent for a long time. He realized he had annoyed me because he
explained that his point of view was based on the way Americans
judge the racial status of the American Negro.

"One eighth of Negro blood in a person is sufficient to be Negro
in this country," he said and then added, "it's the same with Jews.
"The Jews," he continued sounding to me like a speech by Joseph
Goebbels, "have taken over the theater in this country, the movies,
and many businesses; they stick together."

I was a guest in his car, and I did not feel secure enough in the
language to risk getting into an argument. I let the matter drop.

It seems strange now that I don't recall any details of this automobile trip to New York after that lunch. The only thing I remember is checking my purse for Robert Langer's address and telephone number because I had asked him to find me a room.

When we arrived in New York City on March 24, Earl drove to a house East Eleventh Street, where he said he would spend the night before going to his home. He asked me to stay in the car while he and the other two passengers took in their luggage.

While inside, he called Robert Langer. We were, he told me, asked to "come right over." "Right over" was near the East River on Sutton Place. On the way Earl explained that this was a very fashionable neighborhood and enlightened me on the importance of having "the right address."

The traffic overwhelmed me. How could anyone find his way in such a labyrinth of streets and through such anthills of people? Horns blew, buses swerved in and out of lanes, taxis careened around corners, people walked unconcernedly into the path of cars, ignoring traffic lights. By the time we arrived at our destination, I was a nervous wreck.

Earl got out of the car and handed my suitcase and hat box to the doorman (my steamer trunk had been shipped by railway express). He noted that it was a nice house because it had a doorman and a canopy over the entrance. He came upstairs with me to check out my father's friend. On the fourth floor, Robert Langer, whom I had last seen in Vienna, stood in the apartment doorway. Back then he was preparing to flee Europe, certain that he would be picked up by the Gestapo because, as a judge of the high court in Vienna, he had convicted many a criminal, and he knew that some of them were now free and looking for him for revenge. In addition, he was Jewish, an even more pressing reason to get out of Nazi Vienna. Although he had been very wealthy in Vienna, he arrived in America with only the clothes on his back. He was the first of many Austrian friends I would meet again. Since he himself was far from being settled and lived alone in a single room, he felt we should meet in his cousin's home.

Robert introduced us to his cousin, Mrs. Margit Schey-Kux. Madame Schey, a Viennese who had emigrated a year earlier, lived with her divorced brother Gary. She was, oh miracle, a singing teacher! When Earl saw that I was indeed in reliable company, he excused himself after shaking hands all around. He asked me to come for dinner with him and his friends that evening once I was settled in my new living quarters.

Madame Schey's apartment was comfortably furnished with European furniture. She was of medium height, slender and fragile, with a simple hairdo and no make-up. She was very nearsighted and had a soft, almost inaudible speaking voice. She was a trained concert singer who had studied at the Academy of Music in Vienna but was afraid of public performances and, therefore, chose a teaching career. Her brother, who emigrated long before the specter of Hitler darkened the European horizons, was a well-established stockbroker.

Madame Schey's husband, a shadowy figure, rarely in evidence, lived somewhere in New York City and supported himself by some sort of job, but precisely what kind no one ever mentioned. Their marriage was maintained in name only, and I often felt sorry for him in his almost non-existent existence.

When I told Madame Schey that I had sung in nightclubs and hotels in Miami and mentioned my theatrical experiences in Vienna, she opened the piano and said, "Sing for me." There were albums of German lieder on the piano, and within minutes we were knee-deep in songs by Schubert, Brahms and Schumann. I was so joyous singing classical songs under the sensitive guidance of a competent teacher that I almost forgot that I had to move into my room.

This meeting was one of those unexpected coincidences that kept popping up in my life, coincidences that dramatically influenced the course of events. We separated reluctantly and only after agreeing on a regular schedule of lessons.

My room, according to Robert Langer, was located in a "rooming house" uptown on Columbus Avenue and 79th Street. I didn't know what a rooming house was. He called a taxi and we arrived at our destination after a ride that seemed to take an eternity. When we got there after a long taxi ride, I was shocked. The neighborhood was noisy and dirty. I looked in vain for a doorman and canopy. The house was old and had a fire escape running zig-zag all the way down its red brick front. As we entered, my nostrils filled with the pungent smell of disinfectant, and the worn red carpet runners on the stairs were stained and had ragged, torn edges.

A woman in slippers appeared on the first landing and said

something I couldn't understand. She handed me a key, and we climbed four flights of stairs. I arrived breathlessly in a dark corridor lighted by a naked bulb hanging from the ceiling and opened the door. So this was to be my home!

"It's all right for a few days," Robert Langer said after assessing my horrified expression. It's cheap – only five dollars a week – and I thought maybe you didn't have any money."

I thanked him for finding me a place to stay and bade him good-bye. As he departed, he reminded me that he would be available if I needed his help. (A few days later I did need his help, as well the help of two other men, to get my huge steamer trunk up those four flights of steps.)

The room was very small with one uncurtained window looking over the elevated train tracks that ran along Columbus Avenue. There was a bed, a dresser with a mirror over it, a table with no table-cloth, two chairs, and a worn green rug on the floor. The window did have a shade to pull down for privacy. There was a small bathroom, and alongside the wall of the bathroom there was a small shelf with a one-burner hotplate. The telephone was in the hallway.

I had been so happy meeting Madame Schey and singing again. The prospect of working with her and being included in a circle of people interested in the same things had made the immediate future seem bright and promising. But the difference between her apartment and my miserable room was too much of a letdown.

I sat on a chair and stared at the window. Every few minutes, trains thundered by. Discouraged by my surroundings, I slowly walked up and down and around the table. Here I was finally in New York, but so different from the New York I had visualized. I longed for my family and felt the first nagging doubt that perhaps I had been foolish in leaving them.

Then I remembered that Earl Miller had invited me back to his apartment for dinner. I dressed, carefully locked my door, and went down four flights of stairs into a loud, bustling street. It was almost dark. I didn't dare take a street car because I was afraid I would take the wrong one. A taxi was out of the question because it would be too expensive. So I walked. I showed the piece of paper with Earl's address to passers-by and asked for directions, always "straight down south, straight down," they pointed. I walked along Columbus

Avenue and pretty soon arrived at the point where Columbus Avenue and Broadway meet. Ah Broadway, famous Broadway! But up there it didn't look like the Broadway I had seen in the movies. I crossed a big plaza that said Columbus Circle.

About ten more blocks down, Broadway began to look like the street of lights and glamour I had envisioned. It was ablaze with neon signs and filled with people. On a poster high above the street a huge mouth blew smoke into the air – a cigarette advertisement. On one building, a moving band of lighted letters brought information of some sort to the public. I didn't know whether it was news or advertising.

Down around 42nd Street, the street changed with ladies of the night, easily recognizable with feather boas, frizzy hair, and thick make-up. And there were boys in make-up, with earrings and provocative posture. There were some drunks and the slightly rancid smell of fried food. Such a discrepancy between the Hollywood image of Broadway and the reality of Broadway.

I continued walking. Perhaps I walked for two hours. I don't know. I do know I almost collapsed when I finally got to my destination. Earl was very relieved to see me.

When I told him how far I had walked, he gulped for air, "What, you can't be serious."

Then he asked about my room. Embarrassed to tell him how poor it was, I only said, "Yes, thank you, it is fine."

The house on 11th Street was a charming small townhouse. The apartment was comfortably furnished. Deep cushioned armchairs and sofas, books, books everywhere – along the walls on book shelves, on side tables, on coffee tables. There were gilded boxes and photographs of people who were somehow familiar. Photographs on the walls, photographs in good ebony and silver frames everywhere. And flowers in vases, flower arrangements in bowls. It was very obvious that this was the home of a woman.

"Is this where you live?" I asked Earl.

"No, this belongs to the Lady."

On one or two occasions, he had mentioned "the Lady," but my European upbringing made me reluctant to ask personal questions. Now, however, my curiosity got the better of me. "Who is the Lady?"

"Mrs. Roosevelt."

"THE Mrs. Roosevelt, the wife of the President?"

"Yes."

"How can you bring strangers like myself?"

"I don't bring strangers; when I bring someone here I know pretty well who they are. I am Mrs. Roosevelt's bodyguard and friend, so she has given me permission to use the apartment when she doesn't need it herself."

The house was owned by two of Mrs. Roosevelt's women friends, and she and her secretary, Malvina Thompson, "Tommy" to everyone, used it as a New York City residence. Mrs. Roosevelt's apartment had a balcony big enough for a table and chairs so that one could dine there on warm days and summer evenings. The balcony, surrounded by climbing flowers and plants, gave the appearance of a small garden.

The apartment was taken care of by a maid, Georgie, who prepared a dinner for the four of us travelers and served it on the balcony. Although it was only March, the temperature was unusually warm. I was too excited at the thought of being in Mrs. Roosevelt's apartment to even notice what was served.

After dinner, Earl saw that the long walk had taken its toll on me. "I'll get a taxi to send you home," he said. "I'll call you in a few days."

During dinner I had told him about my singing lessons with Robert Langer's cousin. As we descended the stairs to the street he said, "Keep studying. Maybe I can find some work for you." Then he slipped the taxi driver some money and told him to take me to my address on 79th Street.

"Good night, Fräulein." He had taken to calling me that instead of calling me by my name.

Alone in the taxi, I leaned back and took a deep breath. I had been a guest in Mrs. Roosevelt's apartment. Unbelievable, really. Would he really call me? Or was this just a passing incident, a vacation interlude?

"Expect nothing, then you won't be disappointed," was one of my mother's frequent bits of advice. But I couldn't prevent the thoughts from returning again and again to that one theme, "Will he call and will I perhaps someday meet ... "

Climbing the stairs to my room, I thought about March 24, 1939 my first day in New York City. So much had happened. Earl Miller was Eleanor Roosevelt's bodyguard and friend! I had dined in Mrs. Roosevelt's New York City apartment. I had been united with an old family friend of my family, met his cousin, a Viennese singing teacher, and had taken possession of a rather dismal rented room on West 79th Street.

As I entered my room, I couldn't find the light switch. I stood there trying to get my eyes used to the dark. Slowly, details emerged, partly because the neon signs outside my window cast their light into the room. I began to distinguish the furniture and the naked lightbulb that hung from the ceiling. Alongside the bulb I saw a string hanging down from the base of the bulb and remembered that somewhere before I had found out that this was the way to turn on the light: pull on the string. I carefully locked the door and began to get ready for bed. When I stepped into the bathroom, the wall and ceiling were covered with a myriad of insects scurrying for cover as the light was turned on. They were long black bugs with wings and long feelers, quite repulsive. After that, I carefully examined every inch of my bed, but none were there.

It was difficult to go to sleep. The elevated trains were noisy, and neon lights shone through the closed shade. Thoughts of the bugs, and the yelling and clanging from the street contributed to my mounting unhappiness. There must be a better place than this, I thought before finally falling asleep.

The next morning, It took a few minutes to get oriented. When the eyes are busy and the light of the day brings a variety of impressions to the attention of the brain, it is easier to cope with difficulties. Cautiously I approached the bathroom. The bugs were all gone.

I was hungry, so I decided to buy a few cooking and eating utensils and some food. That way I could at least have breakfast in my room. Before I went on my shopping expedition, I called Hildegarde at the Savoy Plaza Hotel.

"Lottie, come on over right away have breakfast with us!" What a lovely reception, and how it immediately buoyed my spirits. Remembering the long walk of the night before, I asked directions.

"Take the subway and then cross town and then . . . "

"Oh no, no, I'll surely get lost. Is there no easier way?"

"You can take the bus, but you'll have to come across town."

Getting around was going to be a problem unless I relied on my two feet. Walking was nothing unusual for me, everyone walked in Europe or took the streetcar. There were still streetcars in New York in 1939, and they looked very familiar to me. But I was unsure of myself, so I asked if perhaps I could walk.

"Of course, it's a lovely day and you can walk along Central Park or even through the park."

I took up her suggestion eagerly. A park, how wonderful! I stepped out into the brilliant sunshine. How many years I had dreamed of seeing the city of the skyscraper canyons, Broadway and Fifth Avenue. And now here I was! I walked to the corner to get a good look at the street's shops, people, and houses in full daylight.

What a difference between Vienna and New York! The houses with their outside iron stairways – fire escapes, I was told – were something I had never seen before. Most people were rushing to get wherever they were going. They bumped into each other without looking and without saying "excuse me." Others leaned idly against the walls of buildings or sat on steps doing nothing, staring into space as I had first seen people doing in the Georgia shacks.

Way over on the other end of 76th Street, I saw the tips of trees and followed their silent invitation. I longed for trees and lawns and shrubs. I had always lived in a house with a big garden. The brownstone houses and red brick blocks moved in on me and took my breath away. Instead of going down Columbus Avenue, I crossed over toward the trees.

A huge park opened its vistas to me. I followed the street that led to its verdant interior. With the unusual early warmth of this spring, the trees were sprouting their first green blush. I looked around and noticed the meadows with great gray boulders. There were spring flowers and a lake where children floated boats. People sauntered along, nursemaids pushed perambulators and held little dogs on leashes; on benches all along the paths sat people reading their newspapers. I walked and walked and couldn't get enough of the pastoral scene. And all of this in the middle of New York City. It was hard to believe! As I went further south, I came upon the biggest surprise, the Central Park Zoo. I promised myself to come back here often. What a blessing to have such a great green reservoir of trees and air in the center of one of the world's greatest concrete and stone conglomerates.

At 59th Street and Fifth Avenue, I saw to my left the impressive structure of the Savoy Plaza Hotel. Straight ahead I saw a big stone fountain in front of another elegant hotel, the Plaza. Along the sidewalk was a row of one-horse cabs and their old-fashioned cabbies, some wearing bowler hats. The people looked prosperous and elegant. The scene was that of an international cosmopolitan city, much different from the atmosphere around 79th and Columbus Avenue where I had my room.

Hildegarde occupied a suite, a living room with a baby grand piano placed in a prominent position and adjoining a bedroom where she and Anna slept. Both women greeted me with warmth, just what I needed to bolster my confidence. I was anxious to get advice from people who meant well and who were as familiar with my profession as were these two women. So often I witnessed the attitude of immigrants who rejected advice because they had been prominent abroad and thought that their reputation and their achievements placed them in a comparable position in America. But the fact was then, and is now, that everyone who comes to this country as an immigrant must first prove himself capable and suited for whatever he wants to achieve. European stars of stage and screen struggling for immediate and automatic acceptance often met heartbreak and disappointment.

Anna gave me Lesson Number One as we sat in the suite. "There are thousands of unemployed singers and actors in New York," she said. "Many of them are extraordinarily talented, but there is only so much room. You must be unique, and even then it's a matter of luck, connections, being at the right place at the right time with the right material."

She walked up and down the room. "Look at Hildy, it took years of struggle to get where she is. And the struggle isn't over. In fact, once you are up there, you have to fight like hell to stay up there."

I told Anna that I was taking singing lessons with Mrs. Schey. She was unimpressed. She felt that kind of singing would get me nowhere.

"It's not enough to be a good singer. You should have a press agent, a personal manager; ideally, you should have financial backing.

And one more important thing – you must be willing to give up your private life to your career and to your success. In other words, you must be married to your career and to no one else."

Nobody had ever talked so honestly to me. Anna continued, "You are a nobody. Getting headlines in Miami Beach doesn't amount to a hill of beans here. You have to start all over again. Learn old American favorites and look for work in hotels, particularly in resort hotels outside New York or in some small continental nightspots here. But please, don't sing your classical songs, don't even sing your Viennese songs unless you sing in a strictly Viennese night club. And even there, you will have to compete with more experienced entertainers from Europe. Lottie, don't expect to be a star overnight – you won't be."

It was a long speech. I know now that it was designed to cushion my fall. But back then I said to myself, "She means well, but I will sing my own repertoire. Why should it be less successful in New York than in Vienna or Miami Beach?" But Anna was right.

"How much money do you have?" she asked, starting Lesson Number Two.

I told her, and while I don't remember it exactly, I think it was in the neighborhood of one hundred and fifty dollars. The hundred came from the sale of my Leica camera to Earl. It was worth four hundred, but he offered me one hundred and I, in need of cash, took it.

She saw my gold bracelet, "Don't sell that, too, for heaven's sake. You won't get anything for it, for in a few years you will be as sorry to have sold it as you should be for selling your camera to Mr. Miller."

Anna knew a lady who was very compassionate to young artists in need, and she would ask her to include me in the circle of her cash recipients. She also told me where to eat.

"Don't go to expensive restaurants. Go to Horn and Hardart. I will take you there and show you how to choose and what to eat. Don't use taxis," she continued, "too expensive. Use the subway, and, if it must be, the bus. But walk too. It's healthy and you get to know the city that way."

Anna closed her introduction to life in New York by saying, "Come any time you like, call us if you need help. Find a job singing; it doesn't matter where, as long as you keep working."

When I rose to leave, she said, "I'll take you to a Horn and Hardart, so you can learn right away how to eat in New York."

I said "Auf Wiedersehen" to Hildegarde, who made me promise that I would come soon again. But she did not invite me to come and hear her sing at the Savoy Plaza's night club.

Anna and I went to the cafeteria around the corner. I was entranced by the variety of food, the cleanliness, and modest prices. We took a tray and utensils and marched up the line, Anna telling me what to take. "The meat is good, but it costs more, take a lot of vegetables – they are clean here and good for you."

When we arrived at the dessert department, my eyes popped. Cakes, pies, puddings, ice cream, everything looked luscious and rich and so inviting. I chose a tall cake with whipped cream and strawberries. We took our food to one of the few empty tables and began to eat.

She was right – the meat was good and so were the vegetables as well as the roll and butter (salty) she had put on my plate. But I could barely wait for the cake. Alas! The whipped cream was not whipped cream but something "Ersatz," and the cake itself was bland and tasteless. The strawberries, while very beautiful, had no taste.

"Do you like it?" said Anna between mouthfuls.

"Very much," I lied. Later on when I came to eat in cafeterias on my own and alone, I ate my way through all the pastries and cakes, looking for one I could compare with the cakes of Vienna. I found none. They all were works of art in appearance but in taste – no!

I soon became such an expert at eating in New York that I could have taught Anna Sosenko a thing or two about it. For instance, one of the favorite practices of the refugee colony in New York was to go to a cafeteria, take a glass of water with some ice, one or two slices of lemon, return with it to the table, add sugar from the sugar bowl – voila! Lemonade – and it didn't cost a dime.

After lunch, I said good-bye to Anna and walked across town to Madame Schey's apartment. I did not know one must never barge in on someone in America without first telephoning. In Vienna, visitors had always come to our house in swarms, usually at mealtime, staying for hours. Sometimes as many as twenty friends appeared at our house on summer weekends when the weather was nice and the fruit trees were ready with their ripe and juicy harvest. They "just happened to be in the neighborhood and wanted to say hello." I remember many occasions when those "short visits" lasted until six o'clock the next morning. I don't recall that anybody ever called to ask, "Is it convenient if we come?"

So I appeared at Madame Schey's home. Luckily, she was not offended. We began to talk about singing.

"You know," I said, "I have no money. I can't pay you anything."

"Who said anything about paying?" she responded graciously. "You will make it eventually; then we will talk about money. Or perhaps, you will give me enough publicity through your success so that I will get a lot of pupils."

When I told her about my conversation with Anna Sosenko, she said that Anna was probably right, but that I would have to look for someone else to learn an American night club repertoire. She could only keep my voice in training and study classical songs with me because she was not familiar with, nor in fact interested in, anything else. Madame Schey was a superb teacher and the year I had spent without training had left its mark on my technique. I was eager to restore what had slipped away.

On the way back to my room, I stopped at a Woolworth's to buy a frying pan, a small pot to boil water, a cup and saucer, a plate, a glass, as well as a knife, fork, and spoon. I also bought some eggs and bacon, bread, butter, and teabags. (I still have that frying pan – it has become a cherished souvenir of my first days in New York City.)

Those first two weeks I spent most of my time exploring. I soon learned that it was easy to find my way in New York by following the checkerboard system of streets and avenues. The avenues went from south to north, the streets from east to west. The only avenue named, rather than numbered at that time, was Broadway.

On the numbered avenues on the East Side the iron scaffolding of the elevated trains lent a somber and compressed appearance to the street. Not surprisingly, I preferred walking along Park Avenue with its elegant town houses, very similar to European town palaces, and its exclusive shops and center strip of landscaped lawn and flowers.

I found myself comparing everything with what I had left behind. This is typical of the immigrant and can cause Americans to become quite impatient with the newcomer, all the more so as the comparison usually tips in favor of the immigrant's homeland. This is, of course, based on homesickness, whether the immigrant admits it or not.

I walked unending miles. I ate in cafeterias and strolled through stores eyeing the merchandise. I was glad that I had brought an ample supply of clothing, because it would be a long time before I could buy anything new.

10

A few days after our meal at Horn and Hardart's, Anna brought me one hundred dollars – a lot of money in 1939 – from an anonymous patron. She also gave me a list of theatrical agents as well as the names of small continental restaurants where I could apply for engagements. It would be utterly useless to try the big agencies like William Morris because they were, she said, only interested in stars.

As soon as I could find my way around, I began "making the rounds." Usually I didn't get past the receptionist. My appearance differed greatly from those who sat with me in the waiting rooms of agents. I wore practically no make-up, my hair fell in natural curls to my shoulders. I wore low heels, and very conservative European dresses. My competitors were very different. Hair in stylish fashions, faces made up for the stage, clothes flimsy but chic. I felt like an earthbound German housewife.

It was always the same: the agent sat behind his desk, hat on head, cigar in mouth and feet on the table. Usually he was in the middle of telephone conversations while I stood as if invisible. Finally, he turned to me, saying absentmindedly, "What can I do for you?"

While I'd tell of my desire to sing, trying to impress him with my Miami Beach successes, he would read some correspondence, interrupting my halting presentation with an occasional grunt. Then he'd say, "Well, ah, I can't think of anything right now, if we have something we'll call you, don't call us." I always left my name and telephone number, just in case. I knew they would never call me.

****

I had been in New York City for three weeks. Only by walking could I begin to understand this new world. So I walked from morning until night, everyday. I gradually covered most of Manhattan, especially the lower section of Broadway where I found the theaters and talent agencies.

The city was not "gemütlich" like Vienna or Prague. In a city of seven million I knew four people – Hildegarde, Anna, Dr. Langer, and Madame Schey. I was very lonely. My friends were preoccupied with their own lives, and while they assured me of their help should I need it, I found out very quickly that I had to depend on myself. Earl had not called, and I was depressed by his silence. Weekends were the loneliest time.

I was also worried about my family in Austria. My father wrote as regularly as he dared, but his letters were guarded and revealed only that fear stalked the land and prevented him from relating any facts of actual conditions there.

What to do when alone in New York without funds? I missed concerts, operas, theater, and even movies. Once I became more familiar with the city, I found pleasurable activities offered to the public free of charge. The Metropolitan Museum did not charge an entrance fee and the Goldman Band offered free concerts in Central Park. For a nickel I could ride the bus all over the city or enjoy a cup of coffee on the terrace in the Central Park Zoo.

During one of my walking tours of the city, I ventured through the elaborate glass door of Rumpelmayers, the famed cafe-restaurant on Central Park South, just to get a whiff of an atmosphere of elegance reminiscent of a time that seemed far away and lost forever. When the headwaiter approached asking me if I were looking for a table, I pretended to search for a friend. Then, sadly shaking my head at the "friend's absence" I left the premises with the scent of rich pastries and hot chocolate still in my nostrils.

****

I wish I could convey what it means to become an immigrant in a strange land. My roots had been pulled out, exposed to the harsh winds of transplantation and planted in the new climate. They had to get a new foothold under new and unfamiliar conditions. The New York of 1939 was something of a cultural shock. The size of the city was overpowering. The immigrants of 1939 did not, as did those of earlier waves, gravitate to ethnic neighborhoods where relatives or friends waited to help them adjust. Instead we scattered here and there all over the city, settling in like flocks of birds wearily coming to roost after a long flight. Lucky ones brought their possessions and moved into apartments with their own furniture, surrounded by the past.

I, like the majority of immigrants, had nothing to ease the sense of separation from my past. I missed an orderly home, belonging to something, to someone. I did have some jewelry, a few photographs, some sheet music, the cherished wool blanket my Aunt Lotte had given me. Under its warm cover, we took naps when I spent my childhood summers with her. (I still have it today.) And I had an extensive array of clothes in my big steamer trunk. To my dismay, I found that my custom-tailored suits and dresses did not fit into the New York scene. The colors – gray, brown, beige, and black – were drab when compared with the vivid colors and prints I saw on American women. My solid low heeled shoes, though expensive and beautifully made, looked clumsy next to the dainty high-heeled footwear I observed on the women who clippety-clopped on the streets. And the hats! My own were felt, severe and devoid of decorations, save perhaps a ribbon. The hats I saw on American women were a fantasy of flower gardens, birds' nests, ribbons, veils, and jewelry.

Still convinced that Anna Sosenko was wrong in her appraisal of my suitability for the New York night club circuit, I stubbornly called on booking agents every morning only to be told, "Nothing now, come back next week." In the afternoons I tried to lift my spirits by walking up and down Fifth Avenue, looking into the windows of Bergdorf Goodman, Lord and Taylor, and Saks. Fifth Avenue and Park Avenue helped make me feel at home because they reminded me of Europe's elegant shopping streets.

Leaving Fifth Avenue to go west toward the river, I saw the seamy side. Street gutters overflowed with debris, people who pushed and jostled, elbowing their way in and out of traffic. Back then I did not look beneath the surface to see that these streets were the heart of the vibrant business centers of the city. I looked only at the loud, vulgar expressions of whatever activity took place there and felt like a drowning victim seeking rescue. My rescue was the green oasis of Central Park.

The third New York Sunday morning opened with a yawning emptiness. How would I spend it? Where would I go? When the phone rang in the hallway, I didn't answer it because nobody called me. But no! I heard someone call "Luddie Kraus."

I was out of bed in a flash, into my robe and slippers

and out to the hall telephone. It was Earl Miller.

"Fräulein, would you like to spend the day with me?"

"Yes, of course, where are you?"

"Listen carefully. Go downtown to Grand Central Station, it's off Fifth Avenue and 42nd. Go to the ticket counter and buy a ticket to Poughkeepsie."

"To where? Just a minute until I get a pencil." He waited while I rummaged for a pencil and returned to the telephone. He spelled Poughkeepsie.

"That's a town?" I asked.

"Yes." He told me the number of the train to take to the town with the funny name.

I dressed and hurried down the stairs. I took a taxi for I didn't have much time to spare. The train ticket cost $1.30. All the way to Poughkeepsie I was nervous. I didn't want to miss the station. I asked the conductor, "Will you please tell me?"

"Yes, lady. Sit down, it will be a while."

But I couldn't relax. I nervously jumped up every time the train pulled into a station. He did forget to call me when the train pulled into the station of Poughkeepsie. Or perhaps, I didn't understand him when he was calling out the name.

Earl was waiting on the platform. He greeted me warmly with a smile and a kiss on the cheek.

"I have a surprise for you," he announced. We walked up the stairs. A tall figure stood next to an open car, a woman dressed in a cloth coat, her hair covered by a beret. The clothes were very simple, yes, one could say plain, but the figure was imposing and the bearing, aristocratic. I recognized the face from pictures I had seen on the cover of newspapers and from photographs in the apartment on Eleventh Street. This was Eleanor Roosevelt, the wife of the President of the United States.

"I am Mrs. Roosevelt," she informed me while putting her arms around me, kissing me on both cheeks. "Welcome dear, I hope you had a nice trip."

Insisting that "we can all sit in front," off we went in the black convertible with the top down in the warm April air. People on the street waved and she waved back. I was in a state shock. How could I not be? It was all so incredible. Would anyone believe me if I told them that the wife of the President of the United States came to the railroad station to welcome a young woman, an immigrant who was neither famous nor important. This could never happen in Europe. This was America!

Although I had been taught never to stare, I could not stop staring. She had a very expressive face with features that constantly moved. It was a warm and kind face. I felt drawn to her, wishing very much that she would like me.

"Earl told me about you," she began, immediately coming to the point. "I understand you are here alone, without your parents. It must be very rough in a strange land dependent entirely on yourself."

I marveled at the interest she took in my situation. I nodded timidly. After all, it isn't everyday that you'd ride "three in front" with the First Lady. How should I behave?

She made it easy. She asked questions. Did I have a decent place to live in New York? How much did I have to pay for it? Did I have an income of some kind or another? Had I begun looking for employment? Did I have any friends?

"Perhaps you could sing for us tonight?" she asked.

"Tonight?"

"Yes, I thought you might like to spend the night with us and go back to the city tomorrow."

"Oh. but I didn't know, I have no night clothes."

"Never mind, I'll give you some, we are always prepared for overnight guests."

It was difficult for me to comprehend how simply all this happened. There were no Secret Service agents. (I realized later that Earl, as her bodyguard, functioned in their place.) No entourage, no formality. Just Mrs. Roosevelt, Earl, and me in a car.

We drove along a two-lane country road for about fifteen minutes until we came to a gravel road on our right. We took a sharp turn between two stone pillars and bumped along over stones and ruts for a few hundred feet. Then the car rattled over a wooden bridge whose loose bridge boards served as the unofficial announcement that someone was arriving.

The car halted in front of a rambling stucco country home, Val Kill, Mrs. Roosevelt's private residence, her own hideaway from her official duties. Earl jumped out to open the door for Mrs. Roosevelt and to help me out too. This was the place she relaxed, invited friends to join her for an evening, a weekend, even a week or two. (I didn't dream then that I would come here often, alone at first and later with my husband and even later with him and my daughter.)

That weekend, there were no other guests – only Earl, Mrs. Roosevelt and me. Later we were joined by Mrs. Roosevelt's friend and confidant, Tommy. Mrs. Roosevelt herself took me upstairs to my room to see that I had everything I needed. She lifted the corner of the bedcover to make sure that there were clean sheets and brought me a nightgown and slippers.

"Now make yourself comfortable and come down at twelve o'clock for dinner. Let me know if there is anything you need," she called out as she hurried down the hall.

I was Mrs. Franklin D. Roosevelt's houseguest! I sat in one of the comfortable armchairs and looked around. The room was furnished in the same cozy style that had impressed me in the apartment in New York. Books rested on every available surface, photographs stood in silver frames and hung on the walls, and flowers graced the little side tables and bookshelves. All sorts of knickknacks, apparently souvenirs, were lovingly put up to testify to the appreciation of the recipient. Clearly the room was used frequently. The desk had writing paper. There were sheets and envelopes; I looked to see if they had a letterhead. They did. Some said Val Kill Cottage, but others said in gold lettering, The White House.

What was it my father had said on that March evening a year ago when I told my parents I was going to America? "Who do you think is waiting for you in America – the President?" I sat down again and the echo of my father's voice overwhelmed me.

"Vati," I wept, "my sweet, wonderful gentle father."

Later that afternoon I asked if she would permit me to use the White House stationery to write my father a letter and explained how much it would mean to him to receive such a letter.

At noon I left the room and got lost in the maze of hallways, stairways, and landings that led to other hallways and corridors that were dead ends. I finally ended up in the kitchen, where the maid, Georgie, whom I had first met in Mrs. Roosevelt's New York apartment, was preparing the meal.

"Where will I find Mrs. Roosevelt?"

"They'll be in Mrs. Roosevelt's sitting room," she said, directing me there. There were so many rooms designed for sitting, relaxing, and cozy gathering, that one never knew which was the designated sitting room.

I finally ended up in the right room, the one where Mrs. Roosevelt was sitting with her knitting – she never was without something to do with her hands. She was talking to Earl and to a lady who was introduced as Miss Thompson, the indispensable Tommy, who made a sour face.

In fact, I don't ever remember Miss Thompson other than with a face that looked as if she had just bitten into a very sour lemon. She was always businesslike, never smiled, and never participated in a conversation, unless asked a question which she answered in monosyllabic terms. I had the impression that she resented anyone who might interrupt what she was doing at that moment. Mrs. R., as Miss Thompson called Mrs. Roosevelt, depended on her and included her in family life, both in Val Kill and in the White House. That familiarity between the two women was kept within bounds by Mrs. Roosevelt, who had a way of keeping people at a respectful distance no matter how great her friendship with them. Even close friends never called her by her first name. The only persons I ever heard address her in a familiar or affectionate way were the President, her sons, and a cousin, former Ambassador David Grey. Everyone else called her Mrs. Roosevelt or Mrs. R.

The maid brought glasses with tomato juice and we chatted for a short while before dinner. We ate in the dining room, at a table set with place mats, flowers in the center, and Franciscan chinaware in the fruit pattern. I remember it because it looked so much like the hand painted china set we used in our family home.

Dinner that first Sunday was delicious – roast chicken, potatoes, beets, and applesauce. There were hot biscuits with butter and later cake and ice cream. Everything was placed within reach of Mrs. Roosevelt, and she served each person at the table asking "dark meat or light meat?" sending the full plate down the line from hand to hand.

She ate very fast. So fast, indeed, that she was finished almost before I had started. She enjoyed her food and took a second helping, asking if anyone wanted more. The salad was served on what I recognized to be bone dishes, half-moon shaped flat plates that are used to hold bones of fowl or fish. But in the Roosevelt household, they were always used for salad. Later the maid removed the dishes and brought fingerbowls filled with lukewarm water. There were tiny little china flowers in the bottom of each bowl.

I watched Mrs. Roosevelt to see what she would do with the fingerbowl, for I had never eaten at a table where one was used. I watched Mrs. Roosevelt lift the bowl and the little doily upon which it rested and place both down alongside the dessert plate upon which it had been served. I copied the gesture nonchalantly as if I always dined with this table accessory.

After the last crumb on her plate was carefully eaten, Mrs. Roosevelt dipped the tips of her fingers into the bowl, wiped her mouth more as a gesture than as a real cleaning, and dried her hands on her napkin. I followed suit.

"We will take the coffee in the living room," Mrs. Roosevelt said as she stood up and nodded to me to follow. In the living room, Earl put another log on the fire while Georgie brought in a silver coffee tray with large cups and small cups and hot milk as well as cream.

"Large cup or small cup?" Mrs. Roosevelt asked. With the large cups she served hot milk, a custom she had learned when living in Europe. I noticed that her strong looking hands shook slightly as she poured.

I sank back into the deep soft pillows of one of the armchairs. On first sight, rooms seemed overloaded with furniture, including odd pieces, such as the table made on an elephant's foot. But one soon became accustomed to the array of personal belongings of a woman who put the stamp of her individuality on the one place she could live as she chose. Val Kill was hers and hers alone.

Mrs. Roosevelt's voice startled me out of my thoughts, "Would you like to go for a walk?"

I nodded. She looked at my city clothes. "I'm afraid you will ruin your clothes in the woods and your shoes will get muddy. I'll lend you some riding britches and boots." She seemed oblivious of the fact that she towered two heads above me.

"Thank you, but I think I can manage in my own clothes." My refusal did not seem to displease her.

She led me up a winding path, that was indeed muddy, behind

the house to the top of the hill where they were building a new house for the President. She told me the President was looking forward to using this house as his own hideaway, as a place to read and study and relax and look out over the Hudson Valley, which he loved. There was an air of tranquility about us and a stillness which made me understand why he would want to seek refuge here.

"It looks like the Vienna Woods," I said more to myself than to Mrs. Roosevelt.

"You miss your home." It was a statement not a question.

"Yes."

"Tell me about it. Tell me about your parents and your life, and tell me if there is anything I can do to help you and your family."

I was deeply moved. Not only because she said it, but because of the way she said it. So quietly. I knew it was not just politeness, she really wanted to learn.

I told her about March 11 when Nazi troops crossed the border of Austria with tanks, guns, planes, and marching troops. About the collaborators, about lifelong friends suddenly turned into enemies overnight. About the beatings, arrests, about university professors having to scrub the streets because they were Jews, about the nightly disappearances of innocent victims of the Nazis, about the songs the Nazis sang, which foretold their intention to conquer the whole world – including America.

I completely forgot about myself and had only one desire, to let her know, to let the American people know of the danger, make them realize that this was no joke, not the passing fancy of a madman. She wanted to know more and more. I told her of the Nazi takeover in Czechoslovakia, of Tante Lotte and her refusal to believe that anything could happen to her, a fatal mistake so many made.

Mrs. Roosevelt listened intently. Her face was grave, and I had the feeling that she understood the gravity of the Hitler menace better than most Americans. Yet, at the same time I sensed in her, as I had in others, an inability to fully grasp the horror of persecution and its cruelty. I was certain that she did not know the panic which all of us who had been victims could not and can never totally abandon.

"You can count on me to help when you need it," she said simply. "I will also see if I can't use you at some of our White House musicales. But I do not know enough about music to make decisions. We have someone who does that. You will find a letter from him when you get back to the city. His name is Mr. Junge, and he will audition you for one of our concerts. His office is Steinway Hall on 57th Street, so be prepared for his call."

After a moment's thought she said, "I will write to our Ambassadors in Vienna and Prague to have them see if there is something we can do to help your family."

"America," I thought. "They said it is the land of unlimited possibilities; you come as a stranger into a strange land, you go up and you go down, roller coasting – one day despair, next day glamour star, down again, nothing today, call next week. And now a walk in the woods with Eleanor Roosevelt, First Lady of the United States of America, who tells me not to worry, she'll help me. She didn't know me a few hours ago, but she gives me hope."

We went back to the warm coziness of the fireplace, to the silver coffee service, only this time it was tea. Afternoon tea was a ritual she had adopted when she was a student in England. "Now you must excuse me," Mrs. Roosevelt said, "I have some work to do. Perhaps you could sing after dinner. Earl plays the piano."

Earl played the piano by ear. He played songs I had never heard, particularly one that was his favorite, "Deep in My Heart, Dear," from *The Student Prince* by Rudolf Friml. Since it was about a European prince and since I was European, he thought I should know it. When I asked him if he knew some Schubert songs he said he had never heard of him. The result, of course, was that we could not succeed together musically, much to his disappointment.

After a while I sat in my comfortable chair, realizing that the thing I longed for most was a place to put down roots, a place such as this – not as grand as Mrs. Roosevelt's, but certainly as individually and personally oriented. I hated to think of going home to my miserable furnished room.

When Mrs. Roosevelt returned from writing her column "My Day," and answering mail, she said that she would change for dinner, and added "But you don't have to worry about it, it's a habit of mine to dress for dinner."

Presently, Mrs. Roosevelt returned, we had a cold supper Georgie prepared. Once more the plates were passed from hand to hand, filled

98

with ham, potato salad, and other cold cuts, as well as some cheese and bread and butter. Ice cream finished the meal. The coffee ceremony was once more held in the living room.

Mrs. Roosevelt loved to read out loud. That evening she read poetry. Although she read with feeling and humor, I was not able to follow very well. Furthermore, I was quite exhausted from the walk in the woods, the ample meals, but mostly the emotional demands of the day. The room with its crackling fire was too much to resist. I fell asleep. If she noticed, she never let on. I dozed only for a few minutes, for she was still reading when I opened my eyes.

Shortly after that, she closed the book and said, "I guess we are all tired today, so perhaps it's better if we go to bed."

She rose, kissed me, and said, "Good night, dear, I'm so glad you could come today. I hope you will come again. You will hear from me concerning the White House musicales."

She also kissed Earl and said, "Show Miss Kraus to her room – she probably doesn't remember the way. Earl's room is next to yours." The latter she said as an afterthought. And then, "Breakfast tomorrow at eight."

I thanked her for the privilege of having been invited to her home. I reached my room ably guided by Earl throughout the maze of stairs and hallways. I kissed him good night and thanked him too for bringing me here and to the attention of this wonderful lady. "I think I have found a true friend," I said to Earl.

"I knew she would like you and, if you behave correctly, she will be your friend forever. Never take advantage of your friendship with her. As soon as people know that you are Mrs. Roosevelt's friend, they will ask you to do something for them. Don't do it. Come to me. If it is worth following up, I'll relay the message. Don't ever try to cash in on your friendship with her. That will end it."

Earl knew what he was talking about. As the years went by and my friendship with her deepened, I was offered thousands of dollars and enticing gifts if I would intercede for this or that. I always refused. My friendship with Eleanor Roosevelt was not negotiable.

On that evening I said, "But she said I could come to her for help?"

"Yes, for you and your family, but not for strangers."

Before going to bed that night I wrote to my parents: "Dearest

Mother and Father, you are not dreaming, this is the real thing. I am a house guest of Mrs. Franklin D. Roosevelt, the wife of the President of the United States. You see, Vati, he WAS waiting for me."

11

The next morning I was at the breakfast table at 8 o'clock. Earl and Mrs. Roosevelt were already there. I later learned that no one was late for meals. She was always exactly on time. She had a very quiet way of exerting authority.

After greeting me, she said "I have to drive to New York. Would you like to come along? It will save the train fare."

I accepted eagerly.

Breakfast consisted of a choice of hot or cold cereal. Oatmeal with brown sugar and honey was a standby. There were also eggs, any style. Georgie took the orders. The coffee was served in the biggest cups I had ever seen. Again my coffee was mixed with hot milk, just the way it was served in Vienna. After breakfast, Mrs. Roosevelt stepped into the kitchen to tell Georgie how delicious everything was.

A bit later, after Earl left for his home in Albany, Mrs. Roosevelt, Miss Thompson and I took our seats in a big black limousine. All the way to New York Mrs. Roosevelt studied papers and official business with Miss Thompson. I sat still and marveled that I was riding in a chauffeured limousine with the wife of the President of the United States, a circumstance which was surely unusual for a citizen, and all the more unusual for a recent immigrant. I sighed.

Mrs. Roosevelt looked up. "Are you all right?"

"Oh, yes, its just that – well, I just can't get quite over it. I mean this whole weekend you must understand is really quite unbelievable for me."

She took my hand, "Don't worry, you'll be all right."

When we reached New York City, I was embarrassed to let her see my rooming house, so I told her to drop me off at Mrs. Schey's. However, the chauffeur took her first to the house on llth Street and then took me to my destination. As she got out of the car, she kissed me good-bye and said I would hear from her very soon.

Dropping in on a startled Mrs. Schey, I asked, "Guess where I spent the weekend?"

"No idea."

"With Mrs. Roosevelt."

"Which Mrs. Roosevelt?"

"THE Mrs. Roosevelt!"

Margit Schey was disbelieving, then amazed, and when I mentioned the possibility of a concert in Hyde Park her eyes opened wide.

"What are you going to sing?" And then, quickly and practically, "Who is going to accompany you?"

It was an important question; the accompanist is crucial. Where would we find one who could measure up. She thought for a minute, and came up with Franz Mittler, another recent refugee from Hitler. No doubt he would welcome this opportunity to play for the President.

In 1939 the cream of the European world of letters, art, and music had moved across the Atlantic as exiles from Hitler's racial madness. There were orchestra conductors such as Bruno Walter, Arturo Toscanini, and the brothers Krips. There were directors and producers such as Otto Preminger, Fritz Lang, Max Reinhardt, and many more. Few spoke English well enough to integrate quickly into the American scene. America was not prepared for the sudden influx of talented immigrants unable to speak English. A few like Lotte Lehmann and Lauritz Melchior landed immediately at the Metropolitan Opera. Some – like Hedy Lamarr (known in Vienna as Hedy Kiesler), Paul Muni, Walter Slezak, Maria and Maximilian Schell, and Theodor Bikel – spoke English well enough to quickly find their niche in Hollywood or on the New York stage. Many others, who had been headliners in their homelands, could not compete and had to be satisfied with small roles.

I remember recognizing the giant of the German-speaking stage, Albert Bassermann, in insignificant parts in several Hollywood films. Bassermann, a Gentile, had refused to stay in Nazi Germany when he was pressed to divorce his Jewish wife. Franz Mittler was one of the best accompanists in Vienna and was now earning money giving piano lessons. (Later, he and three other fine pianists formed the First Piano Quartet, which achieved great artistic and financial success.) He lived, as did most recent refugees, in one of the many rooming houses on the West Side of New York. His room, however, had a special feature, a piano. Franz was about forty-five. He was attractive, gentle, and most importantly, a fine artist. In addition, he had a marvelous sense of humor. As a young man he had fallen in with love American comic books and had learned American English reading those comic books.

Without a moment's hesitation, he agreed to spend hours preparing me for the audition. He knew I could not pay him, but he considered it a labor of love. Once again, a coincidence brought me good luck at just the right time.

When I auditioned for Mr. Junge in Steinway Hall, I was, as usual, very nervous. Looking out over the empty auditorium, I realized I might never have this chance again. The old gentleman was already there, supported and guided by, as I later found out, his niece. He was over eighty years old and blind. But there was nothing wrong with his fine musical ear. I sang one of my favorites – Schubert's "Die Forelle." When I had finished, I waited. He sat motionless. Had he heard me?

"What else do you have?" came the request. I was familiar with the "barometer" of auditioning. Nothing is more welcoming than "do you have something else"; nothing more deflating than "thank you very much, that's all."

I sang "Sonntag" by Johannes Brahms, "Wohin" by Schubert, and again the voice came, "what else do you have?" I sang twelve songs, folksongs, Viennese songs, and one charming song by Franz Mittler himself. With every song, my elation grew.

Finally Mr. Junge asked me to come down. He took my hand and kissed it. "Thank you, my dear," he said in an old and whispery voice. "You have a charming, charming voice and you sing beautifully. It's been a long time since I have heard these songs sung so emotionally and touchingly. I will tell Mrs. Roosevelt you are eminently suited to perform for her guests."

"The Danish Crown Prince and Crown Princess will be here for the opening of the Danish Pavilion at the World's Fair," he continued. "There will be a reception for them at Hyde Park. Prepare a program of at least ten songs."

Could I have heard him correctly?

He went on, "You know that I only suggest. Mrs. Roosevelt makes the decision. But be ready."

I floated out of Steinway Hall on a pink cloud. Mr. Mittler floated right along with me. Finally my repertoire had found appreciative ears and had perhaps won for me a concert at the White

House. I had reached another "high" in the up and down path my life was taking. I didn't even mind my little room and its noisy, dirty neighborhood. I was sure now life had something better in store.

I had just returned to my room when the hall telephone rang. It was Mrs. Schey, eagerly inquiring how the audition had turned out and at the same time making me an offer which justified my optimism: her brother had to go on a prolonged business trip to California and she offered me his room in their apartment.

Immediately, I set about packing my faithful companion – the steamer trunk. How many times I had packed and unpacked it. "Here we go again. You will be just as glad as I to say good-bye to those funny little bugs and the thunder of the elevated train. We are going to live on elegant Sutton Place, and I might be able to completely unpack you for the very first time."

Down the stairs we went, my trunk and I. The landlady had no objection to pocketing a full week's rent. For a good half hour I stood at the corner trying to flag down a cab. None would stop. They took one look at my trunk drove on. Finally one pulled over, but he charged me extra for the trunk.

At Mrs. Schey's the doorman took care of everything. Life is much easier when you live in an apartment "with canopy and doorman." It was a relief to no longer be alone, doubly so when it meant living with someone who was sympathetic to my ambitions and believed in my ability. Unfortunately, Mrs. Schey's sister, Esty, also lived there, and she was less than happy with my presence.

Esty began, like most immigrants, on the bottom rung of the ladder. A successful milliner in Vienna, she had to start in New York as an apprentice on Madison Avenue. Now, as a result of hard work, she was the proud owner of her thriving business. In fact, her hats were no longer called hats, they were chapeaux, and her shop was a boutique. She regarded me as an intruder, all the more so as Mrs. Schey had invited me as a guest and did not expect any money from me. Esty contributed to the household expenses, so why should this singer come along and be allowed to freeload.

To repay their generosity and show Esty that I knew the meaning of hard work, I embarked on a wild housekeeping spree while both women were out of the apartment. Everything was cleaned under, over, and around. The place shone and sparkled when they returned. But what was the reaction? Esty was furious.

"So," she hissed out of her sister's hearing, "you must think we are very dirty if you feel you have to show us how the apartment should look."

I was stunned. I filed it under "another experience." And it did not keep me from continuing to make myself useful around the apartment wherever I saw a chance to do so.

On April 22, two weeks after my visit to Val Kill, the mail brought a letter from Mrs. Roosevelt containing two electrifying items. The State Department found that my parents were still safe and in their own home. In addition, my wish to sing for the President of the United States and his guests would be fulfilled. Her invitation to spend the night again at Val Kill made me particularly happy, for I knew that my first visit was an introductory one. Had I done something to displease her, I might never have seen her again.

Immediately, I submitted a program to Mr. Junge because we had only one week to prepare. We discussed my name and, remembering what a Miami Beach columnist had said about its lack of glamour, I decided to imitate Hildegarde, and call myself simply "Charlotte."

The three of us – Margit Schey, Franz Mittler and I – worked furiously for that week so that when the great day arrived, I was ready. Once more I took the train to Poughkeepsie, this time accompanied by Franz Mittler. As the train rolled toward Hyde Park my heart beat faster and faster. Would I be able to please all these famous people? The President of the United States, The Crown Prince, The Crown Princess, Mrs. Roosevelt herself? Everything, my future career, my reputation as an artist, depended on this concert.

And as I have always done and still do when things seem to be bigger than I can handle alone, I quietly folded my hands and began to pray. It helped. It always does.

Mrs. Roosevelt's invitation to spend the night also included my accompanist. Mr. Mittler, however, was to spend the night at a guest house that Mrs. Roosevelt maintained outside the estate on the main highway leading from Poughkeepsie to Val Kill.

After the chauffeur drove us to Val Kill, we sat down to lunch without Mrs. Roosevelt, who was at the Big House, as she called Hyde Park. Joining us were Earl Miller, Miss Thompson, and Major Hooker, an old family friend who was so much a part of the family that he sometimes appeared at the breakfast table in pajamas, robe, and slippers, even at the White House.

Mrs. Roosevelt had a way of taking care of every detail for her guests. She left explicit instructions, had every minute worked out, took every eventuality into account. I later learned that she applied the same split-second timing and planning to her own schedule which was why she was able to successfully handle her demanding obligations.

The afternoon was spent in rehearsal and relaxation until Mrs. Roosevelt returned. She told me that the Crown Prince was a great music lover and amused me by telling me that it was not at all unusual for him to wander into a rehearsal of the Danish Symphony Orchestra, take off his coat and start to conduct. She was certain he would very much appreciate my program.

She asked Franz Mittler about his own career and plans for a new start in America. She also explained that he would be reimbursed for travel expenses. Mr. Junge told me that Command Performances at the White House are so obviously a circumstance of honor and prestige that they usually were performed without compensation. I don't know if this was the case with others, but in my own case I always received a personal check from Mrs. Roosevelt, with a few motherly words, "I know you had expenses and I don't want you to spend your own money."

While we were having tea, she answered many telephone calls, gave instructions to the maid and Miss Thompson, and told us that we would eat at Val Kill while she was dining with the President and their guests at Hyde Park.

"I'll send the car," she said, "to pick you up after dinner for the concert. Now, please excuse me, I must dress for dinner."

I have never seen any woman take less time to get dressed for a gala event than Mrs. Roosevelt. Within ten minutes she was back downstairs. She wore a long gown that left her arms bare. It could not be called chic and just hung on her. Tommy told me that Mrs. Roosevelt didn't care about clothes and chose whatever was handy at the time. She wore, however, quite a bit of jewelry and all of it genuine. There were rings on several fingers and pearls and necklaces and when the dress required it, she wore brooches.

Her hair was done very simply, just brushed back and up and

pinned with hair pins and combs. She once told me she hated to go to the hair dresser because it was a terrible waste of time. However, she did have beautiful hands and finger nails, oval shaped and carefully manicured and lacquered. That afternoon, Earl had pointed to her pink lacquered fingernails and complained that mine were lacquered with natural clear lacquer.

"I told her she should have them at least pink like yours, its more fashionable." Mrs. Roosevelt seemed a little embarrassed at such an intimate reference to her appearance.

"I think," she responded "that everybody should wear what they feel comfortable with. Miss Kraus has nicely shaped nails and there is nothing wrong with having them natural." Turning to me she added, "The girl at the beauty shop does mine, and I pay no attention to what she puts on. I usually read or doze off."

At six o'clock dinner was served. I was too nervous to eat. Shortly before nine, we were driven to Hyde Park, where we were ushered into a small room off the big entrance hall. In a few minutes, the guests strolled from the dining room to the living room where the performance was to take place. Mrs. Roosevelt appeared in the doorway to greet us.

As usual, I had stage fright. I knew I would forget the lyrics. I shook like a leaf. My eyes wouldn't focus. A lump grew in my throat. I walked up and down, back and forth and began to yawn, great big yawns, one after another. I used to drive my colleagues on the stage crazy with my yawns, but they were uncontrollable.

Franz Mittler recognized my terror and quietly said, "Nothing to worry about. Just look at me, if you get lost, I will supply the missing word."

His words worked like a miracle. When Mrs. Roosevelt took me into the large living room, I was no longer nervous. I remembered not to hold on to the piano. "The piano doesn't need holding up," Mrs. Schey in New York and Harriet Hauser in Vienna had both admonished.

Crown Prince Frederick in his bemedaled uniform and his slender, graceful wife, Ingrid, were in the front row. I recognized the President from pictures I had seen of him. Next to the President was a very distinguished looking old lady, his mother.

Mrs. Roosevelt introduced me as "a young, Viennese friend of mine" and explained why I had left my homeland. I sang well, perhaps because I could feel that this particular audience appreciated my choice of songs. The applause after I had finished the first part of my program told me I had succeeded. When it comes hard on the last note of the song, you know they have been waiting to applaud. It is very different from the slow, polite, forced kind of applause that courteous people extend when they feel obliged to show appreciation.

Mrs. Roosevelt followed me to the room, where I retired for five minutes to relax. "It's absolutely lovely," she said. "We are all looking forward to the second part."

Just before beginning the second part of the program, I looked at the corner of the room where Earl stood, unobtrusively overlooking the scene. I think he was a little bored by the classical music and by the German words.

When it was time to sing the last song, I announced, "There has been a slight change in programming. Instead of 'Dixie,' I will sing a song which most of you know and like. It is a tribute to the city where I was born, a city now lost to us – 'Vienna, City of My Dreams.'"

I sang what I felt, that not just a city, not just a country, but a way of life had been lost. A precious jewel of many facets had been trampled under the heavy boots of the barbaric Nazi hordes. The only place the free spirit of Vienna still lived was here in America, through us, we who had survived and escaped.

Immediately after I finished, amidst the applause, the Crown Prince strode over to me, took both my hands in his own and addressed me in German: "Ganz reizend" he said, "very charming, I loved your songs!" He turned to his wife, Crown Princess Ingrid, and introduced me. She, too, complimented me on the performance.

Mrs. Roosevelt at my elbow said, "I will bring her back to you, but now I would like her to meet my husband."

If anyone had told me during the first trying months that on April 30, 1939, I would be guest of the President of the United States, give a concert for his guests, and stay overnight at Mrs. Roosevelt's, I would have regarded the teller of such a fantastic fairy tale as crazy.

There I was, standing before Franklin Roosevelt and holding his outstretched hand. (I was suddenly reminded of the American Consul in Prague who asked me the name of the President.) He had strong, fleshy, freckled hands. I was shocked to see this powerful man tied to a wheelchair.

I was fascinated by the President's face. It struck me as no ordinary face, but the face of a leader. People who can lead, reflect the power of their leadership in their features. I believe one can see the evil as well as the good in the shape of a mouth, the expression of the eyes, the form of the face. Franklin Roosevelt's face described to me the man and his character. When talking to me he looked straight into my eyes and held them. His chin, strong and slightly jutting, told me of his determination. I was charmed by his voice, and my musically trained ear recognized the tone of his speech as cultured. I knew instantly that I had met an unusual personality, a man of great inner power, a great leader. But a very different sort of leader than the hated Führer. I was drawn to him instinctively, experiencing his charismatic charm which turned opponents to followers.

As Mrs. Roosevelt introduced me to him, he said, "I enjoyed your singing very much. I know your country. I have been there myself, and it is dreadful to realize what is happening there now. But my dear, I would like you not to lose hope because I think that evil will not last. Anyway, I am glad you came to this country, and I hope you will be happy here."

I could not let this moment go by without telling him about my parents. "May I tell you something very personal, Mr. President?"

"Yes, of course," he replied looking expectantly at me.

"A year ago, on March 11, when Hitler moved across the border of Austria and I heard the mad shouting of the mob through the radio, I told my father that I would emigrate to America."

"Yes?"

"And my father said somewhat sarcastically, 'Who do you think is waiting for you in America? The President?'" I continued, "I never dreamed I would actually meet you face to face. Can you imagine what this evening means to me?"

"Yes, I can. Where are your parents now?"

"Still in Vienna, I hope, but one never knows with conditions what they are."

"Don't your parents want to emigrate too?"

"I don't know. They have a house, and my father has a pension.

Here he would have to start all over again. His profession is not one he could use here, a lawyer. There are not many people who have a chance to meet you personally, not even American citizens I would guess, and certainly not immigrants. Mr. President, I want to tell you that America is the hope of the oppressed people of Europe; they know that without America, freedom can not be regained. Do you know, Mr. President, that the persecuted people of Europe are praying for war?"

"No. I did not know that."

But now I could see that this was no topic for an evening such as this. It was to be a gay and carefree evening, and I sensed that my conversation had taken too serious a turn.

"We will do whatever is in our power," he said, and nodded reassuringly. Someone else stepped up to talk to him.

Mrs. Roosevelt introduced me to the silver-haired matron who sat next to the President, "Mama, I would like you to meet Miss Kraus."

Mrs. Sarah Roosevelt graciously commented she, too, had liked my singing and that she loved "that type of music," which she had heard in Salzburg and Vienna.

The image of my parents didn't leave me all evening. I saw their faces before me, ached to be with them, wanted them to know, to see, to hear all that was happening to me now.

After my conversation with the President, I found myself talking with Crown Prince Frederick. He was tall and handsome, and stood straight as a ramrod. Inescapably the conversation turned to Hitler and the threat posed to the freedom of all European countries. His Royal Highness did not seem very worried that Hitler would invade his country, or if he was worried, he certainly did not let on. Not much later, when the Nazis did invade Denmark, the Danish Royal House refused to cooperate with the Gestapo and did not, as did the Dutch and Norwegian Royal families, go into exile in Canada. The Danish King, Frederick's father, and his family stayed in Denmark and, defying the hated conquerors, wore the yellow star of David to show their solidarity with the persecuted Jews.

Crown Prince Frederick personally invited me to the formal opening of the Danish pavilion at the New York World's Fair.

"How will I get in?" I asked.

"Just tell them at the gate that I invited you!" It never occurred to His Royal Highness that the guards at the gate might have their doubts about the plausibility of my claim were I to try to "crash" the party. However, two days later, the lovely Danish Countess Bernstorff, who had been one of the guests, appeared at Mrs. Schey's apartment to take me to the reception. Unfortunately, I did not know she was coming, so I was not at home.

Throughout my conversation with the Crown Prince, I noticed that the Prince's aide-de-camp looking concerned. Suddenly I knew! I realized what a social faux pas I had committed when the officer, looking pointedly at me, addressed the Prince as "Your Royal Highness."

"Oh, good Lord!" I thought, and could feel the red flame of embarrassment spread from my throat to my face. I had addressed him as "you" all evening, never realizing (since I had no previous experience chatting with royalty) that a Crown Prince warrants the title "Your Royal Highness." I decided that the best thing was to ignore my mistake and continue with the correct address, as if nothing happened.

"Is your Royal Highness going to spend the night here in Hyde Park?"

I saw an amused smile cross his face, for he had seen his adjutant's concern, and recognized my attempt to get the protocol right.

"Yes," he replied, "and I do hope I will see you again tomorrow morning. I understand we are going to have a picnic somewhere outdoors. Will you be there?"

Mrs. Roosevelt had come up and overheard the Prince's remark. "Yes, she will be there."

Earl came across the room toward me. "You have made quite a conquest," he said. "He never left your side all evening, you and the Prince." He continued, "I am to take you over to the Lady's house now."

I shook hands all around, saying good night to the President and his mother and to all the other guests, and to Mrs. Roosevelt, who warmly kissed me on both cheeks, wishing me a good night and telling me to be ready for breakfast at eight the next morning. Franz Mittler had already left because he had to catch an early train in the morning. It was a pity that he had to miss the picnic!

It took me a long time to "wind down." While Earl, Tommy, and I sat in Mrs. Roosevelt's living room talking over the events of the evening, my mind was still vibrating from the unusual impressions. Sitting in a deep armchair I must have had a far-away look on my face for I heard Earl say, "Hey, Fräulein, come back! Do you want a nightcap?"

My hand reached up to my hair. Why should I want a nightcap? I thought it was a cover for my head.

Earl laughed, "A nightcap is a drink before turning in."

"Oh! No. thank you, I'm quite content."

But he had one. He said my program was all right for the Danish Crown Prince but that American audiences wouldn't "go for that kind of music, too highbrow, you know." Earl was not much interested in classical music and neither, he assured me, were most Americans, except maybe those who went to the Metropolitan Opera or to Carnegie Hall. "I'm just telling you for your own good."

I should have paid attention to his words. What he told me was, after all, not very different from Anna Sosenko's words. But like many European artists in those days, I was stubborn, and thought I knew all there was to know about success.

After the recital in Hyde Park and its obvious success, I simply smiled and nodded and was convinced that the miracle which had brought me to be where I was at the moment would continue to place me at the right place at the right time.

The next morning I helped Mrs. Roosevelt prepare for the picnic, which was held on the hill above Val Kill where the President's retreat was under construction. Everything had to be transported over a stony unpaved road – food, tables, utensils, and the charcoal stoves that were used to fry hot dogs. Mrs. Roosevelt was in the habit of serving these American favorites to everyone who came to visit, be it a group of disadvantaged boys from Harlem, the Crown Prince of Denmark, or the King and Queen of England. Perhaps it was a welcome change for the latter to be given an opportunity once in a while to be treated as "plain folks." No one seemed to mind eating with their fingers and putting mustard on the food from a kitchen dispenser.

Mrs. Roosevelt herself enjoyed frying the food and serving it on paper plates and in paper cups. On that day, she drove up and down the steep road to the hill, innumerable times for there always was something missing, the napkins, the paper cups, and she was forever being sent down the hill by Tommy to fetch one more thing. It seemed to me that she loved it.

The royal party arrived around noon and so did the President, in his car, which was especially built for him to operate without the use of his legs. I observed for the first time how the President was lifted out of his car and into his chair. It was done with lightning speed.

The place now swarmed with Secret Service men. They were strategically placed behind bushes and trees, and I had to laugh because they were so obvious.

After the picnic, I returned to the city, convinced that my recital for the President of the United States was the sesame which would open every door and skyrocket me from obscurity to sudden spectacular fame. All the more so, as Mrs. Roosevelt had told me she would write about my singing in her column, "My Day." That, surely, I thought, would make me well known throughout the country. It did, in a certain way, but there were other surprises in store for me that I had not anticipated.

12

On the train back to New York City, I thought the passengers should know about my fantastic experience. In fact, I was almost angry that no one seemed to notice the halo which I felt must surround me. But no one paid any attention to me.

At Mrs. Schey's apartment, I finally found interest in my Hyde Park adventure. That day I was also introduced to a gentlemen named Brown, a friend of Lacy Kux, Mrs. Schey's brother, and like Lacy a banker and stock broker. This Mr. Brown wanted to be in show business and was fascinated with the story of the young immigrant Cinderella who sang for the President and the Prince. He called a number of columnists in New York, knowing that newspapers are always eager for unusual material to attract more readers. He was right; the story of Cinderella and the Crown Prince appeared in three hundred newspapers from coast to coast!

I was convinced I would get nightclub engagements. In addition, Mrs. Roosevelt kept her promise to mention my singing her column "My Day." Mr. Brown, impressed with the Roosevelt angle and perhaps hoping to find entry into the world of show business, offered to manage me. So he got busy setting auditions in sophisticated supper clubs. The Blue Angel, one of the most popular, featured such headliners as Pearl Bailey, Hildegarde, Harry Richman, and Edith Piaf. It was utter folly to expect the management to accept me, but because Mr. Brown frequented the place as a well-heeled patron, they politely listened to my songs, and then just as politely said, "Thank you very much. We will call you when we have an opening."

Next on the list was the swank St. Regis Supper Club. Prince Obolensky, the White Russian emigre and manager of the club, listened in the shadows of the darkened club, as I sang in a spotlight in the empty room during one afternoon.

"Sing some French chansons," he asked in his accented English. I had no French chansons in my repertoire, only a couple of French art songs, Bergerette's shepherd songs.

"Very nice for the concert stage," said Obolensky, "but not suitable for a nightclub."

One more try by the determined Mr. Brown, the Rainbow Room in Rockefeller Center. When I auditioned, the chairs were upside down on the tables. The cleaning women swooshed mops, and dishes clattered, hardly a fitting background to my singing for the nameless person sitting in the dark. I heard his voice from the rear, "Thank you very much, we will let you know."

Brown was not a quitter. He arranged for am MGM screen test in Hollywood, but I didn't go. I was afraid of another failure. Perhaps my mother's cautious, and often pessimistic, admonitions influenced my thinking. "Don't expect too much and you will not be disappointed," she warned, putting dampers on my happy-go-lucky optimism. The trouble was that she was often right. Once in a while, when faced with a difficult decision I remembered my mother's words.

Mr. Brown was embarrassed by my failures, and I can't say that I blame him. Suddenly, he became too busy to do anything else for me. I never saw him again.

Anna Sosenko, when informed of my various activities, cautioned me that I was not famous enough, did not have the proper repertoire, didn't look glamorous enough. Further deflating me, she commented that my Hyde Park concert and its resulting publicity didn't mean a thing.

"It takes many things to become successful," she gave the sermon again. "Overnight success takes at least twenty years. People come here, thinking they will find work in the theaters, nightclubs, and restaurants. There are thousands of unemployed actors and singers. You must have unusual talent and, most important of all, do something unusual with it to make it."

****

That May the letters from Austria came infrequently and were written very cautiously. My mother and I developed a code to get past any censor. I invented relatives with names like Maurice to describe the French; cousin Mary, the English; Ivan, the Russians; and Gwendolyn, the Americans. Thus, I could discuss the activities of these cousins and their intentions.

That there would be war sooner or later, none of us doubted it. Hitler's aggressive moves and his belligerent speeches left no doubt that he would not stop. We immigrants could not believe that

France, England, and America conducted business as usual, lulled into a sense of security by Hitler's assertions that he had no more territorial demands. In fact, the opponents of Hitler hoped for war because they saw war as the only rescue from persecution and occupation.

So in my letters I attempted to instill the hope that such a course would eventually be followed and that they could look forward to war as the liberator from slavery. I wrote in a naive, childlike style, so that my letters, though opened and read by the censors, nevertheless reached my parents.

Naturally, I wrote only positive reports about my life and never mentioned my own disappointments and rejections.

****

The weather in New York changed. I was not prepared for such heat. It could be hot in Europe too, but the sweltering humidity, coupled with almost 100 degree temperatures that prevailed during the spring of 1939, depressed me terribly. In addition, Mrs. Schey's brother returned, so I had to find another place. Mrs. Schey recommended the home of a lady physician only recently arrived from Europe. She was renting one room of her three-room apartment in Yorkville, the German section of New York, for six dollars a week, kitchen privileges included.

On a beastly hot day, my large steamer trunk and I took a taxi to a decidedly lower middle-class neighborhood at Lexington Avenue and 86th Street. After I paid him, the driver simply dumped the luggage on the sidewalk and drove off.

The building was gray and impersonal. No doorman, no canopy, no elevator. It was built like a fortress with two courtyards. In each corner a stairway lead to the upper floors. The entrance to the first courtyard was an arched doorway. In the shadows, a prowler could not be seen until you passed directly in front of him. The entrance had been used by countless dogs and the stench was stifling. It was definitely not an address to enhance my prestige. Yet I was grateful I had a place not only to sleep but also to cook, for that would make living cheaper. At that moment, however, my main problem was getting my huge steamer trunk, my suitcase and hat box across two courtyards and up three flights of a winding, iron staircase.

There are moments in life when even a small problem becomes the straw that breaks the camel's back. I looked across the expanse, trying to solve the problem of not leaving one piece of my property unguarded while dragging the other across the two courtyards and up the stairs. People came and went. No one paid attention. No one offered to help. Several times I was tempted to ask a stranger to stay with my suitcase while I dragged the other one upstairs, but then again I was afraid they might steal it. I didn't even notice until later, that my cheeks were wet with tears. My clothes were soaked through from the perspiration that ran in little rivulets down my body. True to my European upbringing, I wore a hat and gloves in spite of the heat.

"Well, you can't stay here all day," I said to myself, "so do something." I began to drag my suitcase, steamer trunk and hatbox, simultaneously across the yards. A pull here, a pull there. One, two; one, two. That worked all right until I reached the stairs. Winding, narrow, iron stairs. Steep. Narrow, almost too narrow for my trunk.

I raced up the three flights of steps with the suitcase and hatbox, hoping no one would have time to steal the trunk. I made it to the third floor, breathless and exhausted. I rang the bell and the lady doctor opened the door. I called out to her, "I'll be right back."

It was hell bringing that monster up the winding staircase. I pulled it step by step, climbing backwards, brump,brump, brump, my face fiery red, my heart beating wildly. "This, too, is America," I thought. "How come no one tells you about this? Only about millionaires, Hollywood, and Cadillacs."

The apartment, while nice enough, was a far cry from the one I had just left. I had a tiny room to myself with a window looking out over small backyards where people hung laundry and children played among garbage containers. The Frau Doctor was hardly ever seen. She studied constantly, preparing for the examination all foreign physicians had to pass before being permitted to practice medicine. The biggest stumbling block was their meager knowledge of English. Often internationally famous physicians flunked the tests several times, not for lack of professional knowledge but for lack of English.

The move to Yorkville lowered my morale. I took stock. The concert in Hyde Park, flattering as it had been to my ego, had not contributed to my career in any tangible way. Mrs. Roosevelt's mention in her column was here today and gone tomorrow. However, I learned a valuable lesson: today's news gets stale very fast.

I still was trying to find work in nightclubs and hotels. Agents said my repertoire was unsuitable, that I needed American songs, semi-classical and popular, which would have to be arranged. I did not understand "arranged." The agents explained that it was not enough to sing a song as the composer had written it. The song had to be taken apart, put together again, the tempo altered, even embellished – in other words, tailored to the singer's personality. This tailoring must be done by a professional arranger, who would be paid a lot. Also, I would need special orchestrations. My arranger would do that for a fee, of course. All of this was very strange to me because I had been taught to respect a composer's work and sing his songs as he wrote them.

The spring of 1939 was also a time of heavy competition in my field. The concert booking agencies had their pick of the finest famous artists, all looking for work and ready to work at depressed fees. My finances were running low. Clearly, I had to find other work to support myself. Margit Schey, aware of my plight, suggested I join a group of Viennese women, all wives of Austrian physicians, who supported their families by making turbans of a knit material supplied by a wholesaler.

We met at the home of Marianne Sorter – an Aryan. She was the organizer of the group. Her husband's parents were Jewish. On the first day of Hitler's occupation of Vienna his "Aryan" colleagues denounced him to the Gestapo. Luckily, a loyal friend warned him. With his wife and two sons, he took the next train to Italy. Fortunately, they had valid passports. In those first tumultuous days, the border guards were not quite up to their later sadistic methods of detaining fleeing Jews. In Italy, the Sorters found what so many of my friends found: the Italians did not harbor any animosity against Jews and were most generous. Because they had spent every summer in Italy, the Sorters had a little money there, and they spoke Italian, both of which made waiting for their American visa easier.

I first met the Sorters in their new home, a brownstone in the Central Park West eighties. Once these houses had been the private residences of well-to-do citizens. Now they were apartment houses or more often rooming houses in which individual rooms, sometimes with kitchenettes could be rented. There was usually one bathroom per floor. Such was the new home of Dr. Sorter's family. They paid ten dollars a week for their room with a kitchenette. The room was divided by four curtains into four cubicles, one for the two boys, one for the parents' bedroom, one for cooking, and one for entertaining. They laughingly called that one their "salon," where we worked on the turbans.

Marianne Sorter was the prototype of the new female immigrant. In Vienna she had household help for every chore. Now she cooked nourishing meals with the few dollars supplied to her by the Jewish Refugee Committee. She washed and cleaned the clothes of her "three boys" by hand and hung them up to dry in one of the four cubicles. She encouraged her husband as he studied, and saw to it that the boys went to school on time, in clean clothes, with a good lunch in their brown paper bags.

And somehow she found work not only for herself, but for four or five other doctors' wives. I, unmarried and very young, was the exception. We did piece work, and the middleman came late in the evening to pick up the finished product, paying fourteen cents per turban. The work wasn't too difficult. Some of the ladies were handier than others and the competition was fierce to see who could make the greatest number. While we were working, we reminisced.

"Do you remember?" was a recurrent phrase. All of us had left loved ones behind. All day long, too, we were surrounded by various "perfumes" circulating from the cooking pots of tenants around us. "Frau Berger is cooking sauerkraut again," "upstairs they are having goulash; I can smell the onions." We brought our own lunches. We made perhaps three dollars a day, which was considered pretty good. I remember that period as pleasant and constructive. Not once did those women express resentment about living in cramped rooms, lacking the comforts they had been used to. Daily I heard expressions of gratitude for having found safety and freedom in the United States. "When the bell rings, I know it is the milkman and not the Gestapo" was the universal description of the reason for everyone's contentment with what, in comparison to their former lives, was a meager existence.

Because the crosstown bus ride was expensive, I walked and

thought nothing of going through Central Park even after dark. I was not aware that it was dangerous to do so, and perhaps in 1939 it was not.

One night a man stepped out from the shadows in my apartment building, exposing himself and hoarsely whispering, "Help me lady, help me lady." I jumped back, screaming. A couple came running to me. By then he had disappeared. I was afraid go through those two courtyards at night, but this was the only incident.

****

Not all refugees arrived penniless in America. Some saw the handwriting on the wall and transferred their assets to banks in Switzerland, Portugal, and South America. The most fortunate of all arrived with their jewels, furniture, paintings, silverware; yes, even with their china, tableware, glassware, rugs, and collections, everything from their former homes.

Among the lucky was Lilly Rona, a noted Viennese sculptress and poetess. My mother had written me about her suggesting that I look her up since she was a distant relative of a relative. I was never shy about calling on strangers and felt that at worst they could say they were too busy to see me, but at best I might win a new friend. The latter was true in the case of Lilly Rona.

A widow, she left Vienna with her two small daughters. After a few months spent in Italy, where so many refugees waited in safety for their immigration quota number, she and her daughters landed in Manhattan. Lilly was a vivacious forty, an unusually intelligent, cultured woman who spoke fluent English, French, Italian and, of course, her native Viennese-German. Her home was a large apartment on Manhattan's fashionable Sutton Place. She found quick entry into Gotham's social circles whose members admired the talented sculptress and attended her sophisticated, celebrity-studded parties.

She was yet another of the women whose friendship and guidance was so important to me. Unfortunately, many women are tempted to look at other women as competitors. Young girls, in particular, look at older women as not being "with it" to use a contemporary phrase. Quite often, they entrust their future to a man who tells them what they want to hear and guides them according to his own advantage, rarely contributing to emotional maturing. At least this is my point of view after years of struggling to survive. But I remember the women who helped shape my life: Harriet Hauser, my singing teacher in Vienna, Tante Lottie in Karlsbad, Hildegarde, Mrs. Roosevelt, and Lilly Rona.

Being included in Lilly's social circle meant a great deal to me. She was not only a sculptress and poetess, she also loved and supported musicians. In her home I found sympathy for my abortive attempts to find theatrical engagements. Moreover, here I found the orderly lifestyle I so deeply missed.

The names in her guest book represented the finest European theater, opera, and cinema had to offer. They came to mix and mingle and seek from each other the homage they had been accustomed to receiving from their audiences, audiences that had turned hostile overnight following the racial edicts of the Führer, Adolf Hitler.

I noticed one thing when I met some of these stars of stage and screen; they retained an air of being unapproachable, an attitude which differentiates European from the American celebrities. This air of superiority as well as their avoidance of "the plebs" caused many failures among European stars. When I observed how studiously they ignored me, an unknown young Viennese, I realized that our common fate had taught them nothing.

Thus, I was truly gratified by the warmth of Lilly's American friends. They came from Park Avenue society and were wealthy people whose portraits Lilly Rona was sculpting and who, like her, were patrons of the arts. It was my good fortune to be included in this circle whose members often asked me to sing for them and when I did, they listened appreciatively. Often I was invited to the homes of Lilly's friends to sing and later found in my purse a check discreetly given "for your expenses."

Now and then I wrote to Mrs. Roosevelt, informing her of my progress (or lack of same) and receiving sympathetic replies. "I do hope you get a summer engagement," she once wrote, "as it may make it much easier in the fall, if you get acquainted with people. Mr. Leigh [her booking agent for her lecture trips] told me that he could not handle a concert tour, but he would be happy to see you and advise you as to the best people in the concert business. Good luck to you."

I saw Mr. Leigh, who was not at all encouraging. "Don't try concert tours, too much competition. Try the summer circuit, the mountain hotels, they are always looking for someone to entertain their guests."

Fortunately, Lily came up with a name. "I have a friend," she said, "Bill Taub. He is a lawyer who knows a lot of people. Perhaps he can help."

A couple of days later she said, "Bill Taub will see you. Go to his office at 444 Fifth Avenue."

Mr. Taub, a tall, elegant man with a kind, gentle face, was waiting for me. He was polite and offered me a chair. I mention this because many times when I went to see people they did not offer me a chair, while they remained seated. Even today this happens.

"I think I have something for you," he said. "Have you ever heard of Grossingers?"

I hadn't. He told me it was a resort hotel in the Catskill Mountains, a couple of hours from New York. It was a kosher hotel. I had never heard of a kosher hotel.

"That's all right," he said, "you'll like it. And I think they will like you there. They will understand your Viennese songs. I got you an engagement for two weeks."

"How much?" I asked.

"Twenty-five dollars a week, and room and board. They'll treat you well, I made sure of that. They know you sang for the President. That helped."

I would have to move again with my two-hundred-pound trunk and give up my room. "And what happens after the two weeks?"

"If you play it right, you'll spend the whole summer there."

I was overjoyed; I had exactly one dollar in my purse. It was like being rescued just before drowning.

"How much will it cost to go up there?"

"A few dollars." He looked at me, reached in his coat pocket, took out his wallet and pulled ten dollars from it. "This is an advance payment," he said, "not to be repaid."
Do you have a lot of luggage?"

"Yes," I nodded, "a big trunk and suitcases."

He thought that over for a moment. "I will arrange for you to go by car." He asked for my address and told me a station wagon would come the next day to pick me up. I was immensely grateful. Why was this man doing that for me? I barely knew him. I learned later that he was always helping refugees. He did it out of a deep love for people and a compassion for those who had left their homeland and lost their loved ones. He remembered his own parents' flight from Russian pogroms.

During the war, when he was in England on a military assignment, he committed suicide. I was told he couldn't take the Blitz. It saddened me deeply for I had hoped to be able to tell him what a momentous event took place as a result of kindness. Overjoyed at the prospect of singing again, I hurried to thank Lilly and tell her of my good fortune. Lilly, practical as she was idealistic, said, "What about that monster trunk of yours? You are not going to take it along with you; you need only summer clothes, leave it here with me."

It was a thoughtful thing for her to do. To keep moving about with all my earthly belongings packed into a steamer trunk which weighed two hundred pounds increased the difficulties that confronted me because it hindered my mobility. That she thought of this without my mentioning it showed me what a kind and thoughtful friend she was.

So often we expect friends to do big important things for us and are tempted to measure their love and affection by the size and expense of their gifts. This is wrong. I measure a friend's value on seemingly insignificant contributions to my well-being, which in reality show that the friend is concerned with my life and contentment.

Thusly fortified and relieved of immediate worries, I returned to my Yorkville room and started packing. I thanked the lady doctor who had rented the room to me for her hospitality. The next morning when it was time for my departure, I was ready.

13

Although nothing had been added, my trunk seemed heavier than before. No doubt it was my frame of mind, my rootless and gypsy lifestyle, and my perpetual financial worries. I dragged that heavy steamer trunk down the winding staircase. Rumpedy-bumpedy from one step onto the next, across the courtyards, one by one, and finally to the street.

I waited by the curb until a station wagon from Grossingers drew up and the stony-faced driver identified himself. We rattled through the traffic and stopped at Lilly Rona's where the doorman took my trunk. And then began the trip to Jenny Grossinger's hotel in the Catskill Mountains where fate waited. Everything seemed rosy again. My Viennese temperament, always looking for the positive side, always ready to quickly change from crying to laughing, took the upper hand. I lived up to the Viennese proverb, "immer lustig fesch und munter, denn der Weana geht net unter," always gay, zesty and in good spirits, for the Viennese don't give up.

Now in a comfortable station wagon, accompanied only by one large suitcase and my hatbox, I sat back and looked around. I saw berthed ocean liners and remembered my arrival only six months before. Then we left New York behind and drove through towns that seemed very European. The scenery changed to sweeping meadows, trees, woods, a beautiful countryside, and a peaceful atmosphere. I had not dreamed this could be so near to one the world's largest, noisiest, dirtiest cities. The air changed; it smelled of fresh-cut grass. That undesirable oppressive heat also diminished. After a while, as familiar curves of hills and mountains greeted me, I knew how much I had missed the mountains. My heart sang.

After a long drive, we pulled into a wide tree-lined driveway and stopped in front of a hotel entrance. "We are here," said the taciturn driver.

The rolling hills and forests surrounding the hotel reminded me of the woods surrounding Vienna. Stretches of meadows, fields and an occasional brook met my eyes. I felt a stillness that was balm to the soul after the mayhem of Manhattan. The hotel was an enormous complex of low-slung buildings, many made of wood, landscaped patches of lawn with flower beds, gravel paths and benches. Along the paths I saw well-dressed elderly guests seated and relaxed, talking animatedly.

I entered the double door to the lobby where I was received by a maitre d'hotel and given a key and directions to my room in one of the nearby cottages. It was a small room, but comfortable and clean. I shared a bathroom with several other guests.

I was starting anew. I liked being away from New York's steel canyons and realized that being surrounded by a landscape similar to my homeland was important. Looking out of the tiny window and seeing trees, lawns and flowers relaxed me and made me hope that I might work there the entire summer.

I dressed for dinner. I did not know what to expect for I had never been in a resort hotel of this kind. I did not know the implications of a kosher hotel. To my knowledge there was no such thing anywhere in Europe.

I walked to the main building where I assumed the dining room was located. I didn't know anyone, and no one talked to me. I stood alone, surrounded by prosperous people who evidently knew each other and greeted each other with little exclamations of joy. It's a lonesome feeling to stand unrecognized in such a crowd. You don't know what to do with yourself, where to look and what to do – should you sit down?

I was relieved when a hotel employee told me to give my name to a woman seated at a table near the dining room entrance. She had a long list of names; I had visions of being embarrassed if my name was not on her list. But it was.

"Oh yes, there you are, Miss Lotte Kraus." And she told me the number of my table and its location.

There were ten people at my table in the huge dining room. We introduced ourselves. Right away they spotted my accent.

"Where do you come from?"

"Vienna."

"How long have you been in this country?"

"Since January."

"You speak English well."

"I learned it in school."

"Oh, do they teach English in school over there?"

"Yes, and French and Latin."

Eyebrows went up. "What do you need that for, who speaks Latin today?" And, "This is a big country, we don't need to speak anything but English."

"Europe is not one country; it is composed of many smaller countries, and in some of them French is the language of the land."

"Oh. Do they speak any English over there?"

"Yes, many people do."

This conversation was typical, as I later learned. Americans have a complex about speaking a foreign language. They refuse, in general, to speak anything but English.

Because of my ignorance of the Jewish food laws, I committed a faux pas. I couldn't find butter on the table and politely asked the waiter if I might have some. He simply stared at me.

"We don't serve butter at this meal," he educated me. Something in his voice made me aware that there must be a reason for the absence of butter "at this meal." I wondered what it could be.

The gentleman next to me asked quietly, "Aren't you Jewish?"

I was startled. "No, why?"

"Because if you were, you would know that butter isn't served when we have a *fleischiges* meal."

I understood the word *fleischig*. It is a German word that means "meat." Thus, I was initiated in the difference between *fleischig* and *milchig* meals. In a kosher home, and in this case hotel, there is a strict separation of meat and dairy products. At Grossingers these laws were strictly observed, down to dishes upon which the food was offered and the utensils. In fact, there were two kitchens. When one was used, the other was locked. The food was delicious. Since it was based on recipes of Eastern and Central Europe, much of it was familiar and welcome to me.

The hotel grounds included golf courses, tennis courts, bridle paths, walking paths, beautifully landscaped gardens, and even a private lake for swimming and boating, all nestled into the gentle curvature of the green Catskill Mountains. I felt like I was in paradise. After the meal was over, as I started to explore all this splendor, a soft, firmly masculine voice said, "Would you mind if I walked with you?"

I looked up. Facing me stood a tall, slender, distinguished looking man, mature, with gray hair, and a face which I liked immediately.

His face was long and narrow, with a finely chiseled nose, and brows tilted toward brown eyes that were warm with a kind and inquisitive look to them. A straight, large, generous mouth and a firm chin completed the picture of the man whom I recognized as "my type." When he laid his hand on my arm to guide me toward one of the paths, I noticed his beautiful, large hands with their manicured fingernails, clean and well shaped. Hands disclose much of a person's character and temperament to me. While I don't profess to be an expert in the art of hand analysis, I do know what kind of hands appeal to me. I could not be on intimate terms with someone whose hands express a coarseness of character.

This man had been at my table at dinner, and I remembered that his eyes had rested on my face almost continuously. But he had been sitting on the other side of the round table and conversation was impossible unless one shouted, a custom we both seemed to abhor.

"My name is Cliff Shedd," he said softly. "I did not quite catch yours."

"Lotte Kraus," and I added, "try to pronounce it Loa-tay, I can't stand the American pronunciation Luddie." He smiled and pronounced my name as it is pronounced in Vienna.

We walked for about an hour until the darkness settled and a honey-colored moon came up over the tops of the trees. His voice began to ring the echo in me that I had been searching for. A gentle man yet there was strength and security in that gentleness. I loved listening to him He seemed to have an accent, his English was very different from the English spoken all around me.

"I am a New England Yankee," he chuckled, "I can't hide it, nor do I want to. I am very proud of Bellows Fall, Vermont. I was born there, and so were ten generations before me. We just missed the boat, the Mayflower, but we came on the next one in 1640 from Essex, England."

I did not know anything about Vermont.

"Some day I'll take you there," he said. "You'll love it if you love mountains and solitude."

I liked him more with every passing minute. His New England English was slightly nasal and seemed very cultured and elegant. He spoke distinctly and slowly so that I had no difficulty following his every word. I was as curious about his reason for being here as he seemed to be about mine.

"I am doing public relations work," he said answering my question, "for Milton Blackstone in New York." It would have been useless for him to explain what the public relations meant; my Americanization had not progressed enough to be familiar with the intricacies of promotion, advertising, and commercialization. Furthermore, it was the man who interested me, his personality and his attitude toward life and people.

Since my arrival in the United States, I had met no man who raised more than a fleeting interest in me. Raymond, in Miami Beach, was more interested in himself and his business than in anything else. Earl Miller, extraordinarily handsome and masculine, did not share my intellectual and cultural interests. His self-admiration and obvious awareness of the impact he had on women created in me a resistance to his charms. I did not wish to be included in his "harem."

I gravitated to men at least twenty years older than myself. Students of Freud might find in this trend a constant search for a father image. I loved my father deeply and admired his character, his honesty, and his loyalty to his family. Perhaps I was searching for the man embodying these traits, but since I had not found them in any of the men who crossed my path, I waited, somewhat impatiently I admit, for the man of my dreams.

That first American summer went by very quickly. I sang my Viennese songs on Saturday nights on the stage of Grossingers Playhouse. I heard the sweet sound of applause and the cries of "more," "encore," and "bravo" and was asked to stay for the entire summer. I swam in the lake, sunned myself on the little beach adjoining it, ate fabulous Grossinger meals, made friends with the guests, saw Cliff Shedd every day.

Mysteriously, he surfaced wherever I happened to be. He said he had to transact public relations business for Grossingers. It was enough for me to see him every day, to listen to his voice, to waltz with him on those rare occasions when the orchestra played a waltz, and to let him tell me about America and Americans. He had substance, a respect and love for tradition and particularly for his country. It was not the flag-waving kind so often demonstrated by people whose patriotism is limited to celebrating periodic festivals.

I talked to Cliff about everything – about my parents, about the

Nazis, about my doubts and fears as well as about my hopes and dreams. He listened attentively and then answered, gently, carefully and always reassuringly. I knew that I could trust him without reservations.

When I emerged from my room each morning, I found myself looking for him and if, by chance, he was not on his accustomed place on a certain bench, I found myself disturbed and uneasy. Could it be that I was falling in love with him?

I knew very little about him, not much more than that he lived somewhere in New York City, drove a gray 1939 Packard car, and was a lot older than I. I was comfortable in his company. When he was not around I missed him.

One morning he sat in his usual bench.

"Good morning," he said. "I have to drive to New York, and I find that I hate to leave you."

"I know the feeling. I will miss you too."

"I have something to tell you. I don't know how to start."

"The best way is to start at the beginning."

He was silent for a moment. "The beginning goes back twenty years."

I felt the heat rising in my throat. Another woman!

"There is someone in New York, and I owe her loyalty and honesty. She has been my friend for twenty years. I never expected this would happen to me. I don't know what in the world has happened to me. I am miserable when I am not with you, and I don't know what to do about it."

I sat very still. I did not say one word, nor did I permit my face to show any emotion. After a long silence, I said, "I do not want to be the cause of someone else's unhappiness. Perhaps we better not see each other anymore."

"I am not married," he said, "but it's as good as being married. Please understand," he hurried to say, "I have never been so happy in all my life. I have never met anyone like you. I – I love you!"

I was not certain of my own feelings. I was sure that I would be lonely without him, but was it love? Who was he really? What could I expect? I did not want to stumble into uncertainty. Life was difficult enough as it was.

"I have my career," I said, "I must think of that first, and I don't want complications."

"I will resolve everything in an honorable manner," he said, "if I just knew that you care for me, too. If I can continue to see you, talk to you, be with you ... my whole world has changed. Someday when everything is clean and orderly, I will marry you."

****

As the days and weeks passed, I knew that I loved him. But I also found out that nothing would be simple. Cliff had lost his money in the Depression by holding on to an advertising display business, paying his employees until all his reserves were gone. He started all over again. Could I, the penniless refugee, afford the luxury of falling in love with a man who had no money? What was more important: emotion or reason?

I had turned down several proposals that had come my way, wealthy men, secure in position and financial resources. Why? Because I did not love them. Silly? My mother would certainly think so. Not my father. He said to me, "Money is not the most important thing – character is most important. Find a man who is decent, loyal, and generous. A man who loves you and has the same interests as you. A man who is kind and gentle." Cliff Shedd fulfilled all those requirements. Yet I could not decide.

"We will wait and see," I said.

"How long will you wait?" he asked.

"As long as it takes."

The summer was filled with the scent of roses blossoming along the paths we walked together, the nights were filled with the sparkle of stars and the light of a moon that shed its beams on two people who had found each other, bewildered, hoping for a miracle to solve the problem of their love. There was music and dancing and laughter and sometimes, suddenly, a stabbing pain – and, "What will happen when the summer ends?"

I was not too preoccupied to forget the political situation in Europe. I received letters from my parents informing me that everyone in Europe expected war. But no one in America expected it. The country was totally unprepared – physically as well as emotionally. Then on September 3, 1939, German planes rained their bombs on defenseless Warsaw and German Panzer divisions blitzkrieged across the Polish border. England declared war on Germany.

Cliff, reading the headlines said, "Well boys, let's polish the guns. Here we go again." No one believed him.

"America will never again be involved in a war in Europe," everyone said. "Let them fight their wars, we have nothing to do with it."

I was at once glad and terrified. Glad because I knew that only a war could end the horror that Hitler was bringing to the world; terrified because of the dangers to my family. I was certain that all communication with them would soon end. As it turned out, I did not get any news for nearly six years!

Immediately after Labor Day we both returned to New York City. Since I did not have a place to live, Cliff suggested the YWCA as a first stop until I could find a room and look for work. We drove to New York in silence, each one dreading the uncertainty that waited for us, hating the prospect of separation yet knowing that there was no other way for the moment.

Within two days I had located a room in a rooming house, recommended by the YWCA, at 139 East 54th Street. It was a good section of town, and the house itself was typical of walk-up rooming houses: a musty-smelling hallway, three flights of stairs, a stained runner on the stairs and dark, windowless corridors – on each floor, a kitchen and a bathroom. I had a corner room on the third floor. It had two windows, one looking out over 39th Street, and the other overlooking Lexington Avenue. The rent was six dollars a week which included all facilities and the use of the kitchen. There was even room for my large steamer trunk.

***

Before telling anyone of my return to New York City, I wanted to get settled and fix up my room so it had some resemblance of home. I got a pail, mop, and a broom in the kitchen and cleaned the place with a vengeance. The kitchen had not been used for a long time and was filthy. I scrubbed until it shone. In my room I washed the curtains and bedspread, polished the windows and the dresser mirror and then bought flowers and a vase in the store around the corner. During this cleaning, doors opened in the corridor and heads peeked out to investigate the unusual goings on.

One by one I met my neighbors: an old lady and her daughter, plus their ancient dog, living in the room next to mine. Two very young girls, farmer's daughters, who had followed the lure of the big city to seek their fortune in New York City; they hadn't found it yet. Then there were George and Jane; he a merchant seaman, she a young English girl who married him, only to find out that he drank and could not support her. They lived several doors down in one miserable room. Next, Helen, a former Ziegfield girl, ill, old, and desperately poor, living on welfare – in those days seven dollars and fifty cents a week, or so she told me. The poverty of their lives, both physically and emotionally, filled me with apprehension lest I end up as they did living in a corridor of abandoned souls.

Therefore I decided to regard this rooming-house existence as a temporary necessity which I would get out of as soon as possible. I had to proceed methodically and not be pushed into quick and hasty decisions by my desire to better myself. I wanted to make my own way and not seek the easy way out – to seek or accept the support of a man, in or out of marriage. As far back as I could remember, I had wanted to be independent, to be successful in show business, to be "someone" purely on my own merits.

When Cliff came to visit, I told him that I wanted time to follow my career. I had to find out how far I could go. In addition, I said I did not want to hurt anyone. Thus, before making any move, we had to do some serious thinking. He was a tenth-generation American, I an immigrant. There is, I told him, a difference in mentality and lifestyle and we needed to be sure that they did not clash. He was neither angry or disappointed.

"I love you" he said. "I have never loved anyone as I love you. I will wait, let things develop in their own time. They will work out, I know it."

For the moment, however, nothing looked as if it would ever work out. I continued my singing lessons with Margit Schey and visited Lilly, who not only offered encouragement and support but also became my confidant, and I discussed my relationship with Cliff.

"Bring him here," Lilly said, "let me see him."

She invited us to dine with some of her European and American friends. It was important to see him blend so easily and comfortably into this cosmopolitan circle. He was a big hit with his quiet, intelligent manner. It is, I think, important that a man and a woman be proud of each other and relaxed in company, alone and with others.

"I like him," said Lilly, "but I hoped you would find someone with money. It makes life easier, you know."

I had written to Mrs. Roosevelt that I was back in town, and she responded immediately by inviting me to dinner with Earl Miller, along with the young woman who was to become his wife, at her apartment.

She wanted to know all about my summer and about my professional progress and was dismayed when I told her I hadn't been able to find work. She suggested I contact the Catholic Refugee Committee for financial assistance, so that I could continue looking for work, making the daily rounds of booking agents.

"I will call them and tell them to expect you" she said, meaning the Refugee Committee. "And I think," she added, "there will be another opportunity for you to sing for us, this time at the White House."

My spirits, once again, rose. The next morning I visited the Catholic Refugee Committee and was told I would receive the usual assistance of $10 per week for ten weeks. That was a lot of money. It paid my rent of $6.50 and left $3.50 for food and maintenance. I cooked my meals in the kitchen down the hallway. They were simple meals – rice and a little ham, vegetables and eggs, milk, bread and cheese – I never starved. My mother's preaching on thriftiness came in mighty handy. I was the only one on the floor using the kitchen, never eating out in the many cheap little restaurants that dotted Lexington Avenue.

Now and then I sang at ladies' luncheons (free lunch there), in nightclubs here and there, at club meetings for women's organizations, and the like. The fees I received – $5 and sometimes even $10 – supplemented my income. But still it was depressing.

My first American Christmas. Everyone was busy with their own lives. Cliff brought me a duck, a bottle of wine, flowers, fruit, candy, and cakes. He was going to New England to be with his family. Lilly

Rona went skiing. On the 24th of December, Christmas Eve, I was suddenly very, very much alone.

I bought a small tree for fifty cents on Lexington Avenue. I found a few real candles and even candle holders, the European kind that clip onto the branches. And I bought some decorations at Woolworth's, late in the afternoon when they were on sale for a few pennies. Then I said to myself, "Stop feeling sorry for yourself! Do something. You are not so badly off. You have a warm room, you are free, and you have enough to eat. Make the best of it!"

I purchased ingredients for cookies – sugar, eggs, butter, flour and nuts and bought a baking sheet. Laden down with my treasures, I went back to my room, put up the tree, trimmed it, and distributed a few evergreen branches about the room. Then I went into the kitchen and soon the tantalizing smell of sweet cookies and Christmas pastries began permeating the entire floor. One by one, the occupants of the adjoining rooms appeared, sniffing and curiously staring at my busy hands and the ever growing mounds of sweets piling up on paper plates. Nothing like this had ever happened before.

When I was done, I invited them all into my room. It was crowded, but we managed. We opened the bottle of wine, and everyone brought a glass to partake in the celebration of Christmas. Someone began to sing American Christmas carols, and then I offered to show them how "Silent Night" should be sung and sang it in German. As I sang, the room became very still, as each one withdrew into himself. I think everyone remembered other Christmases, perhaps happy ones or sad ones, but none as lonely as this one. As I sang "Stille Nacht, Heilige Nacht," I, too, let my thoughts wander to my mother and father, my sister Trude, three thousand miles away. God only knew what kind of Christmas they were having. How strange fate could be. Perhaps it was that loneliness and the tears that streamed over my cheeks as I sang, that made us all understand the deep meaning of this Christmas. It was a Christmas none of us ever forgot.

On Christmas Day a messenger brought me a large basket of assorted fruits, nuts, candy and preserves from Mrs. Roosevelt. These were delicacies I couldn't afford, so I savored the luxuries sparingly and with gusto.

A couple of days after Christmas a letter arrived from Mrs.

Roosevelt inviting me to accompany her to a speaking engagement at the Hotel Roosevelt. She gave me her unlisted telephone number and asked that I call to make arrangements. When I called, I was told to wait for Mrs. Roosevelt in the lobby of the hotel at six o'clock. It was seven before she hurried through the doors, obviously distraught.

"There was," she apologized, "a misunderstanding about the time." She was dressed in a long black fur coat, a hat with feathers was perched on her head, and she carried, as she always did, a large handbag as well as a briefcase. Those last two were always with her. The handbag often held her knitting which she took out at odd moments while involved in conversation.

When we stepped into the elevator, the management wanted to ban other riders. She protested strenuously and insisted that anybody who wanted to use that elevator should "absolutely" be permitted to do so. We then stood squeezed into a corner of that crowded elevator.

Before the dinner meeting, holding my hand, she introduced me to everyone (I do not recall any names, not even the name of the organization, but I do recall her asking that I be seated at the table next to the dais). While the first course of the dinner was being served, she beckoned me to the dais. She whispered to me that she thought it might be a good idea if I were to sing a few songs. She suggested that I go home right after dinner to fetch my music. She, in the meantime, would arrange for an accompanist and a piano to be ready by the time I returned.

It was the most unorthodox, unexpected, improbable arrangement for a concert and caught me completely off guard. But she worked everything out. Someone took me home by taxi and brought me back with my music. Someone else, familiar with my classical repertoire, was found to accompany me on the piano which was wheeled into the large auditorium. Three hundred persons wanted to hear her speak and speak she did while I discussed the choice of my songs in the corridor with the accompanist (I think his name was Bauer). At the end of her speech, Mrs. Roosevelt informed the unsuspecting audience that she had a little surprise.

"A young friend of mine, a Viennese who has only recently come to our country and who has a lovely voice is going to sing for you now."

Today I would know what songs to choose. Back then I did not realize that my classical repertoire by Schubert and Brahms was not what a dinner audience at the Hotel Roosevelt wanted. Yet, they were polite and applauded because it was the First Lady who had arranged for the impromptu entertainment.

Afterwards she said she would take me home. She rejected all offers of assistance, addressing me with a "Come along now." We hurried out through the door onto the street and stood by the curb hailing a taxi. One drove up and a man who had been waiting by the curb was just about to open the car door when he recognized the wife of the President of the United States. He gallantly offered her the taxi. She would have none of it. "No indeed, you waited longer. We can take the next one." When we finally got a cab, she insisted I get in first.

She hoped my singing would help get me a job. Then she promised to write about the performance in her column, thereby giving me added publicity. While, she really knew very little about the complicated and intricate ways of show business success, she helped in the only way she could through letters of introduction and through invitations to perform at the White House.

She delivered me to my rooming house. If she noticed that it was a grubby-looking apartment house, she did not let on but said only, "It's centrally located, you can walk anywhere from here. Be sure to let me know if I can be of help to you. Good night, dear."

14

Dear Miss Kraus:

I know that you are going to sing here on January 16th, and I wondered if you want to spend the night of the 15th or 16th here with us.

If you will let me know what train you are coming on, we will have someone there waiting to meet you. I hope the New Year will be a happier one for you than the past one has been.

Very sincerely yours,
Eleanor Roosevelt

I was to be a houseguest of the President at the White House! I feverishly prepared for the concert, an afternoon musical for the wives of Congressmen. I was to share the stage with a young pianist, Ezra Rachlin. Mr. Greiner of Steinway Hall, the entertainment manager for White House musicales, wrote asking for my program, urging me to write the names of the composers " . . . clearly and to indicate after each piece its duration in minutes. Please remember," the letter continued, "that in making up the program the total time allotted you, including one encore at the end of the second group must not exceed seventeen to eighteen minutes. Also, please give me the name of your accompanist."

I selected a program of light classics, folksongs, and Viennese waltzes and wrote that Professor Franz Mittler would be my accompanist.

On January 15, a liveried White House chauffeur was waiting for me at the Washington station. "Miss Kraus? Follow me please."

A White House limousine waited outside. As an immigrant, I was thrilled to ride in style to the White House. I was truly Cinderella in a gilded coach.

****

The White House, though a large and comfortable mansion, had none of the overwhelming splendor I had seen in Vienna's Hofburg, the former residence of the Austrian Habsburg Emperors. Yet, the White House was awe-inspiring. I sensed history in the hallways, staircases, reception rooms, and even within the living quarters of the President and his family – a history which was at least as important as the thousand-year-old history of the Habsburgs. Even though I was a greenhorn, I was conscious of the crucial role of the American President. I was convinced that the White House held the key to the victory of freedom.

A maid led me to a lavishly furnished bedroom, which I later learned had been the bedroom of their Majesties, King George and Queen Elizabeth of England. The room was also stifling hot with windows that could not be opened. A few moments later, the maid entered with my suitcase and information that the "President regretted not being able to join me for dinner as he had another obligation" and the suggestion that I have my dinner served in my room. I asked the maid if something could be done about the heat, and she said she would see to it. Moments later, a small table loaded with all sorts of covered containers was rolled into the room. I slipped into a comfortable dressing gown to cool off and sat down for dinner.

There was chicken a la king, peas, a boiled potato sitting unhappily all by itself on a small plate, some kind of nondescript pudding, and coffee. Hardly a gourmet meal, but as I learned during subsequent visits, food was a not a noted feature of the Roosevelt era. In fact, at a Hyde Park picnic, I remember the writer and artist, Hendrik Willem van Loon, saying, "They are such lovely people, those Roosevelts. Too bad that they serve such lousy food."

A bit later, Mrs. Roosevelt, just back from New York, knocked on my door to ask if I would like to accompany her to a speaking engagement. I agreed and wondered how she kept up the pace. Did she ever have a chance to spend a few quiet moments at home in the evening?

"No," she laughed. "Not in Washington and not in New York. Only in Val Kill, once in a great while."

I quickly dressed, and we were off to a hall where hundreds of people eagerly awaited her arrival. It was always the same. Like a swarm of bees, the functionaries descended upon her, engulfed her, while she sailed through their midst like a great battleship, towering a head over everyone, shaking hands, smiling, greeting those she had met before and then asking, "Well, what do you want me to talk about?"

She could launch into any subject at a moment's notice, holding her audience spellbound. I marveled at her ability to speak without notes or preparation and studied her technique of adjusting herself to any audience: women, men, mixed, American, cosmopolitan educated, less educated, Park Avenue wealthy, Virginia coal miners – she had the secret that opened the hearts of everyone. Her magic formula was the utter sincerity of her own beliefs and the total absence of desire for personal gain.

When we returned late that night, she took me to my room to make sure that I had everything I wanted, and wished me a good night, with an embrace and a kiss on the cheek. The excitement of sleeping in the White House and in the bed in which English royalty had slept was not conducive to a good night's sleep. Also, the heat was undiminished.

The next morning, we had a large breakfast in the family room. Scrambled eggs, bacon (the dog, Fala, got several slices of bacon), toast, muffins, cereal, and the usual coffee – half milk, half coffee – poured into huge cups. Later Mr. Mittler, who had spent the night at a hotel, and I went on our sight-seeing tour in a White House limousine. Lunch, which included Mr. Mittler, was a light meal hosted by Miss Thompson.

At three o'clock, after testing the piano and my voice, we presented the concert to about three hundred ladies in the East Room. They applauded politely. They were then ushered into an adjoining room for tea and a buffet, while I accompanied Mrs. Roosevelt upstairs to the family quarters to have tea with Mr. and Mrs. J. P. Morgan, who were distant cousins, and a rather disheveled-looking young man, Joe Lash.

While we were having tea, Mrs. Roosevelt said, "Oh, by the way, you don't have to go home tonight, do you? Stay with us, I'm sure you will want to meet the President again."

I accepted with enthusiasm. Later, we went to the Oval Room where we found the President busily engaged in mixing his devastating martinis for his secretary Missy Le Hand, Tommy

Thompson, the Morgans, and Joe Lash. (Those martinis were perfect knockouts; I learned to accept one, stand with it in my hand, and politely refuse to drink up.) We stood in a semicircle around the President, who handed out cocktails one by one while seated behind his enormous desk.

"Frank, this is Miss Kraus. Do you remember when she sang for us when the Danish Crown Prince was in Hyde Park? She sang again this afternoon at our musicale."

"Of course, I remember you," the President smiled as he handed me my martini.

We remained in the study until seven o'clock and then proceeded to the dining room ahead of the President who came down by elevator. To my joy, I was seated at the President's left. Young Mrs. Morgan sat at the President's right. He ate very little. I wondered how such a big man could sustain as heavy a work load on so little food. I hardly ate a bite because of the fascinating man to my right. Several times Mrs. Roosevelt called across the table, "Charlotte, don't forget to eat."

He was a charming table partner. He gave me all of his attention, asking me if I had news from my parents, how I was adjusting to life in the United States, did I have friends to keep away loneliness. Then he asked me whether I had any news about the political situation in Austria. This last question gave me chance to touch on politics and the "destroyer question." Roosevelt had proposed lending eighty of America's mothballed destroyers to the British – a proposal that met with tough opposition from isolationists, who feared the move would involve us in the war in Europe.

I told the President that the destroyer deal should go through and that the United States should give England even more help. I repeated that all of Europe fervently hoped the United States would get involved in the war because that was the only way Hitler could be defeated.

The President nodded and commented that unfortunately it was not up to him alone to make decisions. There were Congressmen who saw the situation differently, and sentiment against involving America in a war was very strong. Then our conversation moved away from politics to his love of trees and the many varieties of berries he grew on his "farm." A bit later, Mrs. Roosevelt moved the conversation back to politics, telling him that Joe Lash wanted to talk more about the destroyers. Lash was prominent in the ADA, Americans for Democratic Action. He was some sort of leader in the student movements and had been in Spain, sympathizing with the Loyalist side against Franco. Lash wanted America to stay out of any European conflict.

At this point Russia was teamed up with Nazi Germany. When Nazi Germany invaded Poland from the west in the fall of 1939, Soviet Russia attacked Poland from the east, ostensibly to help Poland fight the Nazis, a help Poland had not asked for and did not want because the Poles knew the Russians came not as friends but as enemies. In fact, the Russians encircled the Polish armies that had withdrawn to the east and annihilated them. So Poland was split between the two archenemies, the Nazis and the Soviets. Because Russia was not prepared to fight the Nazis, it signed a nonaggression treaty with Germany and promised Germany huge shipments of food and fuel.

The "pink" circles of America were working feverishly to forestall any move which would counteract Soviet Russia's policy at that moment. One such move would be to help Britain in her resistance against the Nazis. Thus, the grotesque situation arose that anyone in sympathy with Soviet Russia had to oppose American help to the Allies.

Lash questioned the wisdom of American interference in the affairs of Europe. He felt, he told the President, that America should mind her own business. Hitler was across an ocean and presented no danger to Americans or the American system. He argued that he was expressing the opinion of millions of young people who didn't want to get mixed up in a European war. Besides, the British Navy would shield us. It was much more important to improve the lot of the unemployed in the United States and it was ridiculous, he continued, to think anybody would attack us with three thousand miles of water between us. The President listened and leaned forward.

"Are you finished?" he asked Lash.

"Yes."

"O.K. Now I am going to tell YOU."

"Let's assume that France does not hold. If we are realistic we must admit that she has only a fifty-fifty chance, England would then stand alone. Let's surmise that England, in all her bravery and courage, could not withstand the onslaught of the Germans and were defeated. Let's even go further and say that the British Navy, or at least part of it, could escape to Canada and so be saved from falling into German hands. But the Germans would then hold all of Europe including the British Isles. Let's assume they would be satisfied with this victory for at least the moment.

"They would make offers to South America to be the main buyer on the South American markets. All South American trade would have to be handled exclusively by the Germania Trade Company, which would buy only under conditions acceptable to the Germans. If the South American countries would not agree, Germania would say, 'All right, so we won't buy, but we will blockade you so you won't be able to sell to anyone else.' Then, with economic submission accomplished, the German infiltration into South America would begin. German schools, German teachers, German businesses, and slowly German political supervision.

"And then German 'tourists' would arrive. South American armies would be wholly dominated by German instructors, radio stations, and newspapers. All cultural, educational, economic, religious, and social life in South America would slowly, but inevitably, be taken over by the Nazis. Airfields would be built in the jungles and the German tourists would all have uniforms in their sacks and one day the tourist armies would be large enough and strong enough to overthrow the legitimate governments of South American countries. And from those airfields the German bombers would easily fly to bomb our own cities."

Lash was no longer cocky. He had not considered the situation as the President had described it.

"Thank you, Mr. President," he said subdued.

Later, I asked Mrs. Roosevelt why she thought it appropriate to bring people who opposed the country's defense system to the attention of the President in such an intimate atmosphere.

"I know people wonder why I do it," she said to me, "but if we don't listen to these people and give them a chance to express their opinions, if we don't bother to explain things to them and try to change their minds, they will go underground and fall prey to all sorts of subversive influences, leaving us with a hidden enemy. It is better to know what you're up against."

Later that same evening, Mrs. Roosevelt asked me to accompany her to a meeting of the Washington Society of Christians and Jews where she was scheduled to speak. Her host was Dr. Frank Kingdon, a friend and supporter. I had watched her all day, following a schedule of activities she adhered to with the punctuality of a Swiss clock. She didn't have a moment's rest except for the half hour at tea time and the hour we dined. Surrounded again by reporters and functionaries of the organization, she asked the question I heard so many times, "What do you want me to talk about?"

That evening she spoke for an hour about the brotherhood of man, the necessity for all religions to work together for the common good of all people. Then she answered questions for a half hour or more. Afterwards, she invited Dr. Kingdon back to the White House for a strategy planning session for the future of the society. My own eyes were heavy and, although she asked me to join them, I begged off. I marveled at her endurance. She seemed fresh and untiring, and I believed Tommy, who said she often stayed up till three o'clock answering her mail.

****

After breakfasting with Mrs. Roosevelt the next morning, I went to my room to pack my bag. She appeared in the doorway, saying, "Listen child, I know you had expenses and I don't want you to spend your own money; I'll send you a check."

Shortly before I left, she returned, having given a press conference in the meantime, to say good-bye and to tell me she hoped I had enjoyed my stay at the White House and that she would see me again soon. On the way to the station, I had the driver stop at a flower shop and ordered a dozen red roses sent to her.

"What a life I lead," I mused on the train. From the glamour and excitement of the White House to my gloomy rooming house in New York City. A concert at the White House but no job, no regular income to bring stability into my life.

When I got back to my room, a letter was waiting. A booking agent wrote that I should immediately call on the owner of a Viennese restaurant in upper Manhattan – Der Wiener Fiaker. I had my first long-run engagement. The restaurant, on West 80th Street, was popular and successful. I sang nightly to Austrian and German exiles, as well as nostalgic Americans, as they ate Wiener Schnitzel mit Gurkensalat, Apfelstrudl and Kaffee mit Schlag. My partner Fritz Spielmann, also a Viennese exile, was a superb pianist and composer whose operetta tunes I knew from my days at Radio Vienna. He played with that sentimental yet exuberant feeling so typically Viennese. Audiences packed the place nightly.

My salary was thirty-five dollars a week and included my dinner. One evening Hildegarde came to hear me sing and was so enchanted with the atmosphere that she played piano and sang. It always adds to the prestige of a place when celebrities appear and enjoy themselves.

Every evening I took the bus to the restaurant and returned to my rooming house at three in the morning. It never occurred to me to worry about walking in the deserted streets at night or waiting at street corners for the bus. Life was safe in those days, at least as it concerned me.

The fact that I sang at the White House was snapped up by several newspaper chains, which helped popularize my name, particularly among the now sizable Austrian colony. Mrs. Roosevelt mentioned my recital in her column. "Miss Charlotte Kraus, who sang for us when the Danish Crown Prince visited Hyde Park, sang again for us very charmingly." Many of the patrons came to see who that Viennese singer was and wondered why, with all the famous refugee artists living in New York, she – an unknown – got to sing in the White House.

One day a Viennese photographer I met at Lilly Rona's pleaded with me to bring Mrs. Roosevelt to the opening of his exhibit at the Gallery St. Etienne on 57th Street. The gallery was famous because Dr. Kallir, also a Viennese exile, had recently discovered Grandma Moses.

I wrote Mrs. Roosevelt about the exhibit and told her that the photographer, Hans Hannau, had been a well-known artist in Vienna who was now trying to establish a new career in this country. Knowing how busy she was, I did not expect her to come. Thus I was astonished to receive a reply by return mail.

"I find," she wrote, "I can spare one hour and will be happy to be at the gallery at the time mentioned. I will, however, have to leave in exactly one hour because I have another commitment later."

We planned a festive program which would do justice to the special visit of the First Lady. I would sing a few songs accompanied by Franz Mittler, and then Mr. Hannau and Dr. Kallir would take Mrs. Roosevelt on a tour of the exhibit. Only a limited number of guests were to be invited and refreshments were to be offered. The time for her arrival came and went. Everyone was terribly nervous. Some of the more malevolent whispered that I had perhaps only imagined her consent. I ran downstairs, looked up and down 57th Street. No sign of Mrs. Roosevelt.

Finally, after half an hour, I spotted her hurrying up the street. I ran upstairs. Everyone took their positions. We expected her to be accompanied by the usual Secret Service protection, but she came totally alone. She had forgotten where the exhibit was and, therefore, dropped in at every gallery on 57th Street to find out where the exhibit was.

She didn't take off her coat and refused the tea and cookies. But she listened to my songs and graciously consented to have her picture taken over and over. She also gave Hans Hannau a very nice write-up in her column, thus helping to publicize his photos of New York and no doubt contributing to his subsequent success.

****

One evening I spotted my old friend Franz Engel, the director of the Literatur Cabaret where I sang in Vienna, among the patrons of the Wiener Fiaker. He wanted me to join some actors, singers, and writers from the Lituratur Cabaret in a Broadway musical appropriately called "Reunion in New York." I was thrilled that all of us, except for those who became Nazis and remained in Naziland, had escaped. Our reunion was joyous. The lure of Broadway was so great that I accepted.

Ezra Stone produced and underwrote the show, which showcased only Viennese actors. It was written by Viennese writers with the help of American experts. Later some of the actors became well-known, including Herbert Berghof who studied at the Reinhardt Seminar the same time I did and was a rising young star until Hitler put an end to his career. Years later he married Uta Hagen, and the two founded a successful acting school in New York. In addition, there was Lotte Goslar, the comic dance genius, as well as Elisabeth Neumann and Bert Silving whose string orchestra had played for the very first radio broadcasts at the RAVAG Radio Vienna.

While rehearsals were underway, I continued singing at the Wiener Fiaker, but once the show opened, I had to give up that job. The revue consisted of blackouts and nostalgic, humorous scenes reminiscent of the Vienna we all remembered and missed. In some scenes we depicted our curiosity about and ignorance of our new homeland, its customs, peculiarities, and strange practices. We sang ditties, danced, and talked and hoped that the audience understood our Viennese humor.

I loved the stage, the footlights, the excitement, and the challenge. What I did not like was the coarse language of some of my colleagues, especially the women who had picked up American four-letter words and a revolting vocabulary. Also, I was not used to the rather shocking informality which existed between the sexes. Even though I had been on the stage with most of these actors in Vienna, they had changed. I was glad I was not on stage much; most of my singing was alone and in front of the curtain.

For the first few weeks the audiences applauded and filled the seats every night. Then they seemed to tire of it. The revue was not spectacular. There were no big chorus lines, no memorable tunes to whistle or hum after leaving the theater. Probably Broadway was not the right frame for it. It belonged in a small intimate cabaret.

As the days went by and audiences dwindled, we faced problems. The stage hands had not been paid. They were union. We were not. We did not have to be paid. To keep the show going, we took a cut – from $50.00 a week to $35.00, then to $25.00, and finally came the day when Ezra Stone closed the show.

On that day I sat in my room. Unemployed again. The Wiener Fiaker would not take me back. The owner was peeved with me for leaving.

15

My second American spring! I had achieved nothing. I was not one iota nearer to my goals. This was a grim time for everyone. The war in Europe was termed the Cold War although for the Poles, Czechs, Austrians, and now, also, the Danes and Norwegians, the war was as hot as fire – from guns, planes, and bombs. No one had stopped Hitler. I knew Holland would be next. I worried about the Schneiders, who had shown me such generous hospitality in Rotterdam. George Schneider had been so confident that the Germans would respect the sovereignty of Holland. I wondered what had happened to the Danish Crown Prince and his charming Princess. Were they safe or prisoners of the Gestapo?

I still received occasional guarded letters from my parents, proof at least that my family was still in their home and alive. I had difficulty reading American newspapers. The headlines, abbreviations, and phraseology seemed like another language. Sometimes I had to read a sentence three or four times before I understood it. So I depended on some of my European friends who were more familiar with newspaper English. All of us, especially those from Austria and Czechoslovakia, were glum and expected the worst and we felt somehow guilty for living under relatively good conditions. Certainly we all savored being free and totally unhampered in the daily pursuit of our lives.

****

Shortly after getting established in New York, I went to the immigration authorities to apply for final citizenship papers. I had applied for first papers in Miami and wanted to make sure that they had been properly transferred. The official sitting behind the desk called my name.

"Nationality?"

"Austrian."

He looked up. "There is no such thing any longer," he said sourly. "Austria has ceased to exist; it is now Germany. You are German."

"Excuse me," I said, trying hard not to scream at him, "I do not recognize the occupation of Austria by Nazi Germany, that is why I am in this country now. I am not German, never have I been a German, and I will never be a German. My country is Austria, and it has been Austria since the year 800."

He was one of those individuals who seemed not to like immigrants, or perhaps he was ignorant of history or possibly he was impressed with the German Reich and Hitler's successes. There were quite a number of those sympathizers back then.

"But now there is no Austria," he said stubbornly.

"Sir," I said, "pardon me, if Hitler should conquer Europe and then come over here and conquer and occupy America would you call yourself a German or an American?"

He looked at me; the color rose in his face. He was silent. He took my papers and wrote on them: nationality – Austrian.

Yes, there were many pro-Nazi Americans in New York. I met them frequently. They talked freely to me because I spoke fluent German, and they assumed I was one of them. They approached me in stores when they heard my accent. One of them, the janitor in my rooming house made long speeches about the glories of the Third Reich and the decadence of "das verjudete Amerika." He was a typical case. He had come to America immediately after World War I, hoping to find a better life. He now lived in Yorktown, Little Germany, and after twenty years could barely communicate in English. He had tried his hand at many things and now swept the dirt from corridors and bedrooms in a rooming house.

He was frustrated and disappointed and looking to the Führer for the salvation of a dream he couldn't fulfill on his own. He was identical to many German-Americans in those days and certainly to his fellow Germans in the Reich itself. I tried to enlighten him about the realities of life under Nazi government and told him about the oppression and horror and the total loss of individual freedom. He did not believe me.

"Greuelpropaganda!" he labeled my tales, "horror propaganda, invented by the Jews and Communists, to destroy Germany once more."

I suggested he contact the German-American Bund, I was sure they would pay his fare back. Perhaps he did get back, I certainly hope so, for there is no cure for fanatics of that kind, except for them to go to the source of their admiration and be cured of their illusions the hard way.

****

While living in New York City during 1939, 1940, and 1941, I was often told that "New York is not America." I wondered why. Was it because New York is the place where immigrants arrive from Europe and go no further? Where is America "more American"? What does it mean to "be an American"? Is it simply a question of one's mentality or spiritual beliefs? Is it a set of habits, mannerisms, attitudes, and customs? When would I be an American?

I knew that I was conspicuous in my appearance, accent and demeanor. I sometimes wished I could camouflage those outward characteristics that labeled me as a foreigner because being a foreigner was not an advantage in those days. I frequently was met with hostility because some Americans were not very sure of their geography and mistook me for a German of the new Germany under Hitler.

When I explained that I came from Austria, I was asked, "What was wrong with Australia and why didn't you stay there?"

I was told that I should "eat correctly" because I cut the meat on my plate and kept the knife in my right hand and ate with the fork in my left and didn't switch back and forth as did Americans.

My European clothes were made of materials designed to last practically forever. The colors I wore were dowdy – gray, black, brown and beige. My clothes were "English cut," severely tailored, no nonsense, no frills. My hats, too, were easily recognizable. They were mannish, simple and practical. (I couldn't believe my eyes when I first beheld the "gardens" American women wore on their heads.) Even my handbags, though made of the finest leather, brought forth invitations to "go and buy something more American." What is an American?

It is easy to understand why immigrants search each other out, live in neighborhoods where they can talk to each other, help each other, keep alive the memories of their homelands, customs, and cultures. It is easier when you have someone who can remember with you, sing and dance and play the melodies of your ancestors. It is not surprising that so many refugees remained in New York, afraid to leave the security of ethnic neighborhoods. I wondered if I could become a "real American" if I stayed in New York.

I was not happy living in the big, noisy city. I yearned for the sun. I found it only on the roof of my rooming house. The roof was full of soot and black dust, and in the sun it smelled of oil and smoke. While it was hot, I felt released from confinement up there among the chimneys and smokestacks. I carried big pieces of packing paper and towels up there, put on my bathing suit and took sun baths. When I got too hot, I went downstairs and took a shower. And then up again for more sun. From my vantage point I could see other roofs, just as black with soot and just as steaming, just as filled with people sunning, holding picnics, sleeping, reading.

Among all the exiles from Vienna, I was the only young woman who had arrived alone. There were families – father, mother and children. There were old people whose children could not get American visas and who had gone to Asia, Australia or even Africa, hoping someday to get the cherished visa. There were young couples. There were older men, alone, their wives unable to follow because their immigration quota based on nationality had been filled. All of them had been uprooted, coping as best they could with a different life and language. They found themselves useless, unrecognized for their life's accomplishments.

Jokes made the rounds among the refugees, "Every Dachshund in New York claims to have been a St. Bernard in Europe." A sadly self-descriptive phrase for the thousands of lawyers, professors, scientists, artists, who had held prominent positions in their homelands but now had only menial jobs. There was no welfare; I doubt those people would have accepted it had there been such.

It was not a good time to be an immigrant. Americans couldn't find jobs. How could the new arrivals hope to integrate into such an economy. The miracle is that America is somehow always able to accomplish the impossible. Somehow all of us survived and most of us, sooner or later, began to prosper.

****

I sang here and there on radio shows, at club luncheons, ladies' meetings and earned enough to pay my modest bills and to eat well. Among my proudest accomplishments during those rather grim months is the fact that I never once went hungry. For a few pennies I was able to prepare for myself tasty, nourishing meals in the rooming house kitchen. The other roomers were either amazed or irritated (perhaps by the aromas of my cooking), but not one of them followed my lead. They ate their meals in cafeterias and restaurants – half as nourishing and twice as expensive.

I lived from day to day in a curious state of suspension, subconsciously aware that this period of my life was a waiting period. I did not know when or how, but I knew that this could be only the beginning, not the end. Cliff went in and out of my life in those months. I was in a strange mood, unable to make up my mind what course to follow. While he called every day, I knew he had not entirely severed his relationship with the other woman, and I rejected the idea of coming between two people.

He also was having financial difficulties. In other words, he had no money. Depressed, he felt he had no right to pursue any future plans for us. To be with him, I eagerly accepted his suggestions to visit the Metropolitan Museum, the Planetarium, the Cloisters, sometimes a movie, or an outdoor concert in Central Park.

He was a rock-ribbed Republican and had none of my enthusiasm for the Roosevelts. He hoped fervently for Wendell Willkie's victory because the economy would improve and he could re-establish himself. I didn't argue because the intricacies of American party politics were beyond my comprehension. All I knew was that I liked the President and Mrs. Roosevelt because they had been extremely kind to me. I considered it an amazing stroke of luck to have met them and been accepted by them on a basis of equality and friendship. If Mr. Willkie won the election, I would no longer be able to sing at the White House; therefore, I hoped he would lose. It was as simple as that.

****

At this point, Otto Wallis was inserted into my life. Several years earlier, he had courted me in Vienna. My parents were happy – here at last was something tangible for their daughter, a well-to-do, handsome, promising physician, someone who might win her away from the stage and give her the right kind of life. Elegant dinner parties were arranged, Papa drew him into a corner of the *Herrenzimmer*, as the study was called, for man-to-man conversations and announced that Otto was charming, cultured, and *angenehm* – pleasant. The only fault Mother found was that Otto was not quite tall enough, she liked tall men.

But then came Hitler and Otto was a gynecologist – a very dangerous profession to practice under the Nazis, particularly when one could not point to a pure Aryan family tree. Otto was a *Mischling* – he had a Jewish father and an Aryan mother. But his mother had accepted the Jewish religion when she married his father and thus Otto was "classified" Jewish under the Nuremberg Race Laws. His Aryan colleagues who had envied his professional success saw their chance to get rid of him.

There was a standard procedure to accomplish this. The nurses in the doctor's office were coerced by the Gestapo into accusing the doctor of abortion, or if this was difficult to "prove," they complained of a pain and asked the doctor to examine them. At a given signal, the Gestapo burst into the office and finding the nurse on the table ready for an examination, they accused the doctor of attempted rape.

Fortunately, Otto had friends who warned him that he was "on the list" and urged him to drop everything and disappear. Before leaving, he called my father who gave him Mrs. Schey's address. After arriving in New York via Sweden, he called Margit Schey and asked for permission to meet me there.

Meetings with friends from the homeland were heartwarming and heartbreaking. I was glad to see that another friend had escaped the danger and found refuge and safety. Yet the monstrous persecution of innocent human beings for no other reason than that they offended a warped and criminal regime ruined what peace of mind I had. Otto's father died when the Nazis took over Vienna. I didn't pursue the why and how. He was trying to bring his mother to America. He was among the fortunate. His future was securely anchored in his medical knowledge. A distant relative promised him the certainty of a new practice in Chicago. We sat alone in Mrs. Schey's living room. He asked me to go with him as his wife. What a shock. Here suddenly was a solution to all my problems. I was offered warm and faithful love, social position, and financial independence. No more struggles, no more worries, a man of my own background, of my own Viennese mentality, an anchor in the ocean of loneliness.

"Come with me to Chicago, forget the stage and the foolish hopes for a career. How can you compete with all the big names? You will have the best of everything, I promise. Come with me, I love you."

But I did not love him. I liked him. I had always liked him. I knew even then that it is necessary to like a man if one is to love him. In Vienna we had listened to music together and discussed the problems we saw on the political horizon. However, I simply could not visualize myself living with this man. There was no longing to touch him, to hear his voice, to be held in his arms. I knew that I could never marry a man without such feelings. It was not enough to be financially secure; it was more important to be emotionally fulfilled, a luxury I could ill afford at this point. Yet my heart has always ruled my head.

"I am so sorry," I told him, "but I cannot come with you to Chicago, and I cannot marry you."

His face fell, "Perhaps you should think it over, perhaps I was too abrupt, I should have taken more time."

"No, I am honored that you wanted me to be your wife and whoever will marry you will be very fortunate, but I cannot. I must do other things with my life."

Mrs. Schey entered the room, and Otto asked her to persuade me to change my mind. I think she knew that she could not.

After he left, Mrs. Schey berated me for being so foolish. I wondered how someone who had married entirely without love, as she had, and had a nonexistent love life could wish something similar for others.

It was very clear that I loved only Cliff. No matter how difficult it would be to solve all our problems, no matter how frugal and modest my lifestyle might be, I could be happy with him.

My birthplace home, Alleegasse3, Klosterneuburg.

Sister Trude 1-year-old, Charlotte 2-1/2-years old, Nanny Mitzie, 1916.

Elementary School 2nd grade (last row).

Tante Lotte, my godmother as a 17-year-old-bride, Karlsbad.

Family portrait: Father, Mother, Charlotte, Trude, 1918.

Earl Miller and I, Miami Beach, Florida, 1939.

My friend and helper Hildegarde, in Miami Beach.

Earl Miller's Cadillac. We drove from Florida to New York together, 1939.

Professional Photo, 1939.

THE WHITE HOUSE
WASHINGTON

December 22, 1939

Dear Miss Kraus:

I know that you are going to sing here on the 16th of January and I wondered if you wanted to spend either the night of the 15th or the 16th here with us.

If you will let me know what train you are coming on we will have you met.

I hope the New Year will be a happier one for you than the past one has been.

Very sincerely yours,

Eleanor Roosevelt

Letter from Mrs. Roosevelt with an invitation to spend the night at the White House. Picture: my first visit to Val Kill, 1939.

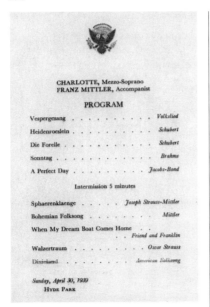

Concert program from my recital in
Hyde Park for the Danish Crown Prince
four months after arriving in America.

Mrs. Roosevelt visits Gallerie St. Etienne in New
York at my invitation. I sang a recital accompanied by
Franz Mittler, 1940.

Invitation to Inaugural luncheon at White
House for Cliff and me, 1940.

I sang at Grossingers, summer, 1939.

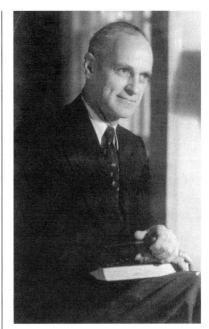

Clifford Shedd, my husband, 1941.

Robert Stolz conducts, New York Symphony. I sang his songs, 1943.

I met Cliff at Grossingers, 1939.

Christobel's christening at my home in
Arden, 1955.

Broadcasting from home while pregnant, 1954.

Christobel's first Christmas, 1955.

List of prominent personalities on my interview roster while I was a radio journalist, 1957.

Otto Preminger, famous film producer and director—and my teacher, 1953.

Invited to meet President Johnson at the White House in response to my broadcast about the Dominican Republic, 1963.

Representing Delaware at the grave of Dag Hammerskjöld of Sweden, 1961.

Reporting from the Berlin Wall.

Mrs. Roosevelt sends flowers to the ship *Gripsholm*, prior to my trip to Sweden, 1961.

Cliff and Mrs. Roosevelt at Val Kill, 1957.

Christobel shares a cookie with her godmother, Eleanor Roosevelt, 1962.

Mrs. Roosevelt and me in Val Kill prior to a trip to Europe, 1957.

I arranged the Democratic luncheon with Mrs.
Roosevelt and Lt. Gov. Alexis du Pont Bayard to
promote Adlai Stevenson's candidacy, 1962.

Ambassador Lemberger pins me with the
Silver Cross of Merit, during a ceremony
in my home in Arden, 1964.

Receiving the *George Washington Medal of Honor* from
Freedom Foundation of Valley Forge, 1964.

162

Charlotte's parents and sister Trude after World War II, 1947.

Mother, Charlotte and daughter Christobel, 1960.

Emma Hale, benefactor and friend.

Gregory Mchitarian, loving companion for 20 years, 1985.

Portrait by Hans Essinger when I was 19, 1932.

Charlotte interviewing Ambassador
Keichiro Asaki, 1954.

From left, Governor Carvel, Mrs. Roosevelt,
Charlotte and Alexis I. du Pont Bayard, arriving at
the Wilmington train station. Fund-raising dinner for
Stevenson 1952.

Charlotte at the Hungarian border, 1963.

16

One of the great blessings of my life is that I can look back over the years and say, "I don't regret anything. If I had to do it all over again, I would choose exactly the same course." Painful and depressing as some of my experiences were, I knew they were necessary, and they helped form my character.

I knew I loved Cliff Shedd. Why him? He was twenty-five years my senior. It is not unusual to hear of young women falling in love with wealthy, older men. This was different. Cliff was devastated by the Depression. What could he offer me? What advantage was it to my security, future, career to tie my destiny to this man?

Still almost penniless, my reason dictated that I choose someone who could make my life more pleasurable, to relieve me of the daily aggravations as I attempted to establish a show business career.

But the chemistry of love is explainable only to those who are affected by it. And sometimes not even to those. One of the mysterious ingredients of love is something in German called "Das gewisse Etwas" – that certain something, or in French "je ne sais quoi" – I don't know what.

I needed his presence to be happy; I felt relaxed and comfortable with him. His even-tempered quiet manner helped me regain my peace of mind when I had moments of panic remembering my parents, their danger, the Nazis, the war, and the fear that I might never see my family again.

He knew no prejudice. His Vermont parents taught him that people must not be judged by their color, religion, or nationality. There were only two kinds of people: good people and bad people. In Bellows Falls, he had grown up side by side with Poles, Czechs, Germans, Chinese, Catholics, Congregationalists, Jews, and heaven knows what else.

He explained, "We only were concerned about living together and helping one another. We attended each other's churches, ate at each other's table, visited each other's homes. I was never made aware that there is any difference in people until I came to New York. At home we were not allowed to 'tag' people. We judged them by their deeds and their behavior and that was all." It was one of the reasons I loved him.

It also appealed to me that he was a tenth-generation American. I sensed a certain patina of traditions and roots similar to my own. His ancestor, Daniel Shedd, had landed in Massachusetts in 1640. The Shedds had remained in New England except for one branch which settled in the Midwest. The generations produced a line of scholars, scientists, ministers, artists, and military men as well as outstanding women whose names are recorded in the Shedd genealogy. This lineage of intellect impressed me more than big money did because I needed to communicate intellectually as well as emotionally with the man I planned to share a lifetime. I had seen enough marriages based only on financial security to recognize that such an arrangement would be disastrous.

Cliff, with his natural nobility, was the leader in our relationship. I could learn from him, follow his guidance, entrust myself to his care. I needed his tenderness, and I admired the tremendous understanding he had – for people, situations, and the complexity of the human spirit. That I judged him correctly was borne out later when, during the war, he performed an outstanding job as War Food Administrator for the Department of Agriculture on the Delmarva Peninsula. However, we were far from those developments in the late fall of 1940.

By then Wendell Willkie had lost. "Now everything is shot," Cliff complained, "I hoped I could reopen my factory. But now with Roosevelt's win, I have no hope."

"Would you mind if I tried to see what I can do for you since I happen to know the wife of the President?" I asked.

He didn't like the idea. It wounded his pride, and perhaps it didn't agree with his political convictions. But I did try. I called the unlisted telephone number of Mrs. Roosevelt's New York apartment and asked if I might come to see her about something very important. As usual, the reply was instantaneous. I met her at her mother-in-law's home on the East Side. She was dressed in coat and hat, but she motioned me to a nearby sofa.

"I don't have much time, but this sounded important, and I didn't want you to wait. I have about ten minutes. You can ride with me in the taxi, I will take you wherever you have to go."

It was like that always. Confiding in her was so easy, much easier than talking to my mother.

"Sit on my left," she said, "this is my good ear. What's wrong?"

"I would like your opinion on an important personal matter. About a year ago I fell in love with a man. I want to marry him."

"Oh, how wonderful!"

"I don't know if you will say 'how wonderful' when you hear the details. He's quite a bit older than I and is a victim of the Depression. He lost his business and has not been able to find his way back to prosperity. Without a secure income and a respectable position we can't get married, and I don't know how to solve the problem. I am coming to you for advice and help."

She was silent for a moment. "Do you really love him?"

"Yes, I really do."

"Well, then here's what we can do. I will have you both come to the White House for Christmas. I would like to meet him, and then we will see what can be done."

Not for one moment did she question my intentions nor did she attempt to dissuade me from doing something which might have seemed quite illogical. She always respected other people's decisions, whether she agreed with them or not. I was overwhelmed by her warmth and understanding.

"I will send you an invitation with the details. Perhaps you can lead us in singing Christmas carols." She continued, "Do you know American Christmas carols?"

"I'm afraid I don't."

"I'll send you a booklet of carols." She thought of everything; it was quite incredible. She reached over and took my hand.

"Don't worry, I think everything will be all right."

I followed my instinct and leaned over and kissed her.

She looked at the huge wristwatch she always wore, "I have to go now, come along."

The maid called a taxi. The driver turned inquiringly, and she said, "I'll give you the exact address in just a minute, it's downtown, go down Park Avenue. "

She began searching for her little black address book in her huge purse.

"Oh dear, my goodness. I must have left it at home." She was distraught. "I can't turn back now, I'll stop at this drug store to get the address from the telephone book."

We left the cab and entered the store. As she approached the clerk behind the counter, his eyes opened wide. "I wonder if I may look into your telephone book for an address?"

"Yes, certainly," he wasn't absolutely certain and looked at me questioningly. His lips formed the words, "Mrs. Roosevelt?"

I nodded. She had gone into the phone booth and was dialing information.

The drug store owner asked, "No Secret Service? She walks around just like that without protection?"

I nodded again. She hated to be followed and if Secret Service agents were shadowing her, I never saw them.

The people she was trying to find had an unlisted telephone. I heard her say to the operator, "Listen dear, I am Mrs. Franklin Roosevelt and I need the address or telephone number of these people. They are expecting me, and I hate to have them think I am rude."

She could not convince the operator. Then she returned to the clerk and put a nickel on the counter. "I found it in the phone booth, it isn't mine." (In those days a nickel bought a telephone call, a bar of chocolate, a subway ride from one end of New York City to the other, an ice cream cone, a day-old loaf of bread.)

The clerk could not pass up the opportunity to talk to the wife of the President. "Mrs. Roosevelt, it's a privilege that you stopped by here today. I am a great admirer of you and your husband."

"Thank you," she said. She was shy about compliments, though by that time she certainly must have been used to them. She thanked him profusely for the use of his telephone and refused his offer to call another taxi for her. We stood at the curb, and a taxi soon drew up.

"No thank you, Mrs. Roosevelt, I will walk home," I replied when she offered to take me home before returning to her own home to pick up her little black address book.

"You will hear shortly from me, dear. Good luck." She kissed me and climbed into a taxi which had drawn up alongside the curb. She was off.

****

It had begun to rain, a slight thin drizzle. I didn't notice. I walked block after block not able to believe what was happening. Christmas at the White House. And with Cliff!

Cliff was torn. He didn't like the Roosevelts, yet he realized that being invited to the White House, particularly for Christmas, was a rare privilege. I also sensed that the lack of a good job weighed heavily on his soul. As soon as Americans meet someone, they want to know what you do. It bothered Cliff, who was a proud man, not to be able to answer proudly. In watching him, I learned about the injury to a man's self-esteem that results from economic misfortune. I hoped I could help him, but I also realized that I had to proceed with caution lest I humiliate him.

To get married, we needed a regular monthly income. At that time, Cliff was producing playground equipment for kindergarten schools, but it brought in very little money. Perhaps it was a carryover from the security I had seen in my father's government job, but I wanted Cliff to have a protected government job and intended to do what I could to achieve that goal.

When the official invitation arrived, it stipulated black tie for Christmas dinner and informed us that a White House limousine would meet us at the railroad station. The mail also brought the booklet of Christmas carols and a letter telling me that I would lead the family in singing carols after dinner.

Goodness! The only carol I recognized was "Silent Night." I took the music to Mrs. Schey, and together we studied the songs. As I practiced, I remembered my last Christmas in Europe when I sang carols with the Schneiders in Rotterdam. Not in my wildest dreams would I have expected that only two years later I would be spending Christmas at the White House and singing Christmas carols with the President of the United States and his family.

On December 25 we took the train to Washington, D.C. – destination 1600 Pennsylvania Avenue, the residence of the President of the United States. The limousine was waiting for us. Because the chauffeur knew me from my previous visit, identification was unnecessary. Once inside the White House, Secret Service agents, looking like ordinary attendants, quickly took our suitcases and disappeared with them.

In the family quarters, I introduced Cliff to Mrs. Roosevelt. Although I had prepared her for the difference in our ages, I saw a fleeting look of astonishment cross her face. She quickly recovered, however, and charmingly greeted him and embraced and kissed me.

A butler guided Cliff to his room. Leading me to the Lincoln Bedroom, Mrs. Roosevelt told me that Mr. Lincoln had slept in the huge bed and I shouldn't be surprised if his ghost appeared during the night. (He didn't.) A moment later, the maid brought my suitcase and asked if I would like to have my gown pressed. Mrs. Roosevelt departed, inviting me for tea in a few minutes.

As I walked down the long hall toward the area where tea was served, I met Cliff and together we gingerly stepped over toys, dolls, trains, and several children playing on the floor. No one bothered them, and they did not pay attention to anyone. Cliff asked, "Who are these children?"

"Oh," said Mrs. Roosevelt, pouring tea into enormous cups, "these are the children of the Norwegian Crown Prince. We are taking care of them while their parents are away on a trip."

Crown Prince Olaf and his wife had left their Nazi-occupied country and were living in self-imposed exile in Canada. They were frequent visitors to the White House, where the Crown Prince acted as a lobbyist for Norwegians who had fled their country to join the British Navy and Royal Air Force.

Suddenly, we heard a voice from the other end of the room, "Eleanor, who sent me those socks?"

"I don't know dear, don't you have the card?"

"No, I can't find it."

The President, quietly sitting by a huge Christmas tree, was unwrapping presents and carefully collecting the accompanying cards so he could thank all the people who had sent gifts. Mrs. Roosevelt helped him go through the pile of wrapping paper, muttering, "Oh, this is terrible. How can we thank those people if we don't know who sent what."

"Mr. Shedd, will you come here to meet the President," Mrs. Roosevelt called across the room.

As we shook hands and admired some of the gifts, he said to me, "I hear you are going to sing for us tonight." Then we exchanged platitudes about how people were so kind to remember him at Christmas but that, unfortunately, the sizes never fit.

On the way back to our tea, we again dodged the children

playing on the floor – it was a very informal, very warm, and very typical American family Christmas atmosphere. The unassuming attitude was having its effect upon my Republican from Vermont.

Later when we assembled in the Oval Office for the President's martinis, he addressed Cliff by his name, "Nice to see you again Mr. Shedd." Cliff was floored.

The dinner in the huge state dining room was formal, with several guests added to the family. Harry Hopkins and his small daughter, Diane; the Morgenthaus; Harry Hooker, the President's old friend; and several others whose names I can't recall. The table, extending the entire length of the room, was beautifully set. Each guest found a small gift package next to the dinner service plate. Mine was a hand crocheted handbag; Cliff's, two very lovely silk ties. Also, there were little match boxes, decorated with a picture of a sailboat forming the letters FDR, and a small white Christmas trees with flowered ribbons.

The President sat at the head of the long table, Mrs. Roosevelt in the middle of the long side. Next to the President sat his mother. Three huge turkeys were brought in: one for the President, one for Harry Hopkins and one for Franklin Junior. All three men now began the serious job of carving the turkeys, calling out across the table, "Who wants white meat, who wants dark meat?"

It was a most informal "formal" dinner. Plates were passed around the table to be filled with meat, potatoes, spinach, string beans, celery, and cranberry sauce. Everything was piled on and then passed back again from hand to hand until it reached the expectant guest. When second helpings were due, Franklin Junior enthusiastically stood up, a piece of meat on his carving fork calling out, "Who wants more, who wants a piece of this delicious meat, come on now, eat some. You'll need your strength later for dancing. Hey, Charlotte, don't you want another piece of meat?"

After pumpkin and mince pie and coffee, the guests went to the East Room where the United States Marine Band was ready to accompany carol singing and square dancing. The President, with his dog Fala, was wheeled in. The President hummed happily and picked up one of the booklets of Christmas carols. I had never led a sing-along and didn't know how to start. Franklin Junior, sensing my quandary, got up from his chair, joined me, arm around my shoulder and said, "O.K., folks, number one." The band began to play and everybody sang "Oh Come All Ye Faithful."

When we got to "Silent Night" I said, "With your permission, I will sing this alone and in the original German." I sang it first when I was seven years old playing an angel in the school Christmas play, and my father had said, "I could hear your voice so clear and silvery, like a bell." I had sung it in Rotterdam, my last Christmas in Europe; I had sung it to the lonely people in my rooming house and at the office of the Catholic Refugee Committee when German and Austrian refugees had gathered for a Christmas celebration. The sweet, gentle tune with its simple message of faith caused that small gathering to weep unashamedly. And now, I sang it for the President. The room was still. Though they did not understand the words, they understood the message.

Mrs. Roosevelt impulsively stepped forward and kissed me and led me to the President. He shook my hand, "A Merry Christmas to you, and may you have happiness from now on."

Mrs. Roosevelt clapped her hands, "Let's dance the Virginia Reel." She told Franklin Junior to do the calling. I felt sorry for the President who sat alone in his wheelchair watching the cheerful hopping and swirling, the laughing and joking because many didn't know what they were doing and had no idea where to go to get their partners. He looked left out.

Fala tried to run among the dancers and slipped on the smooth parquet floor. The President called him back. He let his hand drop on Fala's head, and the dog sat happily, getting his ears scratched. The two of them sat for a little while longer, then the President said, "I think I'll go now," waved goodbye and rolled his wheelchair out of the room.

We danced until about eleven o'clock when the band packed up, and Mrs. Roosevelt bid us good night. It was the signal to go to our rooms.

Before I got to my room, Mrs. Roosevelt called to me, "Charlotte, I have made an appointment for Mr. Shedd to see some people at the Department of Agriculture tomorrow morning after breakfast. Tell him to be there at ten o'clock. Good night dear." Again a kiss, a smile and she was gone, no doubt to attend to some of her mail, even on Christmas.

The next day after breakfast, Cliff went for his interview. The government was just starting the School Lunch Program and needed men with business experience who were good organizers. The job offered to Cliff paid fifty dollars a week. Fifty dollars a week was not bad pay in 1940. Later many of our friends commented that considering the recommendation from the wife of the President of the United States, he could have probably asked for twice that much and received it. But Cliff would not take advantage of connections. He could neither be influenced nor bribed, as some later found to their dismay. He was a man who walked the straight and narrow, even when it was to his disadvantage.

When he returned to the White House and told Mrs. Roosevelt that he had accepted the position, she asked me with a twinkle in her eyes, "Does that solve your problem?"

"Oh yes, Mrs. Roosevelt, I am sure it will."

"All right, then, keep me informed."

Cliff was overwhelmed. "They are such great people," he kept saying over and over. He, a total stranger, had been included in a family gathering at Christmas time by the President of the United States. He had been made to feel welcome, so it was only natural that he became their enthusiastic admirer.

17

Cliff's job made it possible for us to set the wedding for May 17, 1941. I never thought to have a big wedding with all the fuss and trimmings. I didn't even know how to arrange a small formal ceremony. Frankly, I felt that what money we had should be spent on essentials. We bought my wedding ring for five dollars at Macy's, a simple narrow white gold band. I didn't know that black was taboo for weddings. So, the morning of May 17, out of the closet came the black and white wool dress I had worn on my first visit to Val Kill and a big black felt hat with a white ribbon. I slipped my hands into black and white European leather gloves and stuck my feet in my comfortable black and white shoes. I proceeded to City Hall luxuriously in a taxi. Cliff bought me a white gardenia.

The simple civil ceremony was conducted by a judge who was obviously tired and bored by it all. I didn't understand anything until he asked, "Do you take this man?" and when he said, "I now pronounce you man and wife." Suddenly he smiled and said, "Congratulations, Mrs. Shedd."

It gave me a start. "Who?" Oh my goodness, that's me!

Later, when life had become easier, and there was more time and money for the amenities of living, I sometimes wished I could have stood before an alter dressed in a white gown and veil, walked down the aisle to the Wedding March and greeted family and friends between tears and laughter.

Shortly before I got married, a cousin of mine, Hans Peter Kraus, arrived from Europe after spending eighteen months in the notorious Dachau Concentration Camp. Prior to Hitler's occupation of Austria, he had been one of Europe's best-known rare and old book dealers. His success earned him the envy of many competitors as well as the hatred of one of his employees, a Nazi, who denounced him to the Gestapo.

Hans was on one of the first prisoner transports to Dachau. After eighteen months of effort by his friends abroad, he was released and ordered to leave Austria within twenty-four hours. Fortunately his connections to the Royal Librarian in Sweden opened the borders wide enough to let him slip through. He arrived in New York where he found refuge with Lilly Rona.

I will never forget our first meeting in this country. We were at lunch when suddenly a police siren sounded in the street below. Hans started to tremble. "This is how they sound the siren in Dachau," he said hoarsely. But that is all he ever said about his experience for "they" told him that if he ever revealed anything he had seen there, he would be liquidated no matter where in the world he might be.

Hans, penniless but determined, used his enormous knowledge to start a new life in New York. Lilly introduced him to a charming young woman, daughter of a Viennese industrialist who had emigrated to America with his whole family. He married her and step by step they rebuilt the firm of H.P. Kraus. Through him, I met his in-laws, Mr. and Mrs. Herbert Zucker-Hale who took Cliff and me into their home and their hearts. As the years passed, our friendship grew and became a cornerstone in my life.

I wanted to introduce Hans and his story here because he joined us at our wedding dinner at the chic French restaurant, Larrue, in midtown Manhattan, where I betrayed my lack of sophistication by refusing to eat the frog legs he had picked out. But I did enjoy the champagne and the wedding cake which had been thoughtfully ordered for us.

There was no time for a honeymoon, so we returned to our new home in an apartment house properly situated on the East Side with a doorman and canopy. There we sublet a beautifully appointed studio apartment with a disappearing Murphy bed, from its owner, a real estate agent.

When we visited her in her office to discuss the rental, she asked us, "Are you Jewish?" I was speechless. Cliff seeing the expression on my face, put his hand firmly on my arm. He said that we weren't. I could not contain myself. How was this possible in America? I was shocked at finding what I suspected was a Nazi sitting opposite me, so I asked, "Just why did you ask that question?"

"Because," the woman said quite unperturbed, "you rent to one of them and ten move in. This is my own home and I want to be sure my property is not abused. I want to rent to two people and be sure that only two people will live in it."

Cliff later explained that Jewish immigrants had the reputation of moving into an apartment under the pretext of being only two but, as the years passed, wave after wave of newly arrived relatives also stayed there, two, three, and more families, all living in the one apartment.

He assured me that the woman's remark was not synonymous with Hitler's anti-Semitism but rather was a case of simple apartment logistics. But I remained unconvinced. Anti-Semitism by any other name smells just as bad.

****

Toward the end of August, Mrs. Roosevelt invited us to spend the weekend of September 6 in Hyde Park. Arriving in Poughkeepsie in the early afternoon, we found the White House car waiting to take us to Val Kill. Mrs. Roosevelt was sitting on her screened porch with several other guests – her house was forever filled with guests.

As she took us upstairs to our room, she suggested we take a swim in the pool. "Just make yourself at home, I can't join you just yet, I have some work to do, but I'll be here at six o'clock to take you over to the big house."

Our room, large and comfortably furnished with maple furniture in country style, had a little terrace overlooking the gardens. Because it was unbearably humid, we spent a restful, enjoyable hour alone at the pool and on the adjacent lawn.

Remembering that Mrs. Roosevelt always dressed for dinner, I put on my long red lace dinner gown and Cliff got into his newly acquired white tuxedo with its starched shirt and collar, no fun in that heat! Downstairs we met Tommy, who had been delegated to take us to the big house.

Cliff had not been to Hyde Park, so I showed him where I had stood in the living room to sing for the Danish royalty. Then we were ushered to a screened terrace overlooking the lovely hills of the Hudson Valley where we met several people including a young man in a wheel chair. He was a former state trooper who had lost the use of his legs in an accident. Mrs. Roosevelt later explained that he was very depressed, but she believed if he saw the President in his wheel chair, he might develop more self-confidence and hope.

When Mrs. Roosevelt joined us, I was dismayed to see that she had not changed her clothes. I felt very much out of place. Noticing my discomfort, she explained that she just hadn't had the time to do so but that the President would be wearing a dinner jacket. It was so hot and humid that I pitied Cliff in his heavy tuxedo.

After an aperitif of sherry the butler led us to dinner where the President was already seated at the table. The President greeted me like an old friend and cordially shook hands with Cliff. To my delight, I was on the President's left. He was in high spirits, discussing several subjects – politics, current events, and his beloved trees – and ate very little dinner. He didn't touch the dessert of rice pudding with custard sauce. His cigarette kept falling out of his long cigarette holder. I was kept busy retrieving it so it would not burn a hole in the table cloth.

While we were dining, someone entered the hallway. "Who was that?" said the President.

"I don't know," Mrs. Roosevelt answered, "I didn't invite anybody, did you?"

The President put his finger to his forehead, then after a second, shook his head. "No, I didn't." Then smiling to us, "You know, it wouldn't be the first time we forgot we had invited dinner guests, remember, Eleanor?"

"Yes," she said, "I remember, tell them."

"That was in the early years. We lived in New York, and it was the night the cook had her day off, so we decided to have dinner out. We were ready to leave, when the bell rang, and there were two couples, friends of ours, standing in the doorway telling us that my wife had invited them for dinner. Well, what could we do? We asked them to come in, and I took the men into the living room and set about to mix drinks, but there wasn't a drop of Scotch or rye in the house – well, we found something, anyway. Meanwhile the women went into the kitchen to raid the ice box, but I don't think there was much in the ice box either, but they fixed up some kind of supper. By the time they called us, we were in a very good mood and didn't care much about what they gave us to eat anyway.

"Yes," he laughed, "since that night I always get a shock when the bell rings while we have dinner. Maybe Eleanor forgot again that she invited somebody."

But this time it wasn't company, it was the doctor because the President's mother was ill.

As coffee was being served, a maid told the President that his mother wanted to see him. He left hastily, bidding us a good night. We stayed at the table a little while longer, finishing our coffee and then returned to the terrace. Mrs. Roosevelt took up her knitting, a navy blue sweater for an unknown sailor. She knitted beautifully and just attended to it whenever she had a few minutes to spare. The cool of evening brought relief from the heat of the day, so we sat there for another half hour before returning to Val Kill.

Back at Val Kill, Tommy, Mrs. Roosevelt and her knitting, the young man in his wheel chair and his doctor, Cliff and I, talked quietly and feeling very much at home, very relaxed and at peace.

Suddenly Mrs. Roosevelt was called out of the room. She returned saying that she had to go to the village of Hyde Park because her brother, who was very ill, had taken a turn for the worse. She drove off, refusing Cliff's offer to drive her.

Tommy commented, "I'm afraid that's the end of Hall Roosevelt and what with the President's mother so ill . . ." At that moment, the telephone rang, it was the President. We heard Tommy say. "No sir, she just left. Hall got suddenly worse. Yes, sir. I'll tell her as soon as she comes back."

Within a half an hour, Mrs. Roosevelt came back. "Well," she said, "this time, I'm going for good. They are taking Hall to the hospital, and I have to go with him. Then, I'll go to be with my mother-in-law."

Cliff said, "But you can't drive around in the countryside all alone in the middle of the night. Please, let me drive you."

"Oh no, you stay right here and enjoy yourself. I don't mind that at all."

Mrs. Roosevelt was remarkable. With all the events of the previous night, she remembered that I wanted to visit the Roosevelt Library at Hyde Park. While we were having our breakfast, Tommy, who had taken Mrs. Roosevelt's place at the breakfast table, was called away to the phone. She returned to say that the President's mother wasn't feeling any better, that the doctor had given her only a few more hours and that Mrs. Roosevelt was staying with the President. However, she had arranged for a car to take us to the President's library. We also should tell Miss Thompson when we wanted to return to New York so that a car could take us to the station.

As we got in the car to go to the library, Tommy called me aside and pressed a dollar bill into my hand, "Mrs. Roosevelt doesn't want you to have to pay the fee at the museum and you MUST take this, otherwise, she will be angry."

When we returned from the Roosevelt Library, we learned the President's mother had died and Hall Roosevelt was being transferred to a hospital in Washington. Mrs. Roosevelt was going with him.

We went back to New York in a subdued mood. I felt I knew the First Lady better. I had seen firsthand the self-discipline and self-control which governed her every move, even in the most tragic moments.

****

The ring on the fourth finger of my left hand worked its mysterious effect. The stage, show business, the spotlight moved into the background. In their place came a desire to make life comfortable for my husband and to return to the solid, conventional sociability I enjoyed in Austria.

Perhaps those theatrical agents who had so disdainfully suggested that I find myself a nice man, get married and have a flock of kids were right. Perhaps I really wasn't cut out for the stage. I had to choose – career or marriage. I opted for marriage. It wasn't just a preference for domesticity over show business, my love for Cliff made it easy to abandon my dream.

After a year in our comfortable apartment, Cliff was transferred to Wilmington, Delaware. I didn't want to move again. We had no furniture except a radio, toaster, and lamp, all bought on sale. There were also a few wedding presents: a set of dishes from Hildegarde, another lamp from Cousin Hans, a silver coffee set from Lilly Rona. And, of course, from Mrs. Roosevelt, the most precious gift of all, Cliff's job.

In July 1942 we moved. The apartment on North Harrison Street in Wilmington was my first home furnished with my own belongings. It was a remodeled three-room, second-floor apartment in a semi-detached home, belonging to a real estate man named Rearick. On summer evenings the porches were filled with people who waved and talked to passersby or read their evening papers. The sidewalks were laid with old bricks, which roots of century-old trees had lifted, so that we had to be careful not to stumble. In the early morning hours the milkman deposited bottles of milk, loaves of bread, and cartons of eggs on the doorsteps. The milk was rich and yellow. I tilted the bottles carefully to extract the rich heavy cream at the top.

There were no loud street noises; traffic was limited to the arrival and departure of the family car housed in the garage behind each house. It was quite a contrast to the frantic tempo of traffic and pedestrians in the concrete canyons of my three years in New York City.

In 1942 Wilmington was "Small Town America." Market Street was crowded during the day, especially at noon when the people emerged from their offices. The secretaries were fashionably dressed; the men looked very much alike in their suits, on hot muggy days holding their coat over their arm and their ties loose around their throats. The crowds wolfed down a sandwich and a "cup 'o coffee" at lunch counters or if more sophisticated went to a restaurant for the two-martini lunch.

About one or one-thirty, the crowds surged again as if sucked in by a giant's vacuum cleaner into to their desks. At four-thirty, they again emerged, and traffic congested but only for about twenty minutes. Then downtown Wilmington became a ghost town, so different from European cities, thronged until well after midnight with people, walking or sitting in cafes.

Wilmington had no suburbs. The countryside began at the city limits. The highways that now crisscross the state were dirt roads. Only one building qualified as a skyscraper: The Delaware Trust Building. Its distinction, so its owner told me, was that it was the only skyscraper in the world owned entirely by one individual, William "Willy" du Pont.

The shops were attended by unsophisticated sales clerks who stared at me when I spoke because Wilmingtonians rarely heard foreign accents. When I explained that I was from Austria, they thought I was from Australia. Not infrequently I was accosted by fellow shoppers saying things like, "Why don't you learn to speak English better, you are in America, you know!" Also, not infrequently, the challenger herself (it was never a man) could not lay claim to grammatically correct English.

But these incidents could not dampen my spirits. I savored living in a small town because of things like the King Street Farmers' Market. Every Wednesday, Friday, and Saturday, farmers came to King Street. Many of them had horse-drawn wagons which they backed up against the curb, then put planks over two sawhorses forming a long table to display their wares. Shoppers came to buy fresh produce, home-slaughtered pork, beef, poultry, and often game birds. The purplish red carcasses of muskrat and squirrel, considered a delicacy by many (not me!) were scooped up fast. It didn't seem to matter that the meat was displayed without consideration for the hygienic requirements expected of butcher counters in grocery stores.

The market was very similar to markets in Europe. Remindful of Europe, too, were the faces and general appearance of the King Street farmers. Weatherbeaten faces, framed by scarves or old beaten-up hats pulled down over the ears, shapeless work dresses made of calico or dark cloth. In the winter (they came in the coldest weather, too) gloves with half fingers, that permitted a glimpse of gnarled hands. Even their attitude shared a common denominator with their European colleagues: a take-it-or-leave-it-but-don't-touch-it-attitude, (especially during berry season) designed to intimidate the choosy buyer. But their produce was superb. Crisp, light green lettuce competed with green shiny-skinned cucumbers, bunches of carrots next to purple beets and yellow squash. Hands were always busy; the farmer's wives were sitting on small stools shelling peas and lima beans to sell by the pint or quart.

I loved shopping there. I walked ten blocks down Ninth Street; later, laden with heavy shopping bags, I took the 8th Street trolley home. I didn't learn to drive a car until 1947.

****

On December 7, 1941 when the cold war became hot, what little communication I had with my parents stopped. For four years, I didn't know whether they were alive or dead. Awakening in the mornings, I thought, "I wonder how they are now." Sitting down to a good meal, I asked myself, "Do they have anything to eat?" Returning to my warm home in the winter, I visualized the freezing rooms in Klosterneuburg and wondered, "Do they have enough fuel to keep one room warm?"

There were times when I wept uncontrollably. Fortunately, I have always had a very personal relationship with God. I address myself to something that is great and mysterious yet is very near and tangible, outside and inside me at the same time. While I disdain the trappings of what I call "the business of religion" – the dictatorship of organized religion over my private life and over personal decisions – I am conscious of our interdependence with that unknown, existing power which gave us our souls. In the most excruciating moments of my life I have cried out, and it has answered. Of course, there are times of doubt which come when I think of the unspeakable pain and misery visited upon so many millions of innocent people since the world began.

Every day when I walked downtown, I passed Sacred Heart Church. One day I entered it. It was peaceful and silent, a few candles flickered in memory of the departed, and the organist rehearsed quietly. I sat in the church and talked to God. Direct. I don't need intermediaries. I asked for help. I asked, as one would ask a friend, to protect my parents and my sister. I said, "I will come to You every day until the war ends, every single day no matter what." I kept that promise. I was convinced that He would help. It gave me peace.

****

On July 3, 1943 I became an American citizen in the Courthouse in Wilmington. There were several hundred candidates for citizenship, many from nations then at war with the United States. It was a sunny, hot day, and the courthouse room was stifling from the heat from many bodies. Perspiration dripped down my forehead and ran in small rivulets down my back.

One of the requirements for citizenship was a passable understanding of English. During the examination, I stood next to an Italian woman in her seventies, accompanied by her daughter. She could not speak one word of English, though she had lived in this country for forty years. Because she lived in an Italian neighborhood, she had not needed to learn the language. The examiner grew exasperated. Then I heard the daughter say very softly, "She has lost five sons and her husband in this war." There were no more questions.

It was a moving ceremony, short but dignified. In that room stood many who, like me, had lost their homeland. Now by virtue of my newly-acquired American citizenship, I was again a complete person, I belonged. I was jubilant to be an American. Together all of us pledged allegiance to the flag I now could call my own.

I think that those who are born in this country and feel entitled to its freedoms cannot ever appreciate as deeply and emotionally the privilege of such freedoms as do naturalized Americans from countries where those freedoms do not exist.

****

My life settled down to a routine: getting up at seven, cooking breakfast, which Cliff, "the Vermont country boy," as he called himself, deemed very important: two eggs and bacon, hot biscuits and coffee. None of the "coffee and toast" breakfast on the run for him.

He left at eight, and I was alone to tend to the household chores. The apartment was not spacious – living room with dining area, bedroom, bath, and kitchen and a rear balcony large enough for a table and chairs so that we could eat outside in summer. This caused great curiosity among our neighbors. When we ate on the porch, I saw them peeking at us and whispering to each other, shaking their heads at the strange customs of that foreign woman.

I, in turn, shook my head at my neighbors' custom of keeping the window shades pulled down to the half-way mark all day long while keeping the lights burning in their darkened apartments. I kept my shades up and the electric light turned off until dark fell. Sometimes when I got home from shopping, I found my shades pulled down to "regulation length." My landlady had gone up while I was out to set things right. As an excuse, she had left a big piece of apple pie on my kitchen table.

If I had hoped to have an active social life in Wilmington, these hopes were dashed by Cliff's refusal to entertain. Our apartment was not in the right place and not of the right kind to ask people to join us. At least that was his opinion. I did not understand him then, but I do now. I have always loved parties and social gatherings of all kinds. I loved impressing guests with my Viennese cooking and spending an evening among friends in animated conversation, much preferring it to the fishbowl entertaining in a restaurant where one had strangers at one's elbow.

However, Cliff told me that if those wealthy people with whom he came in contact were invited to our modest apartment, their respect for him would diminish. There is some truth in "class differentiation by address." I learned that such phrases as "she comes from the wrong side of the tracks" means just that – someone who was born and raised in the "wrong" neighborhood. The poor lived near the railroad, the rich farther away from it in well-kept quiet sections of town where the noise of the fuming trains could not be heard and where the smoke of the locomotive did not blacken the laundry hung outside to dry.

This was very different from the way I was raised. Perhaps, too, Americans were preoccupied with "the address" because Americans did not place much emphasis on titles as is done, for instance, in Austria. There everybody is a Herr Doktor or a Herr Ingenieur to identify him as being a shade better than the ordinary worker. That the worker quite frequently earns more money than the academician does not count in the European class distinction system. With the exception of European nobility, however, class distinction is not based on snobbism as is the American "address" system. The preference for one's own class is based mostly on common interest; one associates with people with whom one can easily converse on subjects on which all are well informed and well qualified to agree and disagree. In such a social community it is unimportant where one lives.

After our soldiers went overseas, Cliff was appointed War Food Administrator for the Delmarva Peninsula. It was his responsibility to see to it that the soldiers were amply supplied with poultry, a large percentage of which was raised on the Delmarva Peninsula.

18

On April 12, 1945, I was standing in my kitchen, ironing shirts, listening to the radio as usual when I heard, "We interrupt this program to bring you an important message: President Roosevelt died suddenly of a brain hemorrhage."

I stood as if turned to stone. while it had been obvious to everyone who saw pictures of Roosevelt, Stalin, and Churchill at Yalta that the President looked terribly drawn and thin, I did not want to believe that he was so near to his end. I was devastated by the news, as was the whole nation.

The fact that I had known him personally and had been permitted to join so many times in the innermost family circle made the shock so much deeper. I did not know what to do. Cliff came home from his office early, and he too was more disturbed than I had ever seen him. What was going to happen now?

The war was drawing to a close and fate had not allowed Roosevelt to live long enough to see the victorious outcome to which he had contributed so much. I called Mrs. Roosevelt's home to express our condolences and ask about the funeral. Could we attend?

"Only for family members," I was told.

So, it was the radio we relied upon to follow the ceremonies and speeches that accompanied Franklin Roosevelt on his last journey.

****

On May 8, 1945, when the war in Europe ended, I was in New York with Cliff having dinner at a Swedish restaurant. Suddenly all hell broke loose out in the streets. Car horns honked, church bells rang, people screamed and sang "God Bless America." Within seconds, a loudspeaker brought detailed reports about the surrender of Germany. We ordered champagne and fell into each other's arms laughing and weeping for joy. The madness had ended, and Hitler was no more.

I thought about my family. Then a hot flash of fear rose in my throat, "Are they still alive – what will I find out?"

My first action was to write Mrs. Roosevelt for help. My letter was answered by return mail, "There is, at present, no possibility to locate civilians in the Russian occupied city."

On April 13, the Russians, officially our allies, had captured Vienna. Although most Americans were floating on pink clouds of admiration for our "gallant allies," I suspected that the Russians could be as dangerous as the Nazis.

Unlike most Americans, I had read about the Stalin years, the mock trials of the thirties and the executions of millions of Russians in the Siberian slave labor camps. And unlike so many of my naive compatriots, I did not believe the propaganda reports claiming that Stalin's victims were "traitors, criminals, and enemies of the people." I had seen too many similar actions under the Nazis not to recognize the similarity of the methods. I had no illusions about the way a Russian occupation would deal with a captive nation.

There was nothing I could do but wait and worry. Then one day shortly after the surrender of Japan in August, the mailman brought a special delivery letter from Mrs. Roosevelt containing another letter, a letter from my father. For four years I had envisioned this moment. Now that it was here, I was turned to stone. I was afraid to believe that it was true, to awaken and find that it was all a mistake.

"Dear honored Mrs. Roosevelt," my father wrote in his literal translation from German into English, "I beg you to tell my child, Lotte Shedd, that her parents and sister are well and longing to hear from her and see her. I do not know where my child is now, but I know that she knows you and that you will perhaps find her for me. Captain Loewy is so kind to send this letter to you and I thank you for your exceeding kindness to bring us together."

Captain Loewy was a school colleague of mine who had emigrated to the United States, enlisted in the Army, and met my parents on the street in Vienna. Yet another miracle!

My father had laboriously combined his rusted English with the help of his dictionary and put together a letter which tore my heart strings. I fell to my knees and buried my head in my hands and let my tears dissolve the long years of desperate fear for their fate. My prayers had been answered. I went to the church where I had asked the Lord for help everyday. I knelt to say my thanks.

I could barely wait for Cliff to come home. We held each other tightly for a long time, while he whispered, "I knew it, darling, I just knew everything would be all right." And then that practical and generous American said, "Now we have to see how we can help them."

I wrote a reply and sent it off to Mrs. Roosevelt, who, in turn, forwarded it to Captain Loewy's APO address in Vienna. I wrote of my joy and relief to know that they were alive and well. I promised I would send everything they needed as soon as it was possible. I urged them to let me know what was most desperately needed. I added that I would visit as soon as passage could be obtained for civilians.

Getting help to them was easier said then done. The Russians did not permit food parcels or assistance of any kind to reach the civilians under their jurisdiction. It was hard to understand why they wanted to prolong the misery, but they did.

I wrote to Mrs. Roosevelt for help. The answer came back. "Dear Charlotte: I asked the Red Cross about sending parcels and they said packages cannot be sent to Austria. They referred me to the Vatican Information Service and they said the same thing. The only thing I can do is write to the Attorney General about your parents. He will refer it to the Immigration Bureau and I will let you know what reply I get. It is dreadful to think of all these suffering people when we have so much and I am besieged by people here to help. I haven't any way of helping now. Affectionately, Eleanor Roosevelt."

Not even she could overcome the Russian stubbornness.

On August 9, 1945, as a result of a four-power treaty signed in 1943, the Allied Forces divided Austria into four zones and Vienna into four sections. Every four weeks the four powers rotated the military command of Vienna and "Four Men in a Jeep" actually policed the city, one American, one British, one French and one Russian in each jeep. My family's home in Klosterneuburg, unfortunately, was in the Russian Zone; thus its citizens were subject to Russian military authority.

I hoped my family knew about the problems. It is very difficult for people who are cut off from the outside world, as were the people in the Russian Zone of Austria, not to lose all perspective and not to judge the rest of the world. How could you expect people who have been liberated through America's military power to comprehend that America now bowed to the whims and orders of Russia. It just didn't make sense to people who had listened to the BBC and knew that America was liberating Europe and not Russia.

Conditions in and around Vienna remained chaotic, so it was impossible to send any kind of help. European postal communications were minimal. There was, of course, no trans-Atlantic airmail and the only ships were freighters transporting supplies to the armed forces.

The only hope was to catch someone who was traveling in and out of the former war zones and entrust him with personal messages. The Red Cross was overworked and didn't have the facilities to be a post office. It was maddening not to communicate with my parents, particularly since newspapers reported that there was outright famine in Vienna and that the rate of tuberculosis had risen to alarming proportions. No consumer goods were obtainable, not for barter nor huge sums of money.

Finally, in October a letter from Captain Loewy informed me that I could start sending five-pound food parcels to my parents through him. Five pounds! How to choose among the thousands of items on American grocery shelves; five pounds of food which would be most welcome and most needed by people with nothing. Five pounds for the immediate needs of three people: my father, mother, and sister!

"Put yourself in their position," I said to myself, "what would you wish for most?"

I was sure that coffee would be a morale raiser, with it milk in powdered form, and sugar. "If mother has flour, fat, milk, sugar, and powdered eggs, she can bake bread or even cake," I reasoned, and remembered that yeast is needed. Powdered eggs were available through the food assistance programs of the U.S. Department of Agriculture.

I got a small portion of the eggs and enclosed them in my first parcel. When the parcel was carefully packed, we weighed it on my kitchen scale and found there was room for one cake of soap and two packages of Lipton Chicken Noodle Soup. Every item had an attached explanation in German. I was particularly concerned about the can of Crisco, because I assumed (and rightfully so, as I found out later) that my mother would not recognize the creamy white substance as shortening, accustomed as she was from prewar days to lard.

It was such a joy to finally do something concrete. My leaving them, which had left me with huge feelings of guilt, now proved to be a move which might save them from starvation. Since we knew that the packages took at least six weeks to be delivered, we elected every Monday as "package day" and sent parcels every week from then on.

I wrote Captain Loewy alerting him to the weekly shipments of food. He needed to be on the lookout for the packages because food parcels were prime targets for theft, their contents finding their way into the thriving black markets.

That winter of 1945-46 was one of the harshest in Austria's history. There was no fuel to heat my parents' house and the famine was a repetition of the famine years of 1917-1920, but now my parents were almost thirty years older and without physical reserves. So I desperately wanted the first parcel to arrive before Christmas. Every day I waited for the postman to bring me news. Christmas came and went. Then, one day about mid-February, the letter came.

"Dearest Lotte and Cliff: What a wonderful surprise! This was to be our most terrible Christmas. There was absolutely no food left in our house, not even potatoes, and we had eaten the last walnuts from our tree collected in the fall and hidden away in the attic. It was December 24, Christmas Eve. Around four o'clock in the afternoon the bell rang. Papa looked out of the window and saw an American jeep stopped in front of our house. He went out to see what the man wanted. The man had a parcel in his hands and told Papa that Captain Loewy sent it and Merry Christmas! He handed Papa the parcel and jumped back into his jeep and was gone.

"Papa was shaking all over because it was as if Christkindel had come down from heaven with its heavenly gifts. We stood around the precious parcel and for a long while didn't want to open it to prolong the excitement. Then Papa opened the string very carefully because it is also unobtainable and then slowly, carefully the paper, so as not to tear it, and finally the package was open. Oh, my God – real coffee! We haven't seen it in seven years. And real sugar, so fine and white, and real white flour and that beautiful milk powder and the white cream in the can called Crisco – it is similar to our Kokos-fett – and soap, real fine sweet smelling soap. The soup powder called Lipton is wonderful. I cannot make better soup myself even if I had all the ingredients.

"We were so happy we cried and almost were afraid to start eat-ing the good things because we couldn't bear the thought that they would be gone once we ate them. But then we held a 'war council' and decided we would have a Christmas celebration with coffee and kolatschen made with the flour, milk, Crisco and powdered eggs. Everything turned out to be absolutely magnificent and we talked about you all evening and blessed you for giving us such a wonderful Christmas."

Every week I bought easily packed, nutritional items for the Monday package. But I also looked for things in the luxury category because it seemed to me that people who have had absolutely nothing for a long time might also yearn for long-missed delicacies. Every shelf, tabletop, sideboard, chair, and even the kitchen floor was covered with merchandise waiting to be packed. Cliff, a perfectionist in everything, had heavy string, tape, scissors, felt pen and labels arranged within easy reach.

The packages were works of art. Not one of the glass jars containing marmalade, jam, mayonnaise or mustard was ever broken. They were wrapped in corrugated paper, and buffered with Lipton soup, Brillo pads, socks, gloves, etc. As the years went by and the size of the packages increased from five to twenty-two and finally to thirty-five pounds, we became more and more ingenious.

One Thanksgiving I sent the complete makings of an American Thanksgiving dinner to my family: succotash, small white onions (with directions for creaming), corn muffin mix, cranberries, fruit salad, and even a pie plate accompanied by pie crust mix and apple pie mix. I told my parents about the Thanksgiving traditions, about the Pilgrims' landing in New England and the harvest feast they enjoyed. I urged my mother to follow my instructions and cook and serve the Thanksgiving meal in accordance with the American ritual. Albert Loewy played an essential role because he gave my parents the huge Thanksgiving turkey which he, as an American officer, was entitled to.

My mother was speechless when she saw the twenty-pound bird. She wrote how they stood around the American turkey wondering how to cook it. They didn't have a large enough pan; besides the oven was to small to hold such a splendid specimen. Finally and with regret, my mother cut the turkey in half. They followed the American tradition of inviting friends to share the meal, so the Borak family, avowed anti-Nazis and loyal friends, came for an American Thanksgiving.

What I would have given to be there. I could only enjoy the written descriptions of the succulent bird, tasty gravy, the adventure of discovering succotash, and the delight when the corn muffin mix turned out to be "as fine as the finest cake." My mother, a superb pastry cook, did not know how to use the pie plate, since pies are not made in Austria, so she used the mix to make a Viennese apple cake. She wrote, "I cannot imagine that one can eat so many courses at one meal, surely this American Thanksgiving meal cannot contain all those good things at once!"

I could understand that it was impossible for people who had little to eat to indulge in the abundance of an American style dinner. Their stomachs simply could not accommodate that much food. The turkey was eaten in innumerable variations for several weeks!

Once I sent a whole ham and a smoked beef tongue. Because it took six weeks for the package to arrive at Alleegasse Number Three, both meats were covered with a thin layer of mildew. "Never mind," my mother wrote, "I washed it in salt water, scraped it well and boiled it. It was delicious."

When we needed toothpaste, writing paper, aspirin, soap, razor blades, and all such things, we went to the store. The Viennese stores were empty. One of my mother's first requests was for a complete assortment of spices. "Because," she wrote, "with spices you can doctor up anything." I sent every spice the earth had produced. Many of them she did not know and did not use. I found them years later, untouched, on her kitchen shelf.

One day my father wrote, "Would it perhaps be possible for Cliff to spare some clothes he does no longer wear?" And with the request came a list of European sizes in suits, shoes, and socks. When we converted the sizes to their American equivalent, we found to our joy that they coincided with Cliff's clothing sizes. Within a week, a navy blue pin-striped suit, a warm top coat, shirts, shoes, socks, ties, gloves, and underwear made their way across the Atlantic Ocean. They arrived at a good moment. My father had been asked by the Bundespräsident to resume his former post in the Finanzprokuratur and occupy his old desk. It was very satisfying for him, after all the years of deprivation, to be again "der Herr Hofrat," to be respected and honored. No amount of money could have compensated him as much as this reappointment. And to top it all, he appeared among his friends and colleagues in his new American clothes.

The Nazi years tested friendship and loyalty. Most of the "friends" who had enjoyed summer weekends at our house and had taken home bags of fruits and vegetables joined the Nazi party and abandoned my family. Even my mother's brothers had become ardent followers of Hitler's Storm Troopers. Opportunists that they were, they denounced my parents to the Gestapo because they wanted their sister's properties. Fortunately, they failed.

I have the letter my uncle wrote categorically forbidding my mother to ever try to reach him for assistance in any matter. After the collapse of the Thousand Year Reich, he wrote another letter, also in my files, reminding her that she was, after all, his sister and imploring her to let bygones be bygones and help extricate him from his Nazi past. My mother never answered it.

But there was also "das Fräulein Anni," an elderly lady, unmarried and lonely, who had been governess to the children of an Archduke. I never found out how she and my parents met, but she was one of the small group of "anständige Menschen," decent people, my parents kept company with during the Nazi ordeal. My mother asked me to send her a food parcel which I did. Not long after that, I received a small parcel marked "fragile." Unwrapping it, I found a charming baroque mantle clock from Fräulein Anni. A tiny slip of paper attached to the clock said "Schlüssel in Seidenpapier," the key to the clock is in the tissue paper. I carefully unwrapped the paper. To my consternation, I held in my hand not the key but a set of false teeth. Poor Fräulein Anni! The exchange took almost two months, a long time to wait to enjoy the American goodies.

19

Anxious as I was to see my family, I could not get to Austria. Finally in the summer of 1947 I secured a berth on the Waterman Line which allowed 12 passengers on each of its cargo vessels. The cost was high: $500.

It felt strange to stand at the railing waiting to return to a Europe I had left eighteen years before. On the pier stood my American husband, in my pocket lay my American passport. Memories of my arrival here flooded over me. I gazed at the water, thinking, "Why leave now? Why go back? Don't go. Stay in America." The panic, fortunately, passed.

After eleven days we reached Bremerhaven and the maze of sunken hulls littering the harbor. As we approached the docks, I saw that few buildings were intact. To the Americans who had gone through the war without bombs, it was eerie. We were silent, our faces were grim and expressionless. As we disembarked, we saw huge craters and tottering walls, roofless ruins and streets that were mere pathways shoveled through the mountains of rubble.

I had explicit instructions to follow as I continued my journey south toward Austria. I stayed in a hotel requisitioned by the American military which had a lunchroom where I bought a meal with military scrip money that Cliff had secured for me. We were not allowed to use regular greenbacks. After dinner I took a short walk around the block and was immediately besieged by small boys and girls with urgent pleas for "chocolate, chewing gum, cigarettes." I was not expecting this and I felt guilty to be well dressed and well fed. I fled to the hotel.

The next morning, I ventured forth once more. Wandering through the streets or rather what had been streets, walking past houses that were empty shells, seeing for the first time people living in holes in the ground – in burned out cellars – I knew the meaning of war on the home front. I found a square where a farmers' market offered scraps of food. Each table had only a few vegetables. I wanted to know how these people felt about their shattered lives as well as the collapse of the Thousand Year Reich. I stopped at one of the tables. Immediately a crowd gathered. My good clothes marked me as an outsider. They wanted to know where I was from, and I explained I was from Austria.

"Is it bad in Austria?" they wanted to know.

"Yes, it is bad," I admitted, "they have the Russians."

"Ah, yes, that's even worse than the Americans," the voice of the people allowed.

"Na ja," I ventured, "without Hitler all this would not have happened."

A hostile shower of words engulfed me, "The Jews, the American Jews, they got us into that mess. The only thing wrong with Hitler was that he lost the war, but he was right with his ideas, yes!"

I was stunned. Two years after the most horrifying defeat, they still were Nazis. They hadn't learned a thing.

I tried once more, "But it was Germany that started the war in 1939. It was Germany that bombed Poland first."

They screamed at me, "No, this was self-defense, those pig Poles they wanted to attack us."

I retreated to the safety and sanity of my American hotel where I saw several Germans working in the hotel kitchen and later learned that they were among the fortunate. They could feed their families with the food the Americans discarded.

The next day I took the American military train to Frankfurt. Through the window I could see the devastated landscape, town after destroyed town. Frankfurt was one huge heap of rubble. The people were gaunt, obviously hungry, and impoverished. The American presence was overwhelming, everywhere I saw American uniforms, jeeps, military conveyances.

Munich was next. In Munich's roofless railroad station, I saw again what I had observed in Bremerhaven, Frankfurt, and in every other railroad station. The platforms were crowded with people who just sat there. They sat everywhere: on the ground, on steps, on stairs, the lucky ones on benches. They didn't talk, they didn't move, they stared straight ahead waiting, yet not waiting. Now and then, children darted out, bending down for a cigarette butt an American soldier had carelessly discarded, or perhaps not so carelessly. Some soldiers knew cigarette butts were treasures.

On the train to Salzburg I asked the conductor about the people on the platforms.

He answered, shrugging his shoulders. "They have no place to sleep, no food. Some are bombed out, some are displaced persons. In the station they can keep dry, they can sleep, and sometimes someone gives them a piece of bread or permits them to carry a suitcase and pays them a few pfennigs."

As the train neared the Austrian border my heart beat faster. The seemingly impossible had become reality: I was returning as an American citizen, my family had survived the ordeal, and I was soon to see them again. The train stopped. An American Military Control officer entered my compartment accompanied by an Austrian. I handed the officer my American passport, he looked at it fleetingly, looked at me, compared the photograph, handed it back to me. The Austrian didn't say anything. He was only there to interpret should the need arise. When he left, the Austrian put two fingers on his cap, nodded, and said "Grüss Gott" – no longer "Heil Hitler" I thought. "Grüss Gott," I answered. He looked at me with surprise and smiled.

I could not meet my parents in Vienna because the city was surrounded by the Russian Zone, as Berlin continued to be until the early 1990s. Because there were no travel restrictions for Austrians, as there were for Americans, my parents traveled to the American Zone to meet me.

We were to meet in Bad Gastein, a spa in the Austrian Alps where my parents had spent many summer vacations. The Americans had taken over many of the hotels. One hotel, the Bellevue, was set aside for American civilians like me. My room and all my meals were prepaid in the United States. If I wanted extras, they were paid for with military scrip which I could buy in limited quantities at the hotel.

The prospect of seeing my family again was almost more than I could handle. Everything seemed unreal, as if staged for a play. I was embarrassed to be staying in such an elegant place while they lived in war-ravaged conditions. I paced up and down in my room, not knowing when they would arrive. The phone rang. "Frau Shedd?"

It was the desk clerk, "Herr Hofrat Kraus is here to see you."

And then my father's voice, in tears, "Lotterl Lotterl, My child, we'll be up at once."

One more minute, two, three. The door opened, "Vati, Mutti." We fell into each other's arms and held each other tight, so tight. We couldn't bear to let go and wept and laughed and kissed each other and looked at each other and embraced again and again. What had happened to my parents? My tall, straightbacked father had shrunk to a bent, old man. He had been a head taller, now he was a head smaller. His shoulders were rounded, several teeth were missing, his hands – his beautiful strong muscular hands – were bony, gnarled and rough. My mother, hollow-eyed, hollow- cheeked, and gray, was thin and bony. My heart almost burst with pain when I looked at them, but they were alive, they were here, they had lived to see this day. We held each other and stroked each other's faces and hands and for the first hour, we exchanged banalities, "How was your trip, how is Cliff, are you tired?"

Then came a torrent of speech. It was as if a gate had suddenly opened releasing a long-contained stream into an empty river bed. Without let up, hour after hour, the story of those eight years unfolded. My imagination came alive with the tales of treachery and cruelty, of unexpected friendship and loyalty from those from whom it was least expected, of hostility and denunciation from those they trusted. Hunger and cold beyond anything I had dreamed in my comfortable American home. My mother's relatives, weather vanes that they were, had become active Nazis. Under the Nazis they tried to take her possessions. Though the harassment went on for years, they failed, thanks to my mother's indomitable courage.

My parents also listened to BBC broadcasts. The punishment if we were caught was beheading. "We listened to the BBC," my mother related. "We followed the advance of the American Army step by step, and we hoped they would get here first, before the Russians did."

"Did you have a place to hide when the bombers came?"

"No, we became fatalists. If it hits, it hits. We never went into the air raid shelter."

"I stood in the attic window," my mother said, her eyes gleaming. "I heard the sirens but I stayed. I wanted to see the American silver birds. I wanted to see the death and ruin they rained upon the hated Nazis. I was never afraid. I waved to them and sent them my love. They came as liberators."

"It was terrible when the Opera House burned," said my father. "We all wept. The Russians and the SS fought it out all over Vienna and then the Nazis set fire to St. Stephen's Cathedral. That was terrible, too."

It went on and on, the truth, the reality. "And then came the Russians, nobody knew what they would do to us, but the stories of rape preceded them and all the women who could, ran away and hid. And then the Russians came – wild men from the far eastern steppes – asking for the women. 'Where is woman?' they asked, and they raped and raped.

"Across the street from us, they raped the eighty-five-year-old grandmother repeatedly, and the mother and daughters and little girls, and they made the father watch. They had him tied to a chair and made him watch. And when we heard that, we took Trude [my sister] up to the attic and tied her to one of the wood beams under the eaves and pushed a huge wardrobe in front of the door to hide the entrance. Twice a day when we hoped no one would intrude [the doors had to be kept unlocked all the time or the Russians would kick them in], Vater went upstairs to the attic with food and a pot for her to relieve herself and then the wardrobe was pushed back again.

"And once the soldiers came into the house, walked upstairs, found the wardrobe, opened it and pushed their bayonets into the clothes that hung there. But they did not suspect that behind the wardrobe might be a door."

My mother explained that after two weeks, the Russians saw they had antagonized the population. Even though the combat troops were withdrawn and replaced by more civilized occupation troops, everyone knew that the Russians had not come to liberate them from the Nazis but to impose their own kind of dictatorship. In the elections that followed the formation of the new Austrian Republic, the Communists failed to win a single seat in Parliament.

It seemed as if the avalanche of stories about the Russians would never end, as if the opportunity to talk was part of an inner release, a cleansing and healing process. And I listened because I knew that my listening helped them.

My mother explained that when it was finally safe to release my sister, the skin on her stomach was bloody and raw. But she escaped the fate of thousands of her countrywomen – she was not raped. Some of the stories had a dash of humor, such as the one about the soldiers who discovered a strange contraption: the toilet. They washed their faces in the hopper and then, in a burst of exuberance, knocked it over. They took the keys from every door and unscrewed the light switches from the walls.

Strangely, they did not take anything else from our house, did not empty it of its furnishings as they did with other homes on our street. Once a Russian soldier shot at my mother for no other reason than that he was drunk. The bullet missed her and embedded itself in the wall.

"I did not wash myself for weeks," my mother said, "I did not comb my hair and dressed in rags to be as ugly as possible, but even that did not prevent them one day from looking for 'die Frau.' I ran out the back door into the garden, to the back fence and escaped through a loose board. They were running after me, two of them, but I slipped out and ran into a neighbor's house where I hid in the cellar. I thought my heart would burst, but they didn't find me."

Every family in Vienna had a story to tell about the raping of Viennese women, everyone knew that tens of thousands of those violated women had been infected with venereal disease. Seeing soldiers caused women to run and hide as did my sister another time when two soldiers followed her home and demanded "das Mädchen." My parents pushed Trude into their bedroom and placed themselves in front of the door, arms outstretched across the door frame. They knew it could mean death, for the Russian soldiers, particularly when they were drunk, were quick on the trigger. My father summoned all his courage, "You can not go in there, you will have to kill me first."

The soldiers were very young and they were sober. In the bedroom my sister was on her knees. "I have never been one to pray," she later told me, "but I did learn to pray then, I prayed desperately to be spared."

The confrontation between my father and the soldiers lasted interminable minutes. Then they turned and left.

****

No one who has not lived through such apocalyptic times can truly comprehend the impact. A case of condensed milk can become the most prized possession as was the milk the kind grocery owner across the street secretly gave my parents. My father hid the milk under old newspapers in the wood shed. But marauding Russians found it. My father wept uncontrollably. My mother said it was terrible how he wept about that milk.

As I listened to the stories, I was overcome by guilt for not having shared their hardships. I was ashamed of my well-groomed, well-fed condition. I worried that it might create a subconscious resentment when they compared my life with theirs. That I was not far off in my appraisal was proved many years later when my sister unleashed a torrent of accusations about "you running away to America leaving me to cope with all the responsibilities and disasters alone. I always had to do everything alone while you took the easy way out."

It was an understandable reaction, but it hurt me deeply. Clearly though, my difficult times as an immigrant in America cannot begin to compare with the horrors of war and persecution. Only when, or if, she reads this account of my life will she see the hardships facing the immigrant.

20

We were living from paycheck to paycheck, and the cost of the packages to Austria added to our expenses. I did all sorts of things to contribute to the financial coffers. I made lovely leather gloves and sold them to friends and to their friends. I attended millinery courses at the YWCA, and quite often I sold the hats I made right off my head. Never was there any money left over. At times, I feared for our future, which depended so much on a monthly paycheck, especially the time Cliff bought a new Packard car when I thought we should have bought a used car and put aside some savings.

I got a part-time job as sales girl at the John Wanamaker department store in Philadelphia without telling Cliff. This was my first experience dealing directly with people of all types and I found that I loved selling and was very successful. Indeed, within two weeks the management of Wanamaker's wanted to train me for a full time managerial position, but I did not want to give up my independence and continued to sell hats, luggage, jewelry, and anything else for three days a week.

Cliff was not happy about my job. I think he felt my job proved he could not support me. But I told him that my job provided invaluable experience in communicating with the public.

My fellow workers were, in many instances, elderly ladies with very bad feet and worse dispositions. They were jealous because each of my sales brought me a commission. I learned diplomacy and patience while not falling for the shenanigans the ladies invented, such as cutting me off from potential customers. Selling over the counter is an art. While every customer was different, all were very susceptible to courtesy and personal attention. I learned that a smile is the best tool, and I wondered why most of the sales ladies displayed sour faces, which made people believe they disliked customers.

I stayed with Wanamaker's for a year and then transferred to a lingerie shop in Wilmington where I became assistant manager – a high-sounding title given to those gullible enough not to know that such a title meant no overtime pay and a more than forty-hour week. I made twenty-seven dollars a week, much of it used to pay for the food parcels.

All that time I wanted to move into the countryside. My heart was set on a small community, Arden, about five miles north of Wilmington. There on occasional drives, I had seen small houses, winding foot paths, wide green lawns, old trees, and an atmosphere very reminiscent of a European village, unpretentious and intimate.

When I mentioned my desire to live in Arden, I encountered raised eyebrows. "Arden? Heavens! No self-respecting citizen would want to live in Arden. There are nudist camps and free-love practitioners, anarchists and communists, socialists and atheists, and the residents ride about on white horses dressed in Shakespearean costumes. No, Arden is not the place in which to live, if you want to be 'accepted.'"

"It's an artist colony," said hostile Wilmingtonians, as if being an artist were something sinister.

More curious that ever, I embarked on fact-finding expeditions to Arden. Not a single nudist ran across my path, and the horseback riders I encountered on the lovely paths were dressed conventionally. What I did find out is that Arden is a Single Tax Colony founded around the turn of the century on the economic principle of Henry George, a philosopher-economist who believed in the "sanctity of the land as a value common to all people, not to be exploited by profit-hungry speculators." He proposed that all people using the land pay a single tax to a governing body of trustees who administered the income, paying all taxes due and using the remainder for whatever purpose the taxpayers deem appropriate. (The Village of Arden with its approximately 500 families is the only Single Tax Colony to endure to this day and has been placed on the National Register of Historic Places.)

Several famous people had chosen Arden including the writer Upton Sinclair and the sculptor Markus Aurelius Renzetti, who had a small house on the banks of Christina Creek. When the creek crested during spring thaws, the water flowed through his living room, in one end and out the other. He simply moved up to his balcony and lived there until the waters receded. This did not please his young wife who was concerned about the welfare of their three young sons. She left him.

Arden had no building codes, so one-room shacks sat next to elaborate fieldstone homes, but each stood on at least a quarter acre of land, and many leaseholders had an acre or more. The single tax paid for the use of the land. People owned only the buildings that stood on the land not the land itself, which was leased for ninety-nine years. As further proof of the community's worth, I found that Ardenites became so attached to the community they didn't even want to be separated from it in death; therefore, the village has its own Memorial Garden where residents are buried, free of charge, the graves maintained by the community.

Enchanted by everything I learned, I called Cy Liberman, a reporter who lived in Arden and sometimes worked with Cliff, and asked if he could find us a place. Miracle of miracles, he found us a small house that rented for only $45 a month. I took it. Next to coming to America, the move to Arden was the most important move I ever made. Coming to Arden was like coming home after many detours and many wrong exits and entrances. I loved the footpaths crisscrossing the "village," as Arden calls itself. On my walks I met people who smiled, stopped to ask if I were a new resident of "our village," invited me to visit, and offered to help. There was a possessive pride in the speech of the Ardenites, revealing a sense of being part of something special.

Arden was a place that we could afford. We could have a lovely home, beautiful grounds and an extraordinary ambiance and sociability not found anywhere else. For me, it was an oasis. Through the Arden Club with its guilds offering theater productions, concerts, sports, crafts, and community dinners I was engulfed in a whirl of activities such as I had never known before. In the summer we swam in a swimming pool formed by damming the creek. On hot, humid nights we escaped the heat by sneaking down to the pool under the cover of darkness to swim in the cool water in the nude, discovering to our astonishment that others had had the same idea. Perhaps that is how Arden got its reputation of being a nudist colony. For the first time since coming to America, I felt truly secure and really happy.

Shortly before we moved to Arden, my parents sent a shipment of household goods – tagged "Auswanderungsgut" – Emigration Goods. Every emigree from Austria was permitted, on a one-time basis, to export the contents of his entire household. In theory even the Nazis had allowed this, but in practice shipments disappeared on the way. Since I had left Austria with only a suitcase full of summer clothes, my parents could send me three enormous containers full of family heirlooms, china, glassware, linen, rugs, paintings, and other furnishings that had been part of my childhood. It is strange how such seemingly lifeless accessories awaken living memories, adding a new perspective to our lives.

Our house was a small one, living room, bedroom and – because I believe in assigning a separate room to the important activity of eating – I furnished the second bedroom as a dining room. There was a small kitchen and a bath. A few steps led down to a small garden enclosed by a white picket fence.

Cliff became an enthusiastic home decorator. He painted and carpentered; he bought a big saw and tools to "make things." He worked tirelessly on the improvements of our rented house until one day when he was digging out a cellar under our house, he suddenly came into the house looking ghostly pale and breathing hard.

"I have a terrible pain in my chest," he gasped. His face looked haggard and was beginning to take on a greenish color. "You'd better call a doctor," he said.

I had never seen anyone having a heart attack, but I knew that this was what was happening to Cliff. My reflexes operated like clockwork. I called the doctor. He refused to come, but advised me to bring Cliff to the emergency room of the hospital. He should have sent an ambulance. He sat next to me in the car gasping for breath. The hospital had not been alerted; they let him walk in, although as it was later explained, every step could have caused his death. When the doctor arrived minutes later, he put Cliff in an oxygen tent in intensive care.

As I waited in the hallway for the verdict, I felt as if I were encased in a huge glass bowl suspended in midair. I remember an overwhelming sense of loneliness and then desperation so enormous that it was too great to emerge into consciousness. I sat stiff and tearless waiting for the doctor. Finally he emerged from the room.

"Will he live?"

"I don't know yet, I don't know the extent of the damage to his heart. It is a severe coronary thrombosis." He explained that physical exertion must have caused the clot which blocked the main artery and the flow of blood to the heart.

"We have to wait and see it the blood will find a detour and if the heart will be able to withstand the strain."

"I will stay here if you will permit me," I begged.

"No, you go home. If there is a change, I will call you. Go home and sleep."

Sleep? How could I sleep? I left. I walked like a sleepwalker. It is curious to see yourself functioning so automatically. I drove home, parked the car properly, went upstairs, sat in the living room, the silence was vibrating around me. Then the shock broke, and I began to weep uncontrollably. As I had when I was so afraid for my parents, I turned to prayer. "Let me keep him, save him."

I am so grateful for the ability to believe. It is such a tremendous help. Yet sometimes I am reminded of the millions of people who prayed to God for help and they had to die at the hands of murderers. But I prayed and trusted I would be heard. I suddenly felt very relaxed and fell asleep.

At six o'clock the next morning the telephone rang. It was good news, "Mr. Shedd is holding his own, his condition is fair."

I was allowed a five-minute visit. He was completely enclosed in a transparent oxygen tent. When he saw me, his lips formed the words: "Don't worry. I'll be all right."

Two days later he was out of danger. He stayed in the hospital for four weeks and then home for another four. I was with him day and night. It relieved my anxiety to take care of him and watch him get better and, eventually, get well. This traumatic experience made me love Cliff all the more. As the days and weeks passed, we could not avoid the thought which neither of us dared to put into words, "This was a close call. When will it be repeated?"

Cliff began preparing me for widowhood. Little by little it dawned on me why he made me responsible for handling all our finances, why he let me do the negotiations with repairmen, why he so eagerly supported my efforts to establish a career. He knew that sooner or later I would have to take care of myself.

After he had regained his health completely and had returned to work, I found a new dimension in our relationship. I would awaken in the middle of the night and listen for his breathing, then in a surge of love and anxiety embrace him.

The doctor told me, "Ten more years, perhaps eleven, if he guards his health." I hated to see the years roll by. How do you use ten years of grace? What do you do to make every moment count?

"Don't let him know," I thought. "Let us do as much as possible together, let us do things that will linger on as treasured memories."

21

In 1951 when Cliff had recovered completely, we decided to visit Europe and my parents, so we booked passage to Europe on the S.S. Independence. Alas! The voyage was a dismal disappointment. The cabin was nice enough with two berths, but the tourist dining room looked more like a Horn and Hardart cafeteria. No one dressed for dinner. The food was miserable, always cold and badly cooked. There was no choice; you ate what was placed before you. The most infuriating aspect on that voyage was the crew's attitude – arrogant and totally incapable of serving the passengers. One day we asked the captain about the service.

"Simple," he said, "we have to pick up what we find on the pier. We have to hire who the unions tell us to hire. The crews on American ships are not career-minded; ours are just fill-ins, changing every trip and just interested in getting paid."

After crossing the Atlantic and entering the Mediterranean, our first port was Naples. The city was veiled by a morning haze that covered the scars of wars. We began to see the destruction clearly as we neared the dock. This was Cliff's first encounter with the destruction of war – building after building in ruins, bomb craters, valiant attempts to use what was left standing for the business of living. In southern Italy, the misery was softened by the benevolent weather – sunshine is better than ice and snow – but an empty stomach grumbles the same tune in every language. Hungry people do things they would normally not dream of doing. The girls and women who hung around the harbor of Naples waiting for sailors and tourists were a case in point. A piece of chocolate, a cigarette, chewing gum, an American coin were prized possessions. We shooed away the urchins in rags who followed us in a beggars' procession.

We took a tattered 1920s taxi to see the ruins of Pompeii. I could not help but compare the destruction wrought by the eruption of Mount Vesuvius in those ancient times with the havoc visited upon Naples by World War II. So much lost forever, both then and now. Looking at Pompeii I wondered what our modern forces of destruction would leave for posterity.

Genoa, the next stop and our port of debarkation, seemed at first glance to mirror Naples – shipwrecks in the harbor, whole blocks along the waterfront destroyed. Yet Genoa's busy street life, purposeful citizens, and well-stocked shops were quite different from what we had seen in Naples.

It was evening when we got through customs. A porter with the usual European luggage cart took our suitcases, and we followed on foot to the hotel. A concierge greeted us and announced that he had a beautiful double room with bath available. Private baths were most unusual in Europe and could only be found in hotels that catered to Americans. Europeans were satisfied with wash basins in their rooms. Since our room was as big as a dance hall, Cliff took me around the waist and whirled me through the room in waltz time.

By the time we were settled, it was nine p.m. The dining room was officially closed, but they opened it to serve us a cold supper. The waiter, with the prideful demeanor of European waiters, carved a cold roast chicken, arranging the pieces on elegant china plates. A bottle of tangy white wine was presented for inspection to Cliff and a little poured into his glass for his approval. He tasted it and nodded whereupon the goblets were filled half full as is proper. This was Cliff's initiation to European hospitality, and he loved it.

The next day we took the train to Verona where we changed to cross the Brenner Pass into Austria. In the train that sped us toward the border, we met an Italian who spoke good English and was willing to talk about the world situation.

"We are too many people," he said. "There is not enough room for 40 million hungry mouths. There is not enough work. Half of the population wants to emigrate to the United States where they all have relatives. But the quotas are filled for years. Unfortunately," he continued, "not enough people were killed in the war!"

****

The villages of the Austrian Tyrol looked prosperous and the people well fed. The houses seemed to be in good repair, the balconies overflowing with flowers. Our hotel in Innsbruck – set aside for Americans and paid with American scrip money – was comfortable, and the food was plentiful and well prepared. We didn't know then that Austrians didn't have access to such food. Not until we arrived in Vienna did we have the unsettling experience of seeing hungry looking faces pressed against the restaurant window watching every forkful of food as it disappeared into our mouths.

The contrast between the western provinces of Austria occupied by the Allies and the province occupied by Russia was apparent when we took the train from Innsbruck to Vienna. Certainly occupation by foreign troops is never welcomed, no matter how benevolently the occupier might behave. However, in the west the people were clearly free to go about their business, and everywhere the crews were busy rebuilding houses, stores, railroad stations, roads, and churches. In the Russian Zone it was a different story. The roads went unrepaired. Houses were left as they had been when bombs fell. The people were gray ghosts, their clothes drab and shapeless. We saw no smiles.

We had to have a Gray Pass to go through the Russian Zone. At the checkpoint the Austrian conductor, accompanied by the Russian passport officer, demanded our papers. Every page was examined, every picture scrutinized, a grim-faced glance at our faces for comparison, then the papers were handed back to us without comment. We didn't feel safe until the train pulled into the American sector of Vienna.

The Hotel Mozart, where we stayed, was within walking distance of the war-damaged Franz Josef Station where I had said my heart-breaking good-bye to my father. Within minutes of checking in, I was talking on the phone with my father who said that everyone was looking forward to greeting the American son-in-law. Since we needed special permission to visit in the Russian Zone, he said he would accompany us the next day to the American Consulate to get yet another Gray Pass. Only the Russians required entry permits.

Vati got to our hotel early the next morning. While he might have been apprehensive about meeting his new son-in-law, due to the language barrier and the closeness in their ages, the meeting was warm and almost tender. Cliff put his arms around my father. Their immediate ease of communication confirmed what I had suspected: those two were of the same kind. I was immeasurably happy to have them with me and to see that they liked each other. When we got to the American Consulate, we were warned, "You go at your own risk. We can't go in and rescue you if you get in trouble."

My father soothed me, "Don't worry, the Russians are trying to behave. They are only dangerous when they are drunk."

What would I find in Klosterneuburg? Thirteen years had passed. Bombs had fallen, fires had burned. Would I recognize the town the streets, the house, the people? Can one go home again?

Nothing had changed. Everything was exactly as I had left it. The house untouched, dilapidated and neglected, yes, but intact. The ivy had grown higher and now covered the front of the house, the windows barely visible. Our big St. Bernard was gone. Someone had poisoned him during the years of famine. My mother had prettied up the house as best she could – not an easy task when the paint is peeling, the plaster cracked. Everything in the house and outside told the story of neglect.

As he did with my father, Cliff immediately endeared himself to my mother with his warm and affectionate approach, hugging her, fitting in with my family as if he had known them forever. Any doubts I had about my parents' and Cliff's ability to communicate with each other were dispersed within minutes. They understood each other completely – rarely needing me as an interpreter – as they built a linguistic bridge by pointing and illustrating with motions of their hands and, I suppose, with the telepathy of loving hearts.

Cliff molded himself easily into my family. He remained the lover and husband, retaining at all times his youthful curiosity and adventurous spirit, while at the same time talking to my parents at their own level. It was difficult to finally leave them after a stay of two weeks. For both of us the pain of separation was softened only by the assurance that we would visit them again as soon as possible.

****

Returning home on the Dutch ship Ryndam, Cliff experienced the luxury of a well-run ship. After the disappointment of the Independence, the management of the Ryndam was everything I had promised Cliff an ocean voyage would be. The staff in tourist class was superbly trained and polite, our cabin sparkled, the stewards were solicitous, and the service in the tourist dining room was as attentive and individualized as I remembered it from first class on my first journey to America in 1939.

We asked ourselves why the Independence could not produce

service as good as this Dutch ship did. We got the answer from the captain who explained that everyone on ship regarded his job as a career and hoped to stay on for a lifetime. Service as a proud career was apparently alien to Americans who regarded it only as a means of earning money, not for the sake of satisfying the customer.

In later years, I observed that almost all waiters in the better restaurants in America were Italians, French, or German. Americans took waiters' jobs as a stopgap occupation when no "better" jobs were available. When I encountered American waiters or waitresses, they usually emphasized their equality by addressing patrons with phrases like "what's it gonna be, folks" or cozy titles such as "honey" or "deary," a custom annoying and perplexing to European visitors.

****

When we got home, the 1952 Presidential campaigns were getting started. While I was unfamiliar with political campaigning, I adored Adlai Stevenson for his intellect and superb use of the English language. He had integrity and a grasp of the political scene plus tremendous charm. I wanted to do something to ensure his election.

Taking the direct approach because I didn't know any better, I called the Democratic headquarters in Wilmington. "Come on down," they said, and I did. The office was on Orange Street, and I soon found myself sitting at a table handing out campaign leaflets and answering the telephone. That was not enough for me. How would they like Mrs. Roosevelt to come to Wilmington for a big mass rally on behalf of Stevenson, I asked.

The women on the committee looked at me with suspicion, "How do you think you are going to do that? Do you know her?"

I, who had never before organized anything more complicated than a small dinner party in my own home, suddenly found myself charged with organizing a huge political rally for over a thousand people in the Armory in Wilmington. Of course, before doing anything else, I had to secure Mrs. Roosevelt's acceptance. As soon as her acceptance was confirmed, some of the older committee women tried to take over, explaining that my lack of experience would be detrimental to the success of the affair.

When I told Cliff about it, he educated me, "If you don't look out for yourself," he admonished, "they will push you into a corner. Stand up for yourself. You don't need any special experience, just be yourself and follow your instinct." It was valuable advice which rang in my ears many times over the years. I took the reins firmly in my hand and negotiated everything myself. A committee had to be formed, posters printed, invitations sent out, a caterer procured, a menu selected.

On the big day, a reception committee met Mrs. Roosevelt at the railroad station. It included Governor Elbert Carvel and Lt. Governor Alexis du Pont Bayard. Later at the Armory, the caterers served a superb cooked dinner, even if it was the eternal chicken – to the eleven hundred guests.

My introductory remarks were carried over a Delaware radio station as were all the speeches of that evening. When I am asked the circumstance responsible for my success as a radio personality, I hark back to that one moment when I introduced Eleanor Roosevelt. I spoke just a few words, but they contained the phrase "I now give you the First Lady of the World." Later on she was often introduced with that phrase. But I, in fact, created that phrase. It made headlines in Wilmington, was picked up by news sources and used frequently. No, I don't shout plagiarism; I am simply proud I thought of it first.

The response I got from that radio audience was more important. It was a very small audience but large enough to make me realize that I could move people with my voice. We seldom know what triggered a certain turn in our lives, but I know that introduction started a most important phase of development.

The dinner was a success; the Stevenson campaign was not. But for me it was a most important beginning because I found myself involved in all sorts of activities I didn't realize existed. People who heard me on the radio called and told me that they loved listening to my voice and thought my introductory remarks were splendid and did I want to join the League of Women Voters, and all sorts of other groups. I found myself in a spotlight, public attention – though on a modest scale – roused long-buried desires to be in the limelight. Cliff, as always, encouraged me.

****

It was not long before my name appeared again and again in the local newspaper as I was asked to speak before clubs and women's groups. The audiences wanted to hear about Vienna, my childhood, women in Europe, and my friendship with Mrs. Roosevelt. I spoke without scripts. To my own amazement the speeches just poured forth in what was, after all, a foreign language. I loved what I was doing. It did two things for me: with the attention and applause, my longing for the stage was satisfied; and at the same time I could explain events most people knew nothing about, such as the horrors of the Nazi concentration camps, the hunger among war victims, and the difficulties refugees encounter, including hostility from the native-born. Many times I left them in tears, but as many times I myself wept recounting bitter and desperate experiences. It never occurred to me to ask for a speaker's fee, and nobody ever offered to pay me. I spoke because I felt a need to speak and because it was a rewarding emotional experience.

Then the Sunday paper, *The Wilmington Sunday Star*, asked me to write a weekly column about activities in Arden. I had never written for a publication, but I had been at the top of my class in German composition. In fact, shortly after graduating from the Gymnasium I had flirted with journalism. My father, overjoyed at the prospect of weaning me away from the theater, introduced me to the editor of a small newspaper in Vienna who hired me. I was to start with the obituaries. My father was horrified at the thought of my chasing hearses and hanging around morgues. He had visions of by-lined articles and brilliant editorials; it never occurred to him that I might have to start at the bottom. Thus ended my newspaper career.

The pay for my column was nominal but money was not my primary interest. It was the mastery of a task and the chance to communicate that fascinated me. Within minutes I decided on the column's title, "People, Places and Things." My first article practically wrote itself and was printed without a single change with my by-line. When I saw the article in print, I couldn't believe it. Did I really write that well?

When the theater season started at the Robin Hood Summer Barn Theater in Arden, I interviewed the actors, writers, directors, and producers. When I interviewed Arthur Miller, who was directing his own play, *All My Sons*, he confided that this was the first time he had directed a play of his own. He enjoyed, he said, making the cast do what he wanted it to do rather than having another director interpret his play.

I interviewed many actors that summer, including Larry Gates, Anthony Perkins, and Kathleen Widdoes, who also played early roles on the Arden stage. Jack Klugman was a hard worker, a perfectionist who demanded the same perfection from his fellow actors and became quite obscene when others did not live up to his high standards.

As I gained confidence, new possibilities opened up. I found an abundance of topics. There were local painters, sculptors, poets, embroiderers, and doll makers. Of course their work was interesting, but behind each work I discovered a fascinating personality.

It is important to mention a letter I had written some years earlier to Bessie Beatty, who had a talk show on WOR in New York. She had asked her listeners to write letters describing what America meant to them. I wrote describing the importance of the freedom I had found in America and the wide choice of opportunities that offered themselves – even to the greenhorn immigrant. To my surprise, my letter was chosen and I got to visit her program to collect a prize, an imported Majolica hot-chocolate china set from Italy.

On the day of my visit I sat spellbound watching Bessie Beatty conduct a one-hour, unrehearsed interview program. Her guests were actors, artists, politicians. Chatting with them, she extracted all sorts of interesting information. Part way through the program, I was asked to take my place at the microphone and tell about myself. When she saw that I was comfortable before the mike and learned I was a singer, I was invited to sing for the servicemen she entertained every Wednesday afternoon at her townhouse.

Bessie and I became friends. She liked to hear me sing and asked me to appear on her program several times. I, in turn, watched everything she did because I wanted to glean her formula for success. Perhaps there might be a time when I could use it. Sadly, Bessie died while she and her husband were on a short vacation. In the short time I had known her, the imprint of her personality profoundly influenced the future course of my life. I made up my mind that somehow or other, when the opportunity presented itself, I, too, would become a radio personality.

That opportunity arrived when I told Cliff about my desire. "Do it," he said simply.

"What do you mean, 'Do it?'", I asked. "Just like that?"

"Pick a radio station, find out who the manager is, go to his office and tell him you want to do a radio show."

I was not used to the lack of restrictions in a free enterprise system. I feared being asked to fill out forms, bring certificates, and get letters of recommendation from "very important persons," all of which were required in my native Vienna. To walk into somebody's office, ask for a job, and expect to get it was in the realm of the improbable.

Yet I trusted Cliff, so I went to the largest Wilmington radio station, WDEL. The manager, a Mr. Gorman Walsh, was not interested in seeing me, but his assistant, Harvey Smith, listened to me courteously. He knew that I was writing feature stories and interviews, and I told him of my radio experience in Vienna, both as a singer and actress.

"Sorry", he said, "at the moment we have no opening for a woman."

A few days later, while interviewing one of the actors at the Robin Hood Theater, I heard that the radio station planned a weekly interview program with some of the celebrities. Tom Greer, then an announcer with WDEL, was slated to do the interviews. I managed to be there for the first radio interview. In fact, I worked myself into the conversation and within minutes was conducting the interview. Tom Greer seemed pleased to hand the reins over to someone who knew more about theater, plays, and actors than he did.

When the next interview came around, Tom asked me to take over for him. My chance, finally, my chance! It didn't matter to me that I wasn't paid. I regarded it as a heaven-sent opportunity to prove to myself and to the radio station manager that I could do the job and open the door for future activities. The *Wilmington Sunday Star* carried the headline: "New Program Features Star Correspondent."

Thus, I slowly began building a new career, all the while enjoying the comfort and quiet of my home in Arden. I had the best of everything – the theater, with its old magic, yet, with none of its heartaches, frustrations, and demands. I had the spotlight which I craved (my mother was right after all), but I did not have to pay the penalties of a gypsy existence.

When the theater season ended on Labor Day, the radio series ended, and to my chagrin, the *Wilmington Sunday Star* closed its doors. Cliff urged me to stick with radio. "What you have to sell," he explained, "is your very distinct voice, your personal appeal, your background, and your past experience. Others don't have these attributes. Use them to your advantage."

Armed with those tools, I went back to radio station WDEL. Changes had taken place. Mr. Walsh was no longer manager, in his office sat Harvey Smith. Tall, elegant, and soft spoken, Harvey listened to my request. He had heard my radio programs and read my newspaper articles. But he also had a program manager, Dick Ayedelotte, who wasn't going to have any of it. Ayedelotte did a weekly program with Eleanor Parrish, the woman's editor of the News Journal papers. She gave him a hard time. I heard him say to Harvey Smith, "One woman is all we need on this station."

But fate was with me again. Miss Parrish gave up the Tuesday morning show, and I was back in Harvey Smith's office.

"Give me a chance," I insisted, "I heard that in America everyone gets a chance. You don't have to pay me, and if you don't like what I do, I will resign, but let me try, please."

Ayedelotte consented grudgingly, "You're the boss, Harvey, but I still say the last thing we need on this station is another woman."

There was no contract, no conditions, no instructions, no censorship, and, of course, no money. But that didn't matter. This was a golden opportunity to establish myself. How fortunate that I didn't have to worry about making a living. Had I insisted on a salary, I would never have been given the chance.

Cliff's support was wonderful. "First you have to have a title and then a format. You are going to interview successful people because they are interesting. Call the program Spotlight on Success."

Tom Greer was my announcer; all we needed now were guests. To help, I turned to my friend, Jeanette Slocomb Edwards, Poet Laureate of Delaware and teacher of the creative writing class at the Wilmington YWCA. Jeanette, rosy-faced and blue-eyed and with the best disposition, was a splendidly supportive friend. She believed in my ability to succeed in anything I might undertake.

Again a woman! There had been so many. Was it coincidence

that women – older and wiser than I – guided me from one step to the next. It was as if those women handed me from one to another saying, "Here, you take over now." Harriet Hauser, Hildegarde, Margit Schey, Lilly Rona, Mrs. Roosevelt, Bessie Beatty, and now, Jeanette Slocomb Edwards. There would be many more.

When I told her about the radio program, she suggested choosing my first guests from the ranks of the presidents of women's clubs.

"Those women are smart," she said. "They are doing interesting things and are looking for publicity. When you interview them, their club members will listen, so you can build up an audience." Specifically, she suggested Marjorie Speakman, a talented lady, who owned a fashionable boutique. When we sat down in the studio to begin our conversation, I felt at home, as if I had done nothing but this all my life. The fifteen minutes flew by. I loved it. I had found my profession. This was IT – Radio! Not singing, not acting, TALKING. After the program, I hurried to our car where Cliff was listening to the radio.

"Marvelous," he said, "you were great. Like a veteran."

I was distraught that I had to wait a week for the next program. Guests were delighted to be on my program. Harvey was pleased. Dick Ayedelotte sat in the control room when I was on the air and never smiled, never complimented me.

It was a difficult time for a woman on radio. There were no female announcers, and only a very few women on network shows in New York. When I tried to get on Philadelphia stations, I was told "listeners don't want to hear women's voices, they are too nasal and harsh." I was plain lucky to have been able to swim against the stream.

After the first few shows, there was a flood of mail, complimenting me on my style, accent, and subject matter. I showed the letters to Dick Ayedelotte who responded with a non-committal "hm" and to Harvey Smith who jokingly remarked that I must have "lots of relatives in Wilmington."

After six months of success and working without pay, I asked what I could do to get paid.

"There is nothing I can do," said Harvey, "perhaps you can find someone to sponsor you."

So now, I had to go out and sell the program, too. Fortunately,

I had learned how to sell when I worked at Wanamaker's. Cliff came up with a brilliant idea: Why not take the program on a trip to Europe, interview famous personalities there, send the programs back by air and present this package to potential sponsors.

In 1954 Europe was still far from normalized. The Russians were still in Germany and Austria, and no one knew whether they would live up to their commitment to withdraw. No freelance radio broadcaster had tried what we were planning. There were no small tape recorders, and the difference in cycle and electrical current made taping very complicated. The tapes themselves were reel-to-reel, and finally the mail service between Europe and America was still sketchy. Yet we were both enthusiastic.

We asked people at NBC in New York for their expert advice. We were told that no one had attempted this kind of project because "there would be great difficulties with customs and the radio station in Wilmington would have to go to the US Customs House to pick up the tapes there." Moreover, they thought that any tape recorder would be much too heavy to carry.

However, when you have a dream, you try to fulfill it. In the Philadelphia telephone book we found The Magnetic Recorder and Reproducer Corporation. Its president, Albert Borkow, was a pioneer in the field of magnetic recording. He shared our enthusiasm and found us a Crestwood tape recorder, weighing forty pounds, which he altered electronically to match the European currents. We also bought two fine Electro voice microphones – big table models – and a supply of tapes. In addition, Cliff bought a Kodak timer and built a very practical tape editing tool. Finally, he designed and produced a handsome brochure proclaiming in glowing terms my accomplishments.

I wrote Mrs. Roosevelt informing her of the latest developments. I had, of course, kept her abreast of all my activities. She had promised to be a guest on my program when the opportunity offered itself. This time I asked if she could give me a number of introductions to people in Europe whose doors might otherwise be closed to me. Within a few days, I had the copies of letters she had written to the Prime Minister of Luxembourg, the American Ambassador to Italy, Claire Boothe Luce, the American Ambassador to Switzerland, the Director of the American Delegation to the

United Nations in Geneva, and Madame Vaudable, proprietress of the Paris restaurant, Maxim's.

To this impressive list I added several names on my own. Governor Caleb Boggs wrote a letter of greeting to the Mayor of Vienna, a circumstance which gave my trip local publicity, as did a similar letter from the President of the University of Delaware, John A. Perkins, to the Chairman of the Foreign Student Exchange, Professor Pfeiffer in Heidelberg, Germany. In Rome, I added Fontana, a fashion designer, and proceeding on to Monaco, I made a date with Father Tucker, a former Wilmington priest who was chaplain to Prince Rainier and took on, for a priest, the unlikely role of postilion d'amour by arranging the first meeting between Grace Kelly and the Prince.

"I have to find a nice girl for him," Father Tucker confided when we visited him in Monaco. "He is old enough to settle down. He is a little wild now, but I think I have just the girl for him. She will straighten him out."

Everything I did was a novelty for Wilmington. No woman broadcaster had done more than cover fashions, cooking, and club activities. Harvey Smith deserved full credit for giving me my chance and also for letting me discuss any subject. The freedom to say anything without first checking with a superior made me eager to produce the best and to make the station proud of me.

I also wanted to reap financial rewards and, armed with my new brochure, I approached my first target, the advertising department of our bank. The decision turned out to be a lucky one. Charles A. Robinson, a very fine man, was in the advertising office of the Delaware Trust Company. Charlie, as I came to call him, looked at my brochure, listened to my planned European and said, "Fine, I think it's a swell idea. Yes, I'll sponsor you, how much?"

The station and I had already decided on a fifty-fifty arrangement. It never occurred to me that this might be an uneven balance since I had to sell the spot, write the copy, find the guests, and promote the show. All the station had to do was to let me do my show and then collect fifty percent. Had I not been there, they would have played two or three records and read a commercial. However, I was so anxious to take advantage of the opportunity that I gladly agreed to the arrangement. WDEL gave me my chance when no one else would.

Now I had to decide on the value of my radio program. How much? Courageously I asked for ten dollars per commercial: five for me and five for the station. I collected two more sponsors for my once-a-week fifteen-minute show: Marjorie Speakman's Fashion Shop and Marshall & Greenplate Travel Agency. Each signed up for thirteen weeks.

22

Everything had fallen into place. I should have felt fulfilled. Yet something was missing. Something important. One day lying on my bed staring at the ceiling the answer came: a child. I wanted a child. But time was running out; I was forty and Cliff sixty-five. He felt he was too old, but I think he was also concerned lest he lose the preferred spot in our lives.

There were other considerations, including financial ones. We had no reserves. But as I lay on my bed, I was sure that, come what may, I would be able to raise a child, even if I had to do it on my own. I could not tell Cliff about my intention – I had to present him with a fait accompli.

Never was a child conceived with greater love than in that night of love. Within two weeks I knew I was pregnant. I said nothing to Cliff, but I did go to a physician. When I told him my age and that of my husband, he laughed and told me I was going through the change of life.

"I plan to go to Europe in a few weeks, and will be carrying heavy recording equipment, do you really think it's safe?"

"Oh sure," said the doctor, laughing at the silly woman, "do anything you want, if you are pregnant – so am I. Ha, ha!"

I was convinced I was right but said nothing and continued my travel preparations. The forty-pound tape recorder worried me, so when my Viennese friend, Ady Weaver, said she was also going to Europe, I confided my happy suspicions to her and asked her to travel with me. Cliff was to follow a month later.

Trans-Atlantic air travel, in 1954, was in its infancy and using propeller planes. I got permission to take the tape recorder into the cabin with me by interviewing everybody I figured could be helpful to me: the traffic controller, the airport manager, the flight captain. It was good publicity for them and, in return, they made things a little easier for me.

The Hotel Corona in Paris, our first stop, was an old hotel not far from the Place de l'Opera, where Ady and I had an elegant double room. With the telephone help of the hotel concierge, we made an appointment to interview Madame Vaudable, owner of the world-famous restaurant, Maxim's of Paris.

Madame was waiting for us, eager to publicize the rebirth of the restaurant. She wanted to make sure that the restaurant – immortalized by Franz Lehar in his operetta, *The Merry Widow* – would again occupy the number one spot in international popularity. Good business woman that she was, however, she used my radio program not only to promote Maxim's, but also to invite daughters of wealthy American families to enroll in her private school where future society hostesses could learn social graces, manners, and haute cuisine. She did not invite us to dine at Maxims. Ah, well, c'est la vie!

In Paris I took delivery of my car, a Hillman Minx. It was a sturdy, well-constructed small British car which seated five comfortably. On our way out of Paris, we asked another motorist for directions to Luxembourg. He smiled, motioned us to follow him, and guided us all the way out of the city and sent us off with a cheery bon voyage. The French people were extremely courteous and helpful, particularly when I addressed them with formal phraseology in their native tongue.

Not quite as formal, however, was our first confrontation with what is commonly known as a Russian toilet. France had very few gas service stations with bathrooms. So we stopped at one of the small roadside restaurants for a bite to eat and "to wash our hands." Alas, it was a shocking experience which sent us fleeing for the nearest woods. The facility consisted of an open cubicle with a hole in the floor with adjoining impressions for one's feet. It was meant to serve both men and women. The absence of a door confirmed the fact that those who felt the need to use the facility also did not need privacy.

Arriving at our hotel in Luxembourg, we found an invitation from the Ministry of Foreign Affairs to be at the office of Prime Minister Bech the next morning at 11 a.m. It was really quite extraordinary for him to do this, considering that I was not connected with any major network, did not broadcast in a large city, and was unknown outside of Wilmington. M. Bech did it for Mrs. Roosevelt, whom he knew well from the days when they both were at the United Nations. For this interview, he interrupted his vacation, returned to the city, and arrived on the dot of 11 a.m. at his office.

I had brought my tape recording equipment to the Ministry a half hour earlier and frantically looked for an electrical outlet. A handyman was called who, after long thought, found an extension cord so we could hook up the converter and the cumbersome tape recorder. Bech spoke fluent English and was the essence of the charming European diplomat. He graciously spoke with me for almost an hour. When I asked him if he wanted to hear the interview played back he waved his hand and said, "No, no, it is all right."

After he left, we dismantled the complicated wires and electrical connections and returned to our hotel to listen once more to the charming man. Oh, horror! Not a single word could be heard, only a deep low hum – something had gone wrong. To call the Prime Minister and ask him to return for a repeat performance was out of the question. But I learned to check and recheck my machines.

As a result, I was very cautious for my next interview with the American ambassador, Perle Mesta. She was a small, well-upholstered figure in gray, carefully coiffed and made up, wearing spectacular jewelry. She was very friendly and very assertive and, I thought, a real shock to the modestly dressed and discreetly elegant European wives of the diplomatic corps. However, she was very popular with the American GIs because she kept the Embassy open at all times for the "boys." She held parties for them on American holidays and helped them when they had family problems or were just plain homesick. While she didn't speak much French or German, she was a goodwill ambassador for her country and was popular with her colleagues. The musical *Call Me Madame* portrayed her down-to-earth personality well. Yet with all her exuberance in everyday life, she froze before my microphone and was one of those rare guests who answered in monosyllables and made me work for every word.

Our itinerary next took us across the border into Germany to Kaiserslautern where we spent the night on our way to Heidelberg. Tourism was only beginning to revive, and hotel space was restricted to a few buildings that had been spared intensive bombing. We were directed to a hotel which had been assigned to American civilian use. After washing up and changing clothes, we descended to the cozy, wood-paneled dining room where the waitress handed us a menu that made my mouth water. There was deer ragout and saddle of deer, roast hare, grilled partridge in bacon, and roast boar. Ah, what de-light I thought, as I settled down to the luscious meal. And then it happened: I got deathly ill. I had to flee the table. No doubt. I was pregnant.

While I sat nauseated on my bed, Ady came in looking the picture of heavenly bliss, for she had eaten both portions of deer in sour cream sauce, potato dumplings, two dishes of red cabbage, and, in addition, a huge slice of malakoff torte. "You are sick," she groaned. "How do you think I feel? I am sick too, because I can't waste food, so I ate it all."

The next interview was scheduled in Heidelberg with the mayor of the city, the city historian, and a gentlemen from the German tourist office. We stayed at the oldest hotel in Heidelberg, the Hotel zum Ritter. I love those old hotels, preferring them over the new, coldly functional hostelries. Most of the grand old hotels have spacious rooms, large windows that actually open and bathrooms with huge comfortable bathtubs.

The interview was to take place in the hotel restaurant, but no sooner had I sat down than I had to leave the table once more in a hurry. No food for me!

This time the interviewees and the tape recorder had no problems, I was able to tape the story of how the town was saved from destruction by an American general who loved the old houses and streets and the picturesque as well as the historic university.

The autobahn from Heidelberg to Munich was full of potholes. There were very few service stations and those few were reserved for American military personnel, but we could buy gasoline because we had military scrip money. The autobahn ended at the Austrian border. When the border guard in his Austrian uniform looked at our American passports and saw that we were both born in Vienna, he smiled and said "So, you're coming home, are you. Do you like America?"

"Yes, very much," we responded.

Salzburg, the festival city, was making a valiant effort to regain its pre-Hitler status. It was eerie walking through the streets of the city where I had spent summers as an aspiring actress, had seen the specter of Nazism emerging in the arrival of refugees from across the German border, and had met the brothers Bring, who later had helped me to emigrate to America. Looking for the past, I entered the Café Bazar, sat down at one of the marble-topped tables and ordered Kaffee mit Schlag. The waiter brought my order and with it the Salzburger Nachrichten, the local paper; he was the same waiter who had served me in 1937! Was it really seventeen years since I had been here the last time? Had there really been a war, a holocaust? Was this all a dream? It had not been a dream, but in the Café Bazar time had stood still.

I searched my conscience for a reaction to a city that had emerged from the horrors of the past seventeen years with no scars or wounds. Did I belong here or was my allegiance to my new homeland? The city was a part of me, of my soul, and I loved it. But I could not forget that Salzburg was also the willing haven of guilty Nazis who had run away from Vienna and found here a safe refuge. In spite of my love for the city and its glorious atmosphere, I could not overlook the past, and I knew that I had become an "American of Austrian descent."

It is not easy to resolve such a struggle. Almost every naturalized American citizen who has a chance to return to a prosperous homeland is faced with the dilemma of emotional allegiance. We stand for many years as if on a bridge, one foot planted in our new homeland, the other still on tiptoe in the land of our fathers held fast by the roots of culture, traditions, language, and memories. The hold is not easily broken, nor should it be. Fortunately most of us can do both: be loyal Americans and retain a bond to the land of our birth.

I had several interviews lined up in Salzburg, one of them with Karl Boehm, conductor and music director of the Vienna State Opera. He was conducting several operas and although very busy he talked for an hour, describing in great detail the last days of the war when the Vienna Opera was fire-bombed. Now, in 1954, the famous building on the Opernring in Vienna was almost completely rebuilt. The magic moment of reopening was scheduled for 1955, when the last of the foreign occupation soldiers was hopefully to leave Austrian soil.

Maestro Boehm was charming and relaxed, and I, in turn, discovered I could converse with outstanding people – without nervousness or awe – on a basis of intellectual personal equality. I think my friendship with Mrs. Roosevelt and the people I met through her contributed to my ease in interviewing celebrities.

Baron von Puthon, the grand old man of the Salzburg Festivals, was one of my most cherished radio guests. That interview produced a tale about Toscanini – because he refused to play the Italian Fascist anthem, he had had to join the stream of refugees across the Atlantic.

The Herr Baron Puthon had been there at the inception of the Festivals in 1917 and later when the Festivals were abolished by Hitler and now was overseeing their rebirth. In his tired old voice with its elegant Schönbrunner Viennese accent, he spoke of his hope for a rebirth of the splendor of Salzburg.

When it was time to drive to Vienna, we went to the American Consulate to get our Gray Pass so we could drive through the Russian Zone along the narrow corridor on Bundesstrasse #1. We were warned not to stray from the road not even onto the soft shoulder. "Do not stop even for one minute," we were warned, "and do not talk to anyone." An American officer at the checkpoint in Enns told us that he had telephoned Vienna advising his counterpart that two American women were to check in not later than seven hours from the time of his call.

The appearance of the villages and towns we drove through told the story of life under Russian rule better than words could. Everything was gray. The houses were in need of repair. The walls were peeling, roofs had holes, windows were boarded up with wood and cardboard. No flowers graced the window boxes. There were no sidewalk cafes or outdoor restaurants, and the few people we did see walked slowly and with a heavy gait, their heads bowed, their eyes averted. We saw no one working in the fields.

Without incident, we reached the checkpoint where the American Military Police checked our arrival, phoned the guards in Enns that we had arrived and welcomed us to Vienna's American sector. Thanks to the relatively amicable relations among the occupation forces in Vienna itself, it was easy to drive into the Russian Zone where my parents lived. The Russian occupation soldiers loved Vienna, with its easygoing atmosphere. They lived with their wives and children in private homes requisitioned from the civilian population. Here they saw a way of living that was wonderful. As a result, most did not want to return to Russia, so it was standard practice to awaken soldiers scheduled to return home in the middle of the night and immediately send them to Russia. Thus, they had no time to defect.

****

This time I stayed with my parents in the house where I had grown up. After the comforts of my small American home, I found the big house cumbersome and "ungemütlich." Nothing had changed, no modernization. In addition, the house was in terrible disrepair. But I did not complain because I didn't want to hurt my parent's feelings, for they were so happy to have their daughter back home. But when I told my mother I thought I might be pregnant, she was speechless at first.

"Why, why, would you do such a thing, now after fourteen years of marriage – all of a sudden, you decide to have a child. I don't understand you." She was angry and told me I was crazy to "spoil" my life and saddle myself with an added responsibility. I suppose her reaction reflected her own position on motherhood. We decided not to tell my father, in case I might be wrong.

A few days later we left for Switzerland because Cliff was flying into Zürich. Outside the Russian zone, traveling in Austria was easy; there were many gas stations and in the restaurants food was plentiful and well prepared. The Marshall Plan had worked wonders for the Austrian economy. That help was visible in freshly painted houses, tilled fields, newly built roads, and well-stocked shops.

After meeting Cliff in Zürich, the four of us spent several days together. When my parents returned to Austria, Cliff and I toured Switzerland, including a stay in Geneva where I interviewed Dr. Adrian Pelt, Secretary General of the United Nations European Headquarters. Later we went on to Bern to interview the American Ambassador to Switzerland, Mrs. Frances E. Willis. Mrs. Willis' position was unusual because the Swiss regarded women as second-class citizens, not permitting them to vote and relegating them to "Küche, Kirche, Kinder," (kitchen, church, children), meaning that a woman's place is in the home.

The Swiss women we talked to didn't seem to mind their inferior position; in fact, they saw themselves as the power behind the throne. Their men consulted with them privately, and more often than not, carried out their wishes. Thus, the men retained their feeling of superiority yet remained wax in the hands of their wives.

On the way back to Austria, we stopped in Liechtenstein, the tiny principality between Switzerland and Austria, where I interviewed Prince Hans von Liechtenstein, a member of the ruling house of Habsburg. Prince Hans, generally regarded as the enfant terrible of the family, used his connection to the ruler of the principality as an excuse not to pay any bills. When he learned that I would not pay for an interview, he demurred saying that he expected more from "rich Americans." But then, the "ham" in him took over and he talked for more than two hours. With humor and fatalistic resignation, he described his life as an unemployed prince dependent on handouts from his wealthy relative, the Duke of Liechtenstein. We thanked him by inviting him to dine with us.

Back in Vienna I followed my mother's urging to see a physician. Cliff thought I was having some "irregularities."

After the examination there was no doubt. "Well, that's very simple," said the doctor, "you are pregnant." He then added matter of factly, "I will take it from you."

"You will do no such thing. I want it."

"You want it, at your age?"

"Yes. Is there any reason why I shouldn't have a child?" The doctor was noncommittal, "Not really. Everything seems to be all right. You are very healthy, and it is up to you."

When I broke the news to Cliff, he was speechless. He rallied quickly and joyfully began to speak of "him," the son who now would continue the threatened lineage of the Shedd family. He discounted my suggestion that perhaps the baby might be a girl. "No, it will be a boy."

When we told my father, his reaction was quite different from my mother's. His eyes filled with tears and he embraced me whispering that it had been his greatest wish that he might have a grandchild. "I hope it is a girl," he said, "Girls are so wonderful, and a daughter can be so much closer to a mother than a son."

I don't know why he had that opinion. In our family with its two daughters, I was closer to my father than to my mother, and my sister was not close to anyone. Perhaps my father foresaw that I would be alone with the child for many years and that a daughter would be easier to raise.

Then I began to bleed and my mother, notwithstanding her feelings about my pregnancy, did not want to see me and the baby in needless danger. She implored me to give up our travel plans and to return home. But my tenacity compelled me to stick with my schedule of driving to Italy, the Riviera, Spain, France, and then fly home to Delaware.

Outside of Venice I began to bleed again. I thought I might be losing the baby and regretted not taking mother's advice to fly home. Fortunately, the problem seemed to correct itself. I had a number of important interviews in Venice, one at the famous Murano glass factory, and several others describing the art treasures and the cuisine of the city. I could not bear to forego this chance of doing what no one else had done before me – sending home taped interviews from Europe.

In Rome, American Ambassador Claire Boothe Luce, reneged on her promise and was "not in town." But Fontana, the first Italian designer to give Paris serious competition, received me in her palatial salon. She took me through her workrooms where silent seamstresses sat bowed over glittering gowns. These creations were carefully guarded so that they couldn't be copied. One of the gowns, Fontana proudly told me, had been ordered by Margaret Truman.

We traveled all over Italy. Everywhere I had interviews with local personalities who described the wonders of churches, art, the Italian regional cuisines and wines, the poverty and the emerging prosperity, and the thousands of white crosses marking the graves of American soldiers killed in the war.

The interviews were tape recorded on twelve-inch reels and mailed back to the States in cardboard containers which aroused the suspicion of post office employees. We had to explain to post office supervisors and sometimes even quickly summoned security officers that these were not government secrets or spy reports but radio programs to entertain my radio audience and incidentally, too, to stimulate interest in visiting Italy. That usually did the trick, and the tapes were on their way.

In the United States the post office personnel were no less suspicious. The tapes had to go through customs and then be picked up by someone from the radio station who vouched for their contents. Although the war had been over for nine years, the Russians were still occupying Austria; therefore, those tapes could contain (at least someone thought this a possibility) coded messages. I worried that an zealous official might attempt to play a tape and erase it. Luckily, all my tapes arrived in good condition.

We traveled without reservations in hotels, stopping where we found a convenient place. Because Cliff had a grim aversion to asking directions, we often got lost and drove around in circles. Driving with Cliff was frustrating because he reacted to my requests to stop with an absent-minded "hm" and then continued driving for another two hours. In Barcelona this problem was solved when a figure clad in black seated on a motorcycle approached our car to ask if we needed a hotel.

"Yes," I quickly answered before Cliff could decline. The young man, who spoke good English, told us to follow him to a brand new hotel. There the concierge handed us the key to a lovely large room and rewarded our guide with a tip. He refused a tip from us, a circumstance we found hard to believe. "No, thank you," he said, "the hotel pays me, it is enough."

In Barcelona I became very ill. A doctor, trained at Johns Hopkins, examined me. He told me the baby was fine but recommended that I fly home immediately. Again I had to make a decision. I did not want to endanger the only chance I had to have a child; on the other hand, I did not want to cut short Cliff's chance to see Europe or spoil his well-earned, long-desired vacation. Therefore I did stay in bed for the four days we were in Barcelona.

Cliff used one of the days to attend a bullfight. When he returned from that experience, his face was green. "I am glad you couldn't go with me. You would have gotten as sick as I am. The bull doesn't have a chance and the mob is out for blood. I hated every minute of it."

"Yes," I thought to myself, "the mob is always out for blood, be it Auschwitz, the French Revolution, the Spanish Inquisition, nothing has changed and nothing ever will." But to Cliff I said that it is important to see the traditions and culture of a country because only then can one understand the people and their actions.

"At least they eat the bulls after they kill them," he said, and then added pensively, "we kill the steers too, more mechanically, not with such colorful trappings but we kill them, too."

When we left Barcelona, we followed the road to Zaragoza and then across the Pyrenees to France, where I wanted to visit Lourdes. Our faithful Hillman Minx car plowed through the driving rain which turned the roads into mire. We stopped in a dismal village and found a hotel which reminded me of the smugglers' inn from the opera *Rigoletto*. Fortunately it was open, had a room and even some food for Cliff. I only wanted hot tea. We brought in all our luggage and the tape recorder because we were afraid they might be stolen. It was cold and uncomfortable, one of those times when I asked myself why I had the crazy idea of coming here in the first place. But next morning the sun shone, the coffee was hot and sweet, the bread fresh, and the butter aromatic; the whole world looked much better.

At the Spanish-French border, the Spanish customs officer saw the tape recorder in the trunk and became very agitated. He didn't speak English, and I didn't speak Spanish. I had a paper proving I had registered the tape recorder when I entered Spain. Alas, the officer could not understand it. There was much telephoning and consulting and head-shaking. It didn't help that the timer Cliff had designed for me started ticking. After an hour, the gesticulating officer waved us on grudgingly, convinced that he should have put us in jail. It was the only time a customs officer was rude, and it didn't give me a good impression of the Franco regime.

We arrived in Lourdes while the rain was once more playing drums on our windshield. We found a good hotel not too far from the famous grotto where, according to legend, the Virgin Mary had appeared to the peasant girl, Bernadette Soubirous. The grotto houses a spring with miraculous healing powers, according to believers.

My first impression of Lourdes was shattering. Hucksters and souvenir booths selling the cheapest trinkets lined the streets. The grotto was decorated theatrically with colored lights like a third-rate movie set. I was appalled. But then, I turned and saw behind me row after row of pilgrims. They prayed. And in their faces was a light so luminous that it caught me in my throat and made me forget the cheap trappings. Sometimes a miracle actually happened. The doctors who had given them up as incurable could find no explanation for the sudden cure. "It is their faith that cured them," they would finally say and shrug their shoulders.

With all its almost obscene commercialism, Lourdes is justified because it brings peace to so many sufferers. I am not ashamed that I myself knelt to pray for a blessing of the new life that I felt growing inside me.

From Lourdes we drove to Lyons, the gourmet capital of France, but in my condition the huge platters of fruit de mer, the truffled goose liver pate, the fresh raspberries in cream, the incomparable cheeses had to go untasted. Yet, inexplicably as we reached Orleans, the city steeped in the memory of Jeanne d'Arc, I ordered snails in garlic sauce and hungrily, without any ill effects, ate a whole dozen of them. One does things like that when pregnant.

In Paris I had reserved a room for Cliff and me at the Hotel Corona, the same hotel Ady and I enjoyed at the beginning of the trip. This time we were shown to a horribly dirty, dismal room. We were told it could not be changed. Fortunately, I remembered that a public relations man from Pan American had told me to contact the Pan Am office in Paris should I need help. When I called Pan Am and explained that I was an American radio reporter on an interview tour in Europe and in need of a hotel room for myself and my husband, they said they would see what could be done.

Ten minutes later the phone rang, "Mrs. Shedd, we have booked you in the Hotel Prince de Galles, a luxury hotel near the Champs Elysees and the Arc de Triomphe."

I was horrified. "I can't pay for such an expensive hotel." "You will be a guest of the hotel, and perhaps you'd like to interview the manager." I had never thought of such a possibility, and it opened a whole new world for me.

At the hotel we were ushered to our quarters, a luxurious bedroom, with a huge bathrooms with sunken tub and double sinks, heated towel rack and terry bathrobes for HIM and HER. Adjacent to the bedroom, we found a dressing room and a large silk-walled sitting salon. It was incredible. It dawned on me that this was not done as a personal favor. To them, I was an American radio journalist who could spread the word about the hotel, which was in hot competition with its more famous neighbor, the Georges V.

Until this moment, I had thought the people sitting opposite me at the microphone were doing me a favor. Now, I realized that the microphone was a powerful tool, not only for the sponsor, but also for the guest.

****

During those three months travel in Europe, I had interviewed statesmen, diplomats, politicians, artists. One of my favorite interviews was with Robert Stolz, the last of the great waltz kings, who had left Vienna for the sake of his Jewish wife when Hitler invaded Austria. He, like many of the Austrian composers who lived in the United Stated during the Thousand Year Reich, could not compose – in America – the music which flowed like liquid gold from his soul when he lived in Vienna.

"You know," he confided to me, "I need three things to feel inspired to write my music: a glass of good wine, a coffeehouse table where I can meet my friends, and beautiful women."

23

Immediately after my return from Europe, I saw Dr. Hassler, a wonderfully warm gynecologist, who said my health was superlative. He even predicted my baby's birth. "I bet you a bottle of champagne," he joked, "March 9." He added, "Do everything you have been doing until now, you are strong, and happy – everything will be fine."

Those nine months were among the happiest of my life. I felt marvelous, no physical discomfort, no anxieties, only impatience to hold my baby in my arms.

In the meantime I had become something of a celebrity in Wilmington, thanks to my radio program and its impressive guest list. I took my tape recorder to the Playhouse Theater. Tyrone Power, as incredibly handsome and charming off stage as on, received me and my tape recorder in his dressing room. So did Walter Slezak, a fellow Viennese, funny and rotund, and Gloria Swanson, who told me all about her natural food diet. Noel Coward took the microphone out of my hand, talked into it for an hour but held it too close to his mouth. I could have cried afterwards when I could not use one inch of the tape. I was not independent enough, at that point, to insist on my way.

When scientists came to Wilmington to address professional societies, among them Nobel Prize winners, Dr. Linus Pauling and Dr. Peter de Bye, I was there with my tape recorder. Even when I knew very little about the subject, I could make the interview interesting and get the interviewee talking if I showed curiosity, asked questions that my audience would be interested in, and saw to it that the thread of continuity was not cut.

I thoroughly enjoyed interviewing because I met fascinating, successful people. The unrehearsed interviews were conversations such as I would have had in my living room over a cup of coffee. The success of my show was, in part, due its conversational tone.

One day I learned that Leonard Bernstein was to conduct the Philadelphia Orchestra at the Robin Hood Dell in Philadelphia. I found out where he was staying and called his room, expecting a secretary to answer. But no, it was the maestro himself.

"Sure, I will give you an interview. Come to the rehearsal at the

Dell. Ask for me and tell them to call me."

When I arrived with my tape machine, he spied me from the stage, he stopped the rehearsal and sat for a good half hour discussing music, his concerts, European versus American audiences, Vienna, which he loved, and then he invited me to stay for the rest of the rehearsal.

When the Trapp Family Singers were in Philadelphia, I called Agatha von Trapp with whom I had shared a school bench at the Gymnasium in Klosterneuburg. We met for lunch. I remembered her as a delicately aristocratic girl. Now her face was lined and colorless, her hair pulled back straight in a bun at the nape of the neck. As we lunched, I reminisced about our childhood, but she refused to be a part of it. She only told me of the Trapp family's life here in America, about the hectic travel schedule, driven by their ambitious stepmother, Maria von Trapp, who was a very good business woman but was apparently unable to earn the love of the children. Moreover, the Baron was not happy about the gypsy life of the touring Trapps. But they did have the farm in Vermont, she told me, and invited me to visit it, should I ever come to New England. There they spent a sedentary summer running their Trapp Music Camp. Her appearance, as well as the way she spoke, convinced me that the gay and light-hearted manner in performance was just that: a performance.

Not too many years later, I visited the Trapp Family Music Camp with Cliff. Agatha was glad to see me and told me of the difficulties confronting the family when they first settled in Stowe. The villagers distrusted this strange group of foreigners in their quaint Austrian garb, but then the Baroness arranged a concert. The family earned a standing ovation from the audience and the next day many residents turned up at the old barn which the Trapps planned to turn into a home for themselves.

"They looked like gnomes up there, hanging from window sills, roof and walls, working in shifts, helping us to build our house. It was really very moving," said Agatha.

We had been walking past a small chapel the pious Trapps had erected. As we walked by, Agatha genuflected, crossed herself and murmured a short prayer. Perhaps she would have preferred to be a nun.

****

The nearer I came to the date Dr. Hassler had predicted for the birth of my baby, the more I wanted my own home. I wanted to belong, and above all, I wanted my child to have a place to put down roots. Although Cliff was content in our rented house, he wanted to see me happy. However, there was one major difficulty: money. As so often before, I refused to accept the apparently impossible. I had had my eye on a particular house for quite a while. Then I heard that it might be available. I rang the door bell. "Is your house for sale?" I asked the perplexed owner.

He asked me in and said they had toyed with the idea of selling but were in no hurry. I looked around. A parakeet had free flight of the house, so there were droppings in every corner. The upper floor must have been intended for midgets, so low were the ceilings, and the kitchen was terrible. But I could also see some wonderful features: beamed ceilings, three working fireplaces, a separate dining room, and a huge lawn and garden. In short, the house could be just exactly what I wanted.

I knew about buying and selling. "Of course the house needs an awful lot of work to put it in shape. How much do you want?""

"We didn't say that we want to sell," was the answer.

"How much?"

They gave me a price. It was ridiculously low, but I didn't have even that.

I went to my friend in the bank. "I want my baby to live in our own home. Will you help me to buy the house?"

Just like that. It worked. It's a miraculous thing, this determination. Within two days, I had the mortgage and a personal loan for the down payment. Without collateral, just our good name, a reputation, and the guarantee of Cliff's employment.

Every day I called the owners. "Are you ready to sell?"

Finally, "Come on over and bring your checkbook."

The baby was due on March 9. The house was mine on March 1, but settlement wasn't until April 1. And even then we would not be able to move in. The house needed new wiring and plumbing, and a whole lot of cleaning. Cliff planned to do most of the work himself.

March 9 arrived. At six, the pains began. I woke Cliff and said,

"It's March 9; Dr. Hassler was right."

Cliff said, "But I have a meeting in Harrisburg that I can't postpone."

"I can't postpone the baby either, but I can manage."

Cliff left at seven. The pains came at regular intervals. I got dressed and walked to the bus station. A car stopped and a friend said, "Need a ride into town? But we have to stop at the Art Museum first. Do you mind?"

"I'm going to the doctor's office," I said, "but those few minutes won't make a difference."

In the doctor's office the nurse listened to my report, looked at the date and let out a gasp, "You are running around alone! Oh, my God, does the doctor know?"

Within minutes he arrived. After examining me, he said, "Have someone to take you to the hospital. You'll be ready in a short time."

I called Ady who wanted to know where Cliff was.

"In Harrisburg."

She said, "I'll be there in five minutes to take you to the hospital."

Everybody was excited except me. I felt that I was watching myself from the outside, curious to see what would happen next, not in the least apprehensive, very relaxed and in a strange state of efficient preparation. I had a task to perform, and I was going to perform it – orderly and step by step.

Everything went smoothly, an achievement I attribute to Dr. Hassler's skill and, my own strong, healthy constitution. After all, to have a first baby at age forty is a gamble.

The first thing I saw after delivery was Dr. Hassler's face. He was at the foot of the bed, his arms were on the railing of the bed and his chin rested on his folded hands. He beamed. "Remember," he said, "I get a bottle of champagne."

Then I looked at the nurse holding a little bundle in pink in her arms. "Here is your baby, Mrs. Shedd. She is beautiful."

I was overcome. Nothing can compare with the miracle of giving birth. I reassured myself that this was not a mirage, I really did have a child of my own, my little girl.

Cliff called. Ady had told him everything was fine, he had a daughter. I knew that he had hoped for a boy to carry on the name, every man wants that, but he managed not to sound disappointed. I knew, however, that he was. "Wait till you see her," I said, "she is absolutely gorgeous."

Cliff was at my bedside the next morning when I woke up. His disappointment evaporated as soon as he saw his new daughter. It swelled his pride to be able to proclaim his masculinity to the world. Only later did I wonder if this little baby had perhaps made him realize for the first time that in age he was nearer to being its grandfather than its father.

There was also a subtle change in my own feelings. No longer was Cliff the exclusive concern in my life, the baby now was number one. I felt guilty about this. For sixteen years I had loved only him. Now there was Christobel. I chose that name after reading a short story whose heroine, Christobel, was beautiful, intelligent, elegant, and successful. I saw my own daughter growing up to be like her.

After six days in the hospital, I went home with my precious cargo. Everything was ready. My parents sent adorable little baby clothes, and a miniature down comforter for the pram. Friends sent an avalanche of useful gifts, and from Mrs. Roosevelt came a bathinette.

As soon as I put the sleeping baby into her cradle, I took off my coat and prepared dinner. It never occurred to me that I should take it easy. Instead, I resumed my activities. Not once did I ask for help. Not only did I run the house, take care of my radio program, and attend the usual ladies' luncheons and club meetings for promotional reasons, but I also took care of little Chrissy with total devotion. She was a continuous wonder. I wanted to be with her all the time to admire the miracle of her development into an aware and sensitive human being.

The new house was finally empty, so Cliff began to take it to pieces and put it together again. He showed no sign of weakness or tiredness. He removed mountains of trash, installed a new kitchen and a second bathroom. But when we had to move, the house still was not ready. Chrissy was four weeks old, and for the first time my courage sagged. The movers just piled our belongings on the living room floor and left. I had no place to sit, Chrissy's room was not ready, the kitchen did not have a stove, the refrigerator was not hooked up, the hot water not connected.

Ady came to the rescue, taking Chrissy and me home until Cliff could get the basic amenities up and working. I felt miserable because I could not believe we would ever be able to conquer the problems of that house. Alone, I would have pitched in to help, but now I had Chrissy to take care of.

After getting professional help, at my insistence, with the heavy construction, Cliff had the house in a livable condition. We had hot water and clean beds but the stove was not yet connected, so I cooked on a one-burner hot plate for several weeks. I felt like a pioneer woman.

Renovating a house while living in it is not advisable. I had to step around and climb over tools, paints, nails, brushes, and ladders in every room while taking care of a baby. In addition, I had to maintain a hard-working man who left the house at seven and returned at six to eat so that he could work on the renovations until well after midnight. Finally, enough was done that we could arrange for the christening of Christobel.

I decided to ask Mrs. Roosevelt to be Christobel's godmother. Rather than write, I called her. "Mrs. Roosevelt, I have a great big wish to ask of you. Would you consent to being Chrissy's godmother?"

"Oh, my goodness. What do you want with me? I will be dead before I can be of any use to her."

"Please, Mrs. Roosevelt, it will be important for the rest of her life. It will be something to live up to, an example to follow, an inspiration."

"I will do it. Tell me when and where I should be."

We wanted Chrissy baptized in the faith of her father, a Universalist. Since there wasn't a Universalist Church in Wilmington, we chose its affiliate, the Unitarian Church. I did not want Chrissy to join the Catholic Church, my own church, because the American version of Catholicism was so different from the Austrian traditions. In America the Church interfered in private decisions such as the choice of books, movies, and even clothing worn in Church. In Austria the ties between Church and parishioner were much more informal. If you wanted to, you went to Church on Sunday. If you didn't, no one chastised you, nor was there an appendix of social activities connected with church attendance.

Perhaps because the Catholic Church in Austria did not have to go out and catch souls – more than 95% of the population was Roman Catholic – it did not have to be a fighting, competitive church and could afford to be more relaxed. Be that as it may, I did not want to answer for my actions to the Church, although in my own belief, I remained Catholic.

We sent out seventy-five invitations for the christening on June 14. It was to be a formal event in our own home. Not a single regret. Everybody wanted to meet Mrs. Roosevelt.

On June 14, Cliff met Mrs. Roosevelt at the railroad station. She came alone, as usual, and brought a small suitcase with a change of clothes. She went about the house, asked questions about the alterations, and wanted to know about the refreshments.

"Can I help with serving?" she asked, acting exactly as a mother would act at the home of her daughter.

The house was filled with flowers. I think some of my guests did not believe that Mrs. Roosevelt would be present. The newspaper sent a reporter and photographer, the radio station recorded the ceremony, and Cliff was so excited that he forgot to change from his sports coat into his more formal suit coat. Mrs. Roosevelt came downstairs in a lovely brocade gown and took her position in front of the flower decked fireplace. Chrissy was brought down by Mrs. Brown, a wonderfully gentle lady, whom I was fortunate to have as a baby sitter for many years.

Mrs. Roosevelt held Chrissy in her arms and answered Pastor McKinnon's questions with a quiet, "Yes, I will."

She had requested that Chrissy have a second godmother to "take my place when I will no longer be here." So Ady Weaver stood by as the second godmother. It was a lovely ceremony, and Chrissy, dressed in the long baptismal garment of handmade lace I had worn at my own christening, acted as if she knew the very special circumstances that favored her. After the ceremony Eleanor Roosevelt was besieged by the guests, everyone wanted to shake her hand, and she obliged smilingly and courteously in that inimitable way she had.

Later that evening, after all the guests left, she changed back into her traveling clothes to return to New York.. We took her to the railroad station and waited with her until the train arrived. Of course she was recognized. The waiting passengers shook her hand and to told her how much they admired her. She had a friendly smile, a word for everyone. But I was worried all the while lest some Roosevelt-hater try to do her harm. We had no guard, and she seemed not in the least concerned.

As a christening gift Mrs. Roosevelt gave Chrissy a silver cup engraved with her signature. She also started Chrissy on her own pattern of flat silver. A week after the christening, six teaspoons arrived, followed on subsequent birthdays and Christmases by knives, forks, spoons, and finally, shortly before she died, Mrs. Roosevelt had Jensen of New York deliver a large mahogany chest to hold the twelve place settings that had arrived, piece by piece, over the years.

24

The summer came and went, we built a driveway, a double garage, dug the cellar one foot deeper, and installed a new heating and hot water system. Every penny was invested in improvements and there was never any money left, except for Christobel who was cared for like a princess. Cliff built a separate room for her on the second floor. He tore out the walls and floors, put in wood paneling, new closets and light fixtures. Finally with loving dedication, he carved adorable decorations framing the light switches to delight his little girl.

Sometimes as I watched him at his work table in the garage, I worried about his health. He begrudged himself every minute of rest and labored feverishly. Sometimes I felt he was working against time. Although he had no formal training, he was a master at cabinet making and fine carpentry. He was a perfectionist; everything was correct in every detail.

So, in 1957 when my parents asked us to visit them with their only grandchild, I was glad to force a five-week vacation on Cliff. However, I was too embarrassed to tell my parents we hadn't saved enough to see them. Fortunately, my father offered to pay the air fare if we could take care of the rest. We had no choice but to borrow money from the bank once again.

When I wrote Mrs. Roosevelt that we intended to visit my parents, she invited the three of us to come to her home Val Kill for the weekend prior to our departure.

She also wrote that she would be in Wilmington in April at the invitation of the American Association for the United Nations. So, I took advantage of this to invite her to my home for lunch. To have Mrs. Roosevelt as guest was a great honor, so I pulled out all stops to make it a festive occasion. Suzanne Larmore, a French woman who had been a cook at the French Embassy in Washington, now lived in Arden. I asked her to help me. Mrs. Roosevelt loved lobster tails, and I had earned compliments with my lobster thermidor, so the main course was easy to decide. The menu with grilled grapefruit, then the lobster, French fried potatoes and whole, fresh green beans. Suzanne made her superb French salad. For dessert we had my specialty, Viennese malakoff torte, layers of ladyfingers alternating with mocha buttercream and covered with whipped cream.

At the luncheon, Suzanne served me first and then Mrs. Roosevelt. By the time she had served the other six ladies, Mrs. Roosevelt had finished. Luckily the same rules did not apply in my home as applied to the Austrian Imperial Court during the days Franz Josef. That old gentleman ate so fast that none of his guests could keep up with him. Unfortunately, no one was allowed to eat after the Emperor had finished; therefore, everyone left the Imperial banquets hungry.

Mrs. Roosevelt was a little embarrassed, when she saw that she was sitting before an empty plate. I motioned to Suzanne to serve Mrs. Roosevelt a second helping, which she accepted eagerly, saying that these were the best lobster tails she had ever eaten. She ate more slowly the second time around. She was also enthusiastic about my Viennese dessert and put a big heap of whipped cream on her coffee.

Mrs. Roosevelt's appointments were made months ahead of time, so our invitation to come to Val Kill in May and her visit to my home in April had been negotiated in January. When we arrived in May for our weekend visit, we found a full house, as usual. John Roosevelt, his wife, and children were there living in the stone cottage on the grounds. I remember, however, that Chrissy, then two years old, was the only child allowed to sit at the table with the adults. Perhaps, she was granted this privilege because I had trained her, almost from the time she could hold a spoon, to observe table manners, as I regard good table manners as the basis for civilized behavior.

When I was a child, my own mother saw to it that we had good table manners. To get up from the table during a meal was unheard of, and even after the meal was terminated, my sister and I had to get permission to leave the table. We were not allowed to interfere when adults were speaking and had to ask politely for food. To reach out and get anything without my mother's permission was unthinkable. It was equally unthinkable to object to any food my mother put on the table; one ate what had been prepared.

The weather was quite hot, so we ate on the dining porch with the usual array of guests. John Roosevelt kept trying to persuade his mother to take some of the string beans from his garden. There were also many children around. I never quite knew exactly whose children they were, what with all the marriages of the Roosevelt offspring, and everybody bringing children from former marriages into the new unions. Mrs. Roosevelt was loving to all. I wondered how she managed to keep them all apart. Even after their parents got divorced and married again and a new batch arrived, the children kept in close touch with Mrs. Roosevelt.

Shortly after the dinner, Cliff complained of pains in his stomach and went to our room. For the rest of the evening and throughout the night, he was ill. This was the only time I saw Mrs. Roosevelt unconcerned about someone's misfortune, and I could not, and cannot to this day, understand it. She simply ignored the incident. Perhaps it was her own determination to ignore illness which made her regard the sudden illness of her guest as a nuisance rather than a regrettable incident. I believe this because she always pretended not to be ill and kept going against all odds.

I was scared. I had a foreboding that this illness might be more than just an upset stomach, but Cliff insisted that I not stay with him and instead go downstairs to join the party. He sat up in a chair all night because he couldn't get his breath when he lay down. Toward morning both of us fell into a light sleep. Luckily, the crisis seemed to have passed, though he was far from feeling perfect. Mrs. Roosevelt asked only fleetingly how Cliff felt and went about making pancakes at the table.

The guests were on their own at Val Kill. Mrs. Roosevelt did not let guests divert her from her many duties. She disappeared into her office to write letters, write her column, answer the telephone, and now and then, went on errands. She appeared for meals and joined the guests in the evening after dinner and for a short tea in the afternoon.

She had invited us, as she always did, for a very specific time span. We followed her wishes and left on the 11th in the afternoon. I often think of her ability to manage the arrival and departure of her guests. No one ever stayed one minute longer than she wished them to stay. It is a social trick which not many people can accomplish, but she did.

****

We flew from New York to Holland, there to pick up a rented car and drive to Austria. It was a long flight, no jets yet. Again, I combined this trip with radio interviews, so once more the heavy tape recorder accompanied me. At my request Mrs. Roosevelt had asked Queen Juliana of the Netherlands to grant me an interview.

When we arrived in Holland's Schiphol Airport, I heard my name paged and found myself face to face with a delegation from the Royal Palace. Alas! the Queen had refused to fulfill Mrs. Roosevelt's request for an interview. "Her Majesty regrets she will not be able to see you," was the message. This development, however, was not as disturbing to my peace of mind as was the suddenly discovered loss of Pockey, Chrissy's black toy cat.

Chrissy put up a howl. "I want my cat," she sobbed. I went back to the plane and searched. It had disappeared.

At the hotel, hostile glances and a decidedly cold attitude met me. I could not understand why everyone was rude to me and very friendly to Cliff. Finally, I asked the concierge what unforgivable deed I had committed.

"You are Austrian?" was the answer.

"Yes, but now I am an American. I left Austria when the Nazis came to power."

"Ah, then that is different. You are wearing your Austrian costume. We remember the Austrian Nazis here during the war. They were among the worst. They killed our people and terrorized us and dragged our Jews into concentration camps. We have never forgotten and never will."

Once I convinced them that I, myself, was a Nazi-hater, the change was dramatic. The sour faces suddenly beamed with sunny friendliness, the chambermaid, the concierge, the waiters, the busboy couldn't do enough for the lady from America.

We drove to Vienna via the autobahn, in much better repair now than it had been in 1954. Conditions in Germany and Austria had improved dramatically. I had observed the change from the immediate postwar conditions in 1947, to our next tourist visit in 1951, followed by my first extensive interview trip in 1954. Now, three years later Europe had returned to almost normal. No longer did Russian occupation soldiers come to performances at the Vienna State Opera dressed in their ill-fitting odorous uniforms, carrying paper sacks filled with garlicky sausages and black bread to eat during intermission. The wives of these soldiers had worn nightgowns instead of evening gowns and they also had worn their brassieres over the gowns!

When we visited my parents in 1954, we watched the changing of the guards at the Heldenplatz in Vienna. Every four weeks the guardianship of the four sections of the city was rotated among the four powers – France, Britain, Russia, America. When the exchange took place between the Americans and the Russians all of Vienna turned out. The Russians, all spit and polish with their really superb military band, marched to meet the American honor guard, with their battle decorations and spotless white gloves, playing "The Stars and Stripes Forever."

The two cadres stopped, their commanders barked out orders, one of each marched toward the other, saluted, shook hands, turned and the soldiers relinquishing the Kommandatura for the next four weeks about-faced and marched off. The other stayed and played martial music for the crowd. The Viennese obviously loved the Americans. Loud and benevolent comparisons could be heard from the watchers.

In 1955 all occupation soldiers left Austria, and when we revisited the city in 1957, we no longer needed passes to travel anywhere in Austria. My father showed me the old Austrian military barracks where some of the Hungarian refugees from their 1956 revolution were housed by the Austrian government. The Austrians understood what Russian occupation meant, so they offered immediate haven to the Hungarian refugees.

My parents moved out of their bedroom to accommodate us. The concept of a separate guest room, rarely occupied, is virtually unknown in overcrowded Europe. I felt uncomfortable knowing that my parents had, however willingly, chosen to sleep in makeshift beds in two different rooms of the house. Again, as it had earlier, the house seemed cumbersome and uncomfortable to me, yet I didn't want to show my discomfort to my parents. It was their kingdom, they had saved it from both the Nazis and the Russians. It had survived as they had themselves.

My kind father tried to make us comfortable by having gas and hot water tanks installed in kitchen and bathroom, but I sensed that my mother resented my father's desire to please us. What was good enough for her all these years should have been good enough for us. My parents even bought a refrigerator to please the visitors from America, but my mother hastened to say that it would be disconnected when we left because it really was not needed except, perhaps, in exceptionally hot weather.

My father adored Chrissy as he had my sister and me when we were small. He found countless ways to entertain his only grandchild with games and stories told in his quaint, school English. But my mother could not overcome her inability to demonstrate love. Never did she hug or kiss Chrissy, but only sternly watched for something she could criticize. Yet I was convinced that she loved her and was proud of her, but her soul was bound tightly in iron bands of restraint. I know she envied my father his gift of emotional freedom, his ability to give and receive love. As my father so often remarked, "She cannot escape from her skin."

****

When we returned to Arden, we faced a precarious financial situation. Cliff's salary never seemed enough to cover all our obligations. We had loans to the bank, the car still was not fully ours, there was the mortgage on the house, and Chrissy required baby sitters when I had to make speeches and public appearances. My radio broadcasts brought only nominal fees. It was clear that I needed to increase my own income.

One day I heard a Polish language radio program, heavily sponsored, and then a few days later, a German language program from Philadelphia. I could do something like this myself. I approached Harvey Smith, "Would you let me do a musical program of semiclassical and popular foreign music?"

Harvey leaned back in his chair, looked at me, doodled on a piece of paper, sighed deeply. "Who the hell is going to listen to something like that?"

"Oh, there must be lots of people, why don't you let me try? I'll get my own recordings and write my own script, and find my own sponsors. If you don't like it after four weeks, you can cancel it. How about it?"

"We have no time available," said Harvey, and then, seeing my disappointment, "except maybe Sunday afternoon at two."

"Fine," I quickly grabbed the opportunity. "It's a good time. People have just had their Sunday dinner. They sit around and don't know what to do. They'll listen."

The first program was scheduled to go on the air within the week. It was to be a one-hour show. I had neither a record player at home to audition and assemble a program nor did I own a single recording. I went back to my friend, Albert Borkow, of the Magnetic Recorder Corporation in Philadelphia. As usual, he was helpful. He called the Sam Goody store and told them exactly what components to get ready for me and to sell them to me at a special price. I came home with a record player and an arm full of continental records, the likes of which nobody at the radio station had ever heard.

I called my program "Continental Corner" and designed it as a concert taking place in a cafe in Vienna. I wrote a script describing the locale and the music. I timed and arranged the music. On Sunday, I appeared at the radio station, placed a copy of the script before the disk jockey on duty, handed him the records and began my introductory remarks.

As the hour proceeded, the disk jockey began to enjoy himself. The music was totally different from the run-of-the-mill popular tunes he usually played. I played music by Fritz Kreisler, Johann Strauss, Franz Lehar, some Hungarian gypsy music, even Chopin and Edvard Grieg. And, of course, one or two typical Viennese songs.

Did anyone listen at two o'clock in the afternoon on a Sunday? As soon as the program went off the air, the telephone began to ring. Listeners had been surprised to hear such music for the first time and hoped that this was only the beginning. I asked each one to write me a note because this was what I needed to get sponsors.

Within a week I had four sponsors, one for each fifteen- minute segment. While the fees were infinitesimal by national standards, they proved that what I did was salable and that I could judge the taste of an audience.

The program remained on the air for six months; then the hour was sold to a football game. Sponsors or no sponsors, I had to vacate. Nothing is more important than football or baseball. No music can compete with sports because they get national sponsors, an impossible feat for a mere continental music program.

Dejectedly I packed up my records, ready to give up the dream when the manager of WDEL FM asked me to continue the same program on FM. In those days, FM was not as popular as it is today. It was regarded as a highbrow, rather quaint media outlet, designed for the classical elite.

"You fit here much better than over there," said Bill Kline, who had pioneered FM radio in Wilmington. He called his station "The Golden Voice" and played classical music, operas and concerts. I was happy to have my music program on FM, in addition to my interview program on WDEL AM. It was difficult to get sponsors on FM because of the small audience. Fortunately, Bill regarded my program as a prestige item and asked me to add a similar program on Saturday evenings, called Caprice Continental. Cliff built an office for me, wood paneled and equipped with desk, turntable and shelves for the hundreds of recordings I acquired on regular trips to Sam Goody's huge record store in Philadelphia. This office enabled me to work at home while taking care of Chrissy. Slowly our life became easier. The house had become more and more livable, Chrissy grew to be a lovely, healthy, happy little girl, and I was fulfilled with my professional activities.

25

Once again, the sky fell in: one day I found Cliff sitting in his chair in the living room, a vacant stare on his face.

"What is it," I asked, my throat locked in terror.

He slowly moved his eyes. "I don't know," he stammered, "I can't move my arm and my leg."

"Oh, my God, I'll call the doctor."

On all fours, he crawled up the stairs to the bedroom. Not until it happens, can you know the cold terror which holds you in its grip knowing this is the beginning of the end. I ran up to him, held him in my arms and stroked his head, assuring him that everything would be all right, not to worry. Chrissy came in. I told her Daddy wasn't feeling well and to be a good little girl and go play in her room. She did.

The doctor examined Cliff. "No, not a stroke," he said, "a spasm. He will be all right, the paralysis will disappear."

It had been nine years since his coronary thrombosis. What had the doctor said to me then? Ten years, maybe eleven. I went out and wept.

When Cliff retired from his job a few months later, he had recovered the use of his arm and leg. He had reached the mandatory retirement age of seventy and resented his enforced retirement. My happiness was limited by worry. Each time I returned home I was afraid to find him ill or worse.

While he adored Chrissy, she was too lively for him. Yet, he didn't want to admit to any weakness. Through him I learned that retirement can become as poisonous as a disease for some; they feel rejected and do foolish things to prove that they are as good as ever. Cliff was one of those. At that point I realized I had been very selfish to have a baby so late in our life because Cliff needed so much attention, and I could not give it to him.

Another problem was our income, which plummeted with his retirement. This was a financial disaster which he couldn't handle. I thought he had arranged to do some consulting; he had done nothing of the kind. We had no investments, no savings, nothing to fill the gap. Only the money from my radio work and his government pension.

In the midst of all this, a letter arrived from my mother, "My dear Lotte, I have to tell you, to my sorrow, that we no longer have our beloved Vati. He died unexpectedly while walking in the garden." All the grief and despair of the past months finally took their toll and I broke down completely.

But not for long because Chrissy came into the room and ran toward me. "Don't cry Mommy, I love you and Daddy loves you."

I dried my tears. I couldn't let them down, one of us had to carry on.

Cliff's only fault was his refusal to plan for the future. I found out later that he had told his staff at the Department of Commerce that retiring was not a problem because his wife earned a thousand dollars a month. In reality I earned only about two hundred, about as much as his pension. When I tried to talk about finances, he got angry and stopped me. Later I came to believe that his refusal to talk about money was a way of covering his frustration at not providing for us. This frustration, no doubt, contributed to his deteriorating health. At times he became quite irrational, and his usually sweet disposition gave way to fits of aggressive anger and accusations against me.

Today I know that such a character change is a sign of hardening of the arteries. Had the doctor enlightened me, I would not have been so bewildered. All I could think of was that my lovable husband had become a cantankerous, almost dangerously aggressive stranger. But I loved him deeply and felt terribly unhappy for his predicament. He never lost his temper with Chrissy; he always treated her with tenderness and infinite patience.

I tried to keep our living standard on the same level. It was not easy. We were behind in all our payments. My greatest concern was that one of my sponsors would drop out and thus diminish our income even further.

One day while I was preparing a meal in the kitchen, Cliff watched Chrissy play on the floor and said, "She will be a great comfort to you."

He said this with resignation and sorrow. It was a good-bye. I ran to him and buried my head in his arms, and he cried. It is a terrible thing to see a once-strong man cry.

Not long after that, I was working in my office arranging my music program. It was Friday night, January 8, 1960. Cliff came into the room, "Will you come up and stay with me. I am afraid."

I accompanied him to his bedroom. He lay down, and I snuggled up to him and put my arms about him. "Thank you," he said in a very low voice. "Thank you for being with me, you are the most wonderful thing that ever happened to me, and no one will ever love you as much as I have loved you." His breathing was labored. "Stay with me. I am afraid I won't wake up."

Of course, I stayed with him.

The next day was sunny and very cold. Cliff was weak and strangely detached. He did not quite hear when I spoke to him and only smiled wanly, looking far-away. He got dressed, ate almost no breakfast and sat in his chair. I suggested we go for a walk.

"No, you go with Chrissy, I will stay here."

Chrissy and I went. We had walked once around the village green when I saw Cliff, dressed in his warm coat and hat, coming down the path. Chrissy ran toward him with squeals of delight. He picked her up and kissed her.

"I came looking for you," he said, again in a far away voice. "I don't want to be without you." We walked together for a few yards, chatted with some friends and continued on, I one step ahead of him. I heard a swishing sound and a heavy thump. Turning around, I saw Cliff, unconscious on the asphalt road.

I screamed for help, kneeling by his side, holding his head in my hands. The blood was oozing from a scalp wound. Doors opened and people came running. I cried for an ambulance and gave them the name of our doctor. I begged neighbors to take Chrissy to a friend's house. No ambulance came and no doctor. But Cliff's best friend, Frank Herzog, happened by in his car. By then Cliff had regained consciousness and asked, "What happened? I want to go home."

Although it was probably the wrong thing to do, we helped him up, and Frank drove him to our house.

He sat in a chair. Frank held a towel to the wound. Still no ambulance and no doctor. Cliff's breathing grew ragged. And then, he was very still. I did not know that he was dead. So when the ambulance finally came, I urged the two attendants to be careful and gentle, so as not to hurt him. The men said nothing.

Frank put me in his car, and we followed the ambulance. He

didn't say one word. When we arrived, the nurse said, "Oh, Mrs. Shedd, you don't want to go in there, do you?"

I did not know what she meant until she led me to the room where my husband lay, covered with a white cloth. She left me alone. It was very quiet. I lifted the cloth and saw the man I had loved so deeply and lived with for seventeen years. His eyes were closed and his mouth was slightly open. Such stillness! I put my head on his chest and stroked his face and kissed his hands, his wonderful, caressing, strong, beautiful hands. I kissed his face and his forehead, and I could not believe that this would be the last time I would see him. He would never talk to me again, never hold me again, never tell me again that he loved me. So many years, so many difficult, wonderful, loving years. Now, it was over.

Shock took over and covered my consciousness with a merciful veil. I did not cry. I had no tears. I moved like a robot. As I entered the house, I saw Cliff's eyeglasses on the dining room table. I left them there. It was almost as if he was still in the room.

A strange thing happened. I sat down at my desk and began to play the music for Sunday's radio program. I sat at my desk, wrote the script on my typewriter, played gay waltzes and sentimental ballads, like a zombie. I heard Cliff say, "Finish your job, first things first. This is going to be your only support now, do your work." And so I did.

Then came a knock on the door. Frank returned, and he wept. I said, "Will you please take that stack of records and my script to the radio station for me. I have to take care of Chrissy." He looked at me as if I were some crazy ghost.

"You worked?"

"It had to be done." He nodded and went out.

Then I called Charles Robinson, whose bank had been my first sponsor, and now was a reliable friend. His wife answered. My voice began to break, "It's Cliff."

Almost clairvoyant, she asked, "Did he die?"

"Yes."

"We will be over in twenty minutes."

I moved as if locked in an insulated bubble. Whatever I did was done automatically. Then I remembered: Chrissy, I have to tell Chrissy – the hardest assignment of all.

I called the neighbors who had Chrissy. "Cliff has died. Please bring Chrissy back to me."

A few minutes later her small figure appeared at the door. I could not believe how composed I was. No tears. I took her on my knees. "Chrissy, my love, you know how ill Daddy has been and how he had to stay home and couldn't play with you and hurt all over?" She nodded. "Well, you see, now Daddy no longer has to suffer. He has no more pain and he is happy. He has gone to heaven. While we can no longer see him and be with him, I am sure he can see us and watch over us and love us as much as he did when he was here."

Her big eyes filled with tears. "But I want my Daddy. I want to be with my Daddy, will he never ever come back to me?"

I held her tightly pressed to me. "He is with us. It's just that we can't see him."

The next day, Sunday, we had tickets for the Ice Follies Show in Philadelphia. Should I go? Could I bring myself to go to a place full of gaiety, fun and glitter? I heard Cliff's voice, "You take her for me."

I drove to Philadelphia, walked in the crowd holding Chrissy by her hand, climbed the steps to our seats, and watched her face glowing with joy as the splendor of show unfolded. Children with fathers and mothers surrounded us. I wondered whether Chrissy had the same thoughts I had, "They have a Daddy." If she did, she never showed it. She was five; one adjusts more easily then.

For the first time I knew what it meant to be the only parent. Half of me had been cut off. I was fulfilling a duty to my dead husband. It was a most difficult assignment. Never before had I faced death in the family. My father had died far away in Vienna, and I hadn't been able to help with the funeral arrangements, something for which my sister has never forgiven me. Now, I had to handle the arrangements. No one of Cliff's family helped me. They had stayed aloof all these years. His older sister in New England had never once come to see us, and they did not even want to come to pay their last respects. When I told them about Cliff's death, they simply said, "sorry" but no word of compassion, and no offer of help. My own family was too far away to come to me, as I had been too far to come to them. I was alone, except for my friends. I found out how many compassionate, loving friends I had. They came to my assistance with tactful unobtrusive steps, to ease the painful decisions about the sad details of the last rites.

Buzz Ware stood by and helped me through the conversation with the funeral director who kept referring to my husband as "the body," wanting to know how much I would be willing to spend "to give the beloved a beautiful ceremony." He got very upset when I selected the simplest. I knew Cliff had wanted to be cremated and his ashes buried in Arden's cemetery.

Cliff died on January 9 and our home was still decorated for Christmas. The tree sparkled with tinsel and candles, and I could not bring myself to dismantle it. I didn't have to. The morning of the second day, two friends came to take down the Christmas tree. Silently and carefully, they took down the decorations, put them in their boxes (which they had found in the cellar) and tiptoeing around the house, they removed all reminders of Christmas. Kissing me tenderly, they left as gently as they had come. For the funeral, the Robinsons took over my kitchen, prepared every detail and served the guests. I don't know what I would have done, how I would have managed without my friends.

It was a cold, drizzly afternoon when Cliff's ashes, in a bronze urn, were lowered into the earth. The Unitarian pastor spoke simple, warm words about the eternity of life and love, and I stood there by the small grave that held my life's love. So near to our home he rests, I can see the spot from my window and I feel that he is still near. I was once again on my own, except that now, thank God, I had my Chrissy.

26

I removed all Cliff's belongings immediately. When I was packing the suits and coats, I buried my face in the folds and wept bitterly. I knew that I had to separate myself physically. I couldn't keep everything untouched for decades. That was unhealthy and an obstacle to accepting the inevitable: living alone, on my own.

Then there were so many decisions. For many years I had discussed everything with Cliff, but now it was all up to me. My friends urged me to sell the house and move to smaller, cheaper quarters. To me it was important to give Chrissy a place where memories lived on, where she belonged emotionally. No matter how difficult, no matter how great the sacrifice, I would stay in my home. Too much of my own effort and too much of Cliff was built into this house. If I had to starve for it, I would not give it up.

The next decision dealt with finances. There was a small pension, just enough to pay the mortgage. That would insure the roof over my head. I had to earn the rest. But how? Radio? Since I was not employed by the radio station, I had no health insurance, no salary, no bonuses at Christmas, no Social Security was paid for me. My livelihood depended on my ability to sell my programs and to look for other sources of income.

We needed food, clothing, electricity, the telephone, health insurance. Cliff's pension stopped with his death, and my widow's allotment got hung up in red tape. For several months I received no money at all. Finally I contacted my representative in Washington, Harris B. McDowell. It arrived within two days.

When Cliff died, we had been in the middle of extensive renovations. Two new bathrooms, a new guest room and the total renewal of my own bedroom had been started. I needed a loan to complete the renovations. To my surprise I had no difficulty getting a personal loan. Even more to my surprise, the contractor agreed to finish it at cost.

I had so little money for the daily expenses that I became an artist in closing one hole by opening another. I could never pay all my bills, and my most persistent dream was to earn enough to live without owing anybody any money. I hated to be hounded, but I did not resent the pursuers. They simply did their duty, even when they turned off the electric power and cut off the telephone without warning, although the bills were only one month in arrears.

I was in a peculiar position. Everyone believed I had received a large insurance payment. It was inconceivable that I was left without financial protection. My doorbell and my telephone rang with all sorts of characters wanting to invest my money.

I asked myself whether it might not be wise to abandon my radio career and take a regular job. I earned so little with my radio show that I was ashamed to reveal it to the friends who asked about my future plans. Advise was given freely: rent your house, rent one room in your house, sell your house. Take a job (but no one offered one), go to New York, go back to Europe, get married again.

****

For the first few months Chrissy and I were invited out frequently. Then, almost overnight, I found myself abandoned. I was no longer part of "a couple." I also represented a threat; some women were afraid that I might be on the prowl for another husband: their husband. I was no longer invited out, and no longer – with a few memorable exceptions – did my former friends inquire about my well-being. This is not unusual. Any widow will tell you that she has had the same experience. So, I decided to create my own world.

I sent a telegram to Vienna immediately after Cliff died and asked that my mother come to stay with me. Luckily Ady Weaver was in Vienna at that very time, and she agreed to bring my mother with her on the Dutch ship, Ryndam. I stood at the pier of the Holland America Line awaiting my mother's arrival – the same pier where I had first set foot on American soil. While I stood there in my black garments, the past emerged before my mind's eye. I saw once again the girl with the huge trunk and an empty purse. I remembered my bewilderment in this new and strange land. Now it was twenty-one years later. A war had been waged and won, I had been so happy and now I was alone again.

So many times I had begged my parents to come and visit me, but they had always declined. Now my mother came, but it was to come to a sad house and to visit a grave. But I was pleased that we could help each other in our new loneliness.

In the two months my mother stayed with me, we grew closer than we had ever been. She liked my home and was sweet and kind to Chrissy. She picked up English with amazing speed and marveled at the comfort and practicality of American households. When I took her to the supermarket, she stood stunned at the variety and abundance.

America was very different than she had imagined. She had expected nothing but Hollywood clichés. She found my friends charming and warm, and my home in Arden had a setting even better than her home in Klosterneuburg. She loved American food, particularly the muffins and pies I made for her, but she did not like steak because she could not bear the sight of rare meat with blood on the plate. She realized the stories she had been told about Americans living exclusively on canned food were exaggerated.

At the same time she did not want me to be alone. She knew life was going to be hard for me. So, she wanted me to come back to Vienna where she could help with Chrissy. She couldn't understand that America, and Arden in particular, was home to me. As a special treat, Mrs. Roosevelt invited us to lunch at her apartment in New York City. My mother was thrilled to visit Mrs. Roosevelt's house because Mrs. Roosevelt had visited my parents in Austria. There were several ladies from the United Nations. While the food was rather bland, the conversation was exciting because each of the ladies had special project to discuss. My mother tasted the international and fascinating world Mrs. Roosevelt lived in and saw that I had become part of it.

"All my life I have had a great desire to see the world," my mother once said to me, "but I was never able to get away. One disaster after another kept me at home. My duties and obligations were to my family. World wars, famines, foreign occupation, and twice the collapse of Austria stifled any possibilities. Now at the end of my life I have come to America."

This sad statement made me aware of the frustrations she had endured. Nothing could be worse than looking back upon the years and saying, "Now it is too late. I can never catch up with my dreams. I can never do what I had so much hoped to do. It has been a wasted journey." I know that this is what my mother felt, so I tried to fill a fraction of that dream. We went to Washington, New York's

Chinatown, and Philadelphia's historic places. While she couldn't do much walking, she drank in every detail and every nuance. My sister told me later that she couldn't stop describing everything she had seen. After her return to Austria, she wrote,, "Now I can see every place and every person when you tell me about it. I loved America."

My house was doubly empty after my mother left. Chrissy missed her Oma. Twice now, the people she loved suddenly disappeared, and she began to fear that the same would happen with me. When she began asking if I was going to leave her alone, I realized I needed to give her an orderly life and create as few emotional problems as possible. What I could not give her was something she evidently missed very much: a father. She asked every male who approached our home – the mailman, the electrician, the plumber – "Will you marry my Mommy?"

I wanted her to remember her father and kept his presence with us. I also thought his authority, even if in absentia, would help me to instill important principles and attitudes. So, I cited Cliff when establishing rules for Chrissy, saying "your father would expect you to do such and such," or "your father wouldn't like that" or very often "your father would be so proud of you!"

****

One day I realized how much I had neglected myself. Worries and cares had taken their toll; there had been little time left to think of myself. As a result I lost weight, took care in the way I dressed, kept my hair well coiffed and my hands soft and manicured.

The change was so drastic that often people who knew me did not recognize me immediately, and the phrase "my goodness you look ten years younger" gave me a badly needed lift. I was torn between a not easily forgotten loyalty to Cliff and the realization that I was now alone and free to choose again. I enjoyed the admiring glances and attentions of men and at the same time felt guilty about my reactions.

Several of my friends told me that if I wanted to get married again I had to do so soon – no longer than two years. I thought they meant that men want younger women. Today I know that this is not so. The difficulty lies in the fact that the widow becomes more independent, so that in most instances the advantages outweigh the disadvantages.

While in this limbo, one of my sponsors – Marshall and Greenplate Travel Agency – offered me a week's cruise to the Bahamas on the Swedish ship, Gripsholm. It was a promotional press trip, so it was free. All I had to do was tell my listeners about the cruise and the Bahamas. Heavenly! Mrs. Brown, my wonderful baby sitter, agreed to stay with Chrissy, so I was all set.

When I went on board, I found that my cabin was far below deck, and I had to share it with two others. My first chance to assert myself! I ordered my suitcase returned to the lounge and asked for the purser. A portly gentleman asked what the problem was.

"I am here as an invited guest and find myself quartered in most unsuitable circumstances," I said. "There must be a mistake, and if there isn't, I will immediately return to the shore and, albeit regretfully, cancel the trip."

"Madame," said the gallant purser, "please wait here for one minute." He returned shortly and with and inviting gesture of his hand said, "Follow me, please."

I did and found myself in a suite on the sundeck in a spacious cabin. "I hope this is more to your liking," said the well-upholstered uniform, "if there is anything you wish, you only have to ring the bell." He departed with a kiss on my hand and a deep look into my eyes.

"Aha," I thought, "watch out, Charlotte."

Cruising is perhaps the best vacation. No telephones, no newspapers, no effort, only relaxation, fabulous food, dancing, and – if one is lucky – a bit of flirting. While we were docked in Nassau, I interviewed the Governor of Nassau and his wife. This interview brought me fame on the cruise ship; I had become a "personality." In the meantime, the purser tried to interest me in some "treasures" in his cabin (how naive men can be!). One day he cornered me in the ship's elevator and pushed the up button while I pushed the down button. This went on until I finally convinced him that a shipboard romance was not for me, that I was only interested in my career.

Near, the end of the cruise, the purser, who now seemed to respect me, said, "I think you could do some travel publicity for this line and Sweden." That one sentence opened a world of possibilities.

I asked, "How am I going to do this?"

"I'll give you a letter to the President of the Swedish American Line in New York. Ask for an interview and tell him what you did on this cruise."

I never doubted this new venture would be successful. I had a built-in success indicator. I could feel if a project had possibilities. When the indicator pointed to "yes," I worked with such enormous confidence that I convinced people I would succeed. In those early days of my independence, I began to develop a fierce determination not to be taken advantage of. Some called me "pushy" behind my back and accused me of being selfish and aggressive, but they themselves were securely anchored as wives of successful husbands. There were also men who didn't like to see a woman succeed on her own two feet, standing up straight and not on her knees. With my new self-assurance I accepted every opportunity, never doubting that I could succeed.

When I look back at both the obstacles and miracles in my life, I saw that my approach to communicating with people was part of my strength. If I employed this gift correctly – in honesty and without false pretenses – people would trust me, and I could achieve almost anything I truly desired to achieve. Thus, whenever I presented myself or submitted a curriculum vitae, I never exaggerated, never tried to impress anyone with false statements, and invented stories. Frankly it wasn't necessary; my experiences since were so unusual that they stood on their own merits.

Not long after returning from the cruise, I met with the man in charge of the Swedish American Line public relations, Birger Nordholm, who was also chairman of the Scandinavian Travel Com mission. Mr. Nordholm, a charming gentleman who was very conscious of the importance of publicity, listened intently as I recounted my happy experiences on the Gripsholm. Then I showed him the purser's letter suggesting that I be invited to Sweden.

Well," he said, smiling charmingly, "I think that is a good idea. When would you be ready to travel?"

I was excited at the prospect of yet another journey. I decided to try one more step while luck was with me. "I am a widow, you know. My husband died only a short while ago, and I have a six-year-old little girl. I can't leave her at home alone, could she come with me?"

He didn't waste a minute, "Of course, bring her along."

It was unbelievable. Within a few days I had confirmation that we had a cabin for two in first class on the Gripsholm.

When I wrote Mrs. Roosevelt telling her about the trip, she invited us to spend the two days prior to our departure at Val Kill. Mrs. Roosevelt had already written a letter on my behalf to the headmaster of Friends School in Wilmington and to Clarence Prickett, director of the Friends Service Committee in Philadelphia, a personal friend of hers, supporting Chrissy's admittance on scholarship to Friends School. I had asked her help after I observed the quiet and respectful behavior of the students, the dignified appearance of the staff, the absence of rowdyism during recess. Unfortunately, the school's tuition was way beyond my means; therefore, I turned to Mrs. Roosevelt for help. She promoted Quaker causes and helped them wherever possible. If ever there was a spokesman for me in a Quaker school it was Mrs. Roosevelt. And I was right. In my letter, I explained that I couldn't give Chrissy a very elaborate life, but I knew that education is the only thing which can't ever be taken away.

With the invitation to Val Kill came complications involving getting the two of us and all our luggage from Wilmington to Val Kill then to the Gripsholm. Very thoughtful friends, Mr. and Mrs. Joseph Naczi, volunteered to drive us to Mrs. Roosevelt's home and then drive us to New York to board the ship. When I informed Mrs. Roosevelt of the offer, she invited the Naczis too. There was always room in her home or, in this case, in a little guest house not far from Val Kill. In addition she had arranged for all four of us to spend Friday night at her apartment in New York City so that we would not be late for the boarding scheduled for 11 o'clock Saturday morning.

All went well with our plans, the Naczis were overwhelmed at the cheerful hospitality at Val Kill. Mrs. Roosevelt relied on my judgment, knowing that I would have never brought anyone to her home who would not have measured up to her standards.

Friday morning, after two lovely days spent at Val Kill, we drove to New York. Mr. Naczi parked his stationwagon on Madison Avenue, and we walked the short distance to Mrs. Roosevelt's residence. When we got back to the car – it hadn't been even twenty minutes – we found someone had broken into the car and had taken the suitcase with my clothes. Luckily, the rest of the baggage, including my tape recorder, remained in the car.

What to do? Without my clothes I could not go, and I had neither the money nor the credit to purchase new clothes. Dejectedly we returned to the apartment where we telephoned the police, and I hesitantly telephoned Mrs. Roosevelt to inform her of the disaster.

She lived up to the occasion as always, "You go to Arnold Constable's," she instructed me, "I have an account there. I'll telephone them and tell them to give you anything you want, don't worry and enjoy yourself."

Never before had I been able to order a whole new wardrobe. I was almost grateful to the thief. I bought a coat, a suit, a sleek black evening gown, a short kelly green cocktail dress, and a black wool day dress with a jacket to match. I was a perfect size 12, and everything fit like a glove.

Fortunately, I always believed in insurance and kept up payments even when I had to forego other necessities. Thus, I was certain my home owner's insurance would cover the loss, particularly when it occurred during a visit with Mrs. Roosevelt. I was correct. Thanks to Mrs. Roosevelt's assistance, I was able to travel to Europe attired in a style to match our first-class accommodations – much more elegantly than I would have been without the incident.

Once aboard the ship, we found a huge bouquet of flowers and a box of candy in the cabin from Mrs. Roosevelt. I was overwhelmed that she thought to do these lovely things for me. I have resigned myself to the fact that very few people offer such gracious gestures. Yet sending or bringing flowers never fails to create joy, even if the recipient is surrounded by a blossoming garden. Being remembered is so important. Mrs. Roosevelt had been raised in an era of well-defined courtesies. One did certain things if one had breeding, and she knew and followed the rules of her social class. Her rules were very similar to the social rules by which I had been raised, and I know that she appreciated this.

While there could be no doubt that the friendship and support of Eleanor Roosevelt helped me in opening doors that may have been difficult to open without her name, I was aware of my own contribution to my success. I remembered the letters of introduction she had written when I was attempting a singing career and how I had failed although I was known to be the First Lady's protegée. I simply did not have what the market demanded no matter how much she tried to help me.

But now I had discovered my own metier. I had learned to use the right tools at the right time in the right manner and slowly but surely the wheels of success began to turn in my favor. My interest in politics, art, industry, and human relations, my knowledge of the theater, music, and the dance, my familiarity with European manners and customs, my fluency in German and English and my passable French contributed to my self-assurance. Thus I could sell my services as a roving radio journalist and travel writer to agencies anxious to promote the tourist attractions of their countries.

I was an independent agent working with a station with which I had a loosely knit verbal contract, a nonsalaried, totally unprotected position. This paradoxically was an advantage because I could accept invitations to travel which I could not have justified had I been an employee.

I did not embark on this new career with any preconceived plan. I followed the opportunities as they offered themselves, step by step, obeying my instinct and learning all the time.

27

To succeed, I knew I had to prove I had a following. Thus I sought out activities offering publicity. On the Voice of America I told listeners behind the Iron Curtain about freedom and happiness in America. Using my radio program to corral the support of local landscape architects, I arranged for an American atrium garden to be part of the Vienna Flower Show.

I had a scrapbook with articles about me, clippings of my articles in the *Wilmington Sunday Star*, and letters from my listeners. Then there was my voice. People liked to listen to me. Nearly everyone told me that success can only be found in places like New York or Hollywood. But big cities are where you can get lost in the shuffle, where competition is overwhelming, where living is expensive and unhealthy. As for becoming rich – I was not interested in becoming rich but in earning enough to live comfortably and, above all, peacefully. Independence was what I wanted, and I could only achieve that if I worked for myself.

By giving my community something no one else offered – a local program with international personalities as well as radio programs from abroad – and by involving myself in the community, I had become a "personality," a big frog in a little pond.

That all of this gained publicity and fame and almost no money was the other side of the coin. But it did convince foreign tourist bureaus and travel agencies that I could be useful. The advantage in visiting foreign countries as an official guest of government tourist offices was not monetary. The advantage was that Chrissy and I traveled under luxurious conditions. Wherever we arrived – airport, train station or harbor – we were greeted by a representative of the country's travel ministry. We stayed at the best hotels and ate at fancy restaurants. English-speaking guides arranged for interviews, tours, and visits to museums and theaters. No one knew I had almost no money, a circumstance I carefully hid.

Sometimes I was able to borrow – not rent – cars to drive throughout Europe. It was quite remarkable, really that complete strangers entrusted me with their cars. I told the rental agencies, "You lend me your car and I will tell my friends and listeners about you." And I did get customers for them.

My first trip included all three Scandinavian countries – Denmark, Norway and Sweden. Mrs. Roosevelt had written the American Ambassador in Copenhagen announcing my arrival and asking him to be of assistance. She also wrote King Olaf of Norway requesting an audience for me.

The ambassador arranged for Chrissy and me to take the overnight boat from Copenhagen to Aalborg on the north tip of Denmark to attend the annual Fourth of July celebration at Rebild Park. This event began in 1912 when a Danish American named Max Henius bought the land with money he had made in America and gave it to King Christian X with the stipulation that each year a genuine Fourth of July celebration must take place there.

It was a moving celebration. Twenty-five thousand people sat on the slopes of the hill waving American flags, eating hot dogs, speaking mostly Danish but singing along in English with the band playing American songs. There were many speeches, including one by Dr. Ralph Bunche then American Ambassador to the United Nations.

I interviewed him that evening. This was shortly after he had been denied membership in a tennis club in New York because of his race. He allowed how pleasant it was not to be discriminated against in Europe. We discussed the incongruity of a situation whereby a man could be his county's high diplomatic representative and yet be barred on racial grounds from playing tennis in a social club.

"But it will change," he said, "it will soon change."

After we checked into the hotel in Oslo, Norway, a lady of impeccable manners from the Norwegian Tourist Office took charge of us and advised us that we would have to curtsy to King Olaf. "When in Rome . . . " and the same goes for Norway. So the three of us practiced curtsying in our hotel room until we had it right.

The next day at precisely twelve the king's adjutant opened the door to the king's salon and in we went. I was apprehensive about interviewing royalty. The king, resplendent in his uniform with medals and decorations, was charm personified. With a perfect curtsy Chrissy handed him some flowers she had bought and then sat and watched him intently. We reminisced about the war, and I told him how I had stepped over his children as they played on the floor of the White House living room during a visit there. We talked about the political situation, about the proximity of the Russians and the precarious balancing act that involved. King Olaf spoke with great affection of Vienna and the Viennese, and perhaps that was why he waved away the adjutant who came to remind him that another caller was waiting.

"Never mind," he said, "I am enjoying this. Let's talk some more." We talked and talked, and the quarter hour I had been allotted grew into an hour.

As we were leaving he said, "Give my warmest regards to Mrs. Roosevelt. I hope you and Chrissy [he remembered her name!] have a wonderful time on your trip and particularly during your stay in our country."

We curtsied again, shaking hands with King Olaf. As soon as we had left the room, Chrissy looked up at me and started to imitate the sound of a baa-ing lamb. The king's little laugh indeed sounded a bit like the "baa-baa" of a lamb. I was glad she had waited until we had left the royal presence to display her theatrical talents.

****

Traveling with Chrissy had its advantages. A woman traveling on professional assignment accompanied by her small daughter was very unusual. More than once I was asked cautiously, yet curiously, "Where is your husband, Madame?" When I replied that my husband had passed away there was an embarrassed silence and then the obligatory, "Oh, I'm sorry."

Being a widow made people respectful, and they lavished particular attention upon Chrissy. She was given gifts and was treated with extraordinary loving kindness. Our collection of dolls grew, and she often found candy and small toys on her pillow in our hotel rooms. A fishmonger in the Bergen fish market entertained her with his "talking fish," manipulating its mouth to make it appear that the fish was talking, and in English yet! In Stockholm, my life got a little simpler when the Runges – friends we had made on the ship, who had a home in Stockholm – invited Chrissy to spend the rest of our stay with them. She didn't hesitate to leave me. I trained her to get along well with people and to be independent. Of course I called her every day. She was enthusiastic about staying with Grandma #2 (as she called Mrs. Runge) her daughter, Virginia, and Peter, Virginia's son, who was the same age as Chrissy.

Now, it was easier to travel and interview – in English of course – people like Karl Birger Blomdahl whose opera *Aniara* was being performed with soprano Elizabeth Soederstroem. I also interviewed Tore Wretman, owner of a Stockholm restaurant, who gave me a mouthwatering account of how to eat at a smörgasbord, the traditional Swedish buffet.

"When faced with the hundreds of variéties of food," Mr. Wretman lectured, "one should be aware that it is untasty to mix foods on your plate that don't go together. Eat each category separately. Seafood first, then salads, meat and hot dishes, each on a clean plate. Then cheeses and breads or crackers. Finally, desserts and fruits."

The Swedes drink a lot, so when they go out for dinner they leave their cars at home. "And no one," I was told, "not even the King, would be exempt from being put in jail if caught while driving under the influence of alcohol."

Every morning someone from the tourist office was waiting to take me wherever I wanted to go, show me whatever I wanted to see, arrange interviews with whomever I wanted to interview. I had no visible proof to show the Swedes that their hospitality would bring them results. I wondered if they treated everyone as gently and graciously as they treated me.

So I asked them point blank, "How do you know that I really am what I claim to be?"

The answer came, "It is quite unmistakable who you are. You have the kind of manners we appreciate, you are an experienced interviewer, and your Viennese charm makes people like you and want to do things for you. If you met some of the journalists who come here, arrogant and pushy, you would understand why we all like you." I marked that tribute down as a guideline for future ventures in the field of public relations.

****

One terrible day Sweden was thrown into despair. Dag Hammarskjöld, Secretary General of the United Nations and one of

Sweden's most famous sons was killed in an airplane accident. Every Swede was in tears. Most believed that it was not an accident but murder.

The state funeral was to be in Upsala, the ancient university town where Dag Hammarskjöld lived for many years. I wanted to represent Delaware – the state where, in 1638, the Swedes had been the first settlers – at the funeral. I sent a telegram to Governor Carvel of Delaware, "Would like to represent Delaware at funeral of Dag Hammarskjöld." Carvel had been my guest one of the times Mrs. Roosevelt visited me. The answer came immediately, "Would like you to represent Delaware at State Funeral of Dag Hammarskjöld."

I contacted the American Embassy and arranged to be a member of the official funeral party. I was sent an assortment of cards enabling me to enter areas reserved for official guests only. The Swedes are extremely formal in their observance of traditional rules and regulations. It would it have been unthinkable to attend the funeral in anything but black clothes. Fortunately I had a black dress, hat, shoes, gloves and pocket book but no stockings. I bought black silk stockings, an expense I had not counted on. I knew a wreath would be proper, so I dug even deeper into my empty pocket for a wreath with blue and yellow ribbons – the colors of Delaware and Sweden. I hoped the State of Delaware would reimburse me for the expense. (It never did.)

A special train took the official guests to Upsala. There the several hundred guests walked silently through the streets of the old university town, a black snake winding its way on narrow cobblestone streets. At one point church bells began pealing, and everyone stopped. It was thus all over Sweden, a moment of silence in memory of the great man. When the church bells pealed again, the walking resumed. At the cemetery, each mourner approached the grave. I saw my wreath prominently displayed with the inscription "from the State of Delaware, USA." As I walked up to the grave, cameras flashed. Afterwards there was a reception in the castle where Hammarskjöld had grown up. Several American representatives were there including Senator Javits from New York and Vice-President Lyndon Johnson. And Charlotte Shedd of Delaware. But nobody knew me, and I did not know anyone so I walked back to the train.

The next day Chrissy and I left Sweden to drive to Vienna. We stopped for the night in Jönköping where Chrissy picked up a newspaper and shouted, "Mommy look you are on the front page!"

I was dumbstruck when I saw the picture of a woman standing with bowed head at the grave side of Dag Hammarskjöld and recognized the woman as me!

I couldn't translate the Swedish caption and had to find someone to translate it. "We don't know who the woman bowing her head at his grave was," it read. "We only know that many women would like to do the same. Women and peace belong together. Peace and Dag Hammarskjöld also belong together. Longing for peace was the link that joined the women with Dag Hammarskjöld, and women all over the world felt as if that link broke within them when Dag Hammarskjöld left us."

So! I had represented the women of the world! I later learned that Dag Hammarskjöld was not interested in women, but the journalists decided that indeed there had been a woman in his life, that he had kept this a deep secret and that I was the woman. Well, I quickly dispelled that assumption. I wrote a letter to the Stockholm newspaper telling them who I was and that I was not a mystery woman.

After visiting my mother in Vienna for a few days, we returned to Wilmington where I found that the interviews I had sent home as well as the newspaper reports of my activities abroad had greatly increased my prestige and established my position more firmly.

28

It was not easy to keep afloat. My radio programs brought in fifty dollars a week, and now and then I earned a little from speaking engagements. Yet my style of living was such that everybody thought I must be rich. "She must be loaded," they whispered. But it was simply a question of priorities. I did everything myself to maintain an orderly and cozy home. I wanted Chrissy to grow up in an atmosphere of civilized living, so I used all the lovely furnishings my mother had sent me, linens, silverware, china and crystal. Sometimes neighbors dropped in as I was setting the table, and they thought we were having company. They were surprised when I explained that Chrissy and I warranted the same amenities I would offer guests.

Often I was quite desperate about money. Yet we never wanted for food. My childhood training implanted by a mother who had coped with famine and scarcities came in handy. I didn't rely on steaks or roasts, but with a few ounces of meat I prepared tasty casseroles. Instead of buying desserts and sweets, I made them myself. I trained Chrissy to distinguish between well prepared, fresh food and the commercial concoctions so many of her friends preferred. I also taught her to be frugal and let her be witness that no leftover food was discarded. Everything was utilized and in one form or another used over again.

The same was true for her clothes. My cousin Hans Kraus in New York had four daughters. Since he was in very comfortable circumstances, the girls were always dressed beautifully and never in each other's hand-me-downs. Twice a year a huge carton of clothes arrived for Chrissy. Coats and dresses made in London and Paris, sweaters and skirts and even handbags and gloves. It was a tremendous help. Although Chrissy did not object to her cousin's clothes, she felt somehow not on a par with her classmates whose parents bought them the latest fads. She never told me – until years later when our fortunes had improved – how hard it had been in the world of status symbols that surrounded her.

"You don't know how cruel kids can be," she told me, "how they can tease and hurt you. I never told you because you were doing the best you could and I didn't want you to be sad."

I also remembered how depressed I was when I had to wear hand-me-down coats from my male cousins, although there was really no comparison between those and the beautiful clothes Chrissy received. It is simply a question of owning something which is yours and yours alone.

I remember how disappointed I was when my mother refused to attend school functions and avoided mingling with other parents, so I attended every school affair. I drove Chrissy to school every morning and waited for her every afternoon as did all the other mothers. Once or twice a year I waited in the school parking lot until one or two o'clock in the morning until the students returned from skiing trips in Vermont.

My life revolved around Chrissy. I loved watching her grow, unfold, and develop, and I was deeply grateful to have her with me. I felt guilty, however unjustifiably, that she had to grow up without a father, but I also rejoiced in being able to bring her up without interference. I believe her father would have indulged her with too much, too early. I wanted her to grow up in the knowledge that everything has to be earned, nothing comes easy and obstacles are there to be overcome.

The desire to raise Chrissy without interference was also the reason why I chose not to marry again. I had the chance several times. But each time I weighed the pros and cons with regard to Chrissy and decided against it.

There was Professor Hans G., who was from Berlin but was teaching at the University of Delaware. He was a charming man, attractive, with good strong manly hands. We liked each other immediately. He had escaped from East Berlin before the Wall went up. He didn't understand American women and felt they didn't mean the nice things they said to him. While he enjoyed the American abundance, he felt guilty for having so much while his relatives in East Germany had so little. He was indeed quite neurotic. But he was wonderful with Chrissy, spending hours building sand castles with her when we visited the seashore.

He was twelve years younger than I. He did not realize it, and I doubt it would have made any difference to him. He eventually asked me to marry him and move to Berlin. I explained that America was my home, and I was fortunate to be an American citizen. I would not give that up for an uncertain fate in encircled Berlin. He was angry.

He said he would return to Berlin and wait for me to change my mind.

****

My only vacation in 1962 came when Mrs. Roosevelt invited us to visit Val Kill for a few days. While there, I took her place as hostess – she was called away to New York – for a party of East Indians invited for lunch. Although I am certain they were disappointed not to see Mrs. Roosevelt, I considered it an honor to pinch-hit for her. We had an animated conversation about India and its problems so that I felt I had justified Mrs. Roosevelt's confidence in electing me as stand-in.

She returned in the evening from New York quite exhausted and feeling ill. Nevertheless, she hosted another dinner party that same evening although everyone could see that she could barely keep herself upright. Her breathing was labored and her voice hoarse. Yet as I went to bed – my room was next to her writing room – I heard her shuffling papers and knew that she was doing what she did every evening, no matter how late: reading her mail and writing the answers for her secretary to type the next day.

Breakfast had been called for eight the next morning, and I was surprised when she joined us, her breathing still rasping and obviously painful. She took her place at the head of the table, making a stack of perhaps twenty-five pancakes for the five or six guests. She served herself last, and she was just about to sit down and eat, when the butler announced that a son of a former employee was at the main entrance gate, hoping to have a few words with Mrs. Roosevelt.

John Roosevelt said, "Let him wait, Mommy, eat your breakfast first."

Without a moment's hesitation she got up, pushed her plate back and hurried out to speak to the young man, saying, "If he came all the way to see me, I can't send him away or let him wait." It was a lesson in human behavior.

She was gone quite a while, and when she returned she just drank some coffee and motioned to me to join her in a corner of the room. "Now tell me how you are making out."

I told her I wasn't making ends meet with my radio program.

Maybe she could establish some contacts to include lecturing and appearing on the NBC weekend show, "Monitor." She promised to send letters of introduction to her own lecture agency. But as happened in 1939 and 1940 when she had tried to open doors for me, nothing happened. The gentlemen received me, out of courtesy to Mrs. Roosevelt, but I could not offer them what they were looking for.

On that day, Eleanor Roosevelt gave me the last of many interviews discussing human rights, the United Nations, the political future of the United States and the world. She spoke slowly and in a voice which indicated her illness, tuberculosis.

"They want me to give up my work and go to Arizona," she said, "but I would rather die than spend my days doing nothing."

She wrote me twice more. Once in August and once shortly before she died. When I read reports of her hospitalization and saw a photo of her leaving the hospital, I called to inquire how she was doing. "Oh Mrs. Shedd," Maureen, her personal secretary, said with a broken voice, "she is dying. Mrs. Roosevelt is dying."

Somehow you do not want to believe that people close to you can and will die. I didn't want to lose her, too. Her death was the end of an era. She had been a towering figure in my life almost from the time I arrived in America. While there might be long intervals between meetings, we corresponded regularly, and she had been the decisive factor in many of my most important decisions. To have been befriended by her, to confide my most intimate thoughts to her discreet wisdom, to consult with her in times of crisis and to know that she would always understand, never criticize made her a pillar of strength in my life. She shared both the difficult and the happy hours of my life.

There was now a vacuum where she had been. I was glad I had her voice on my tapes. Her inner and outer elegance continued to be my guidelines. When faced with difficult decisions and questions of attitude, I still ask myself how she would have behaved or what she would have done.

I once asked her definition of success in the life of a woman, "If she has a family, children, then I think the upbringing of the children is the most important success a woman can have. A woman who is a mother can have no greater success than children who turn out well." It was said rather wistfully, I thought perhaps with a slight intonation of self-accusation.

I asked, "Did you spend all your time with your children?"

"No, I did not. In those days we had governesses and nannies, but I tried to have a certain time each day which was devoted to the children. And then," she continued, "success in a woman's life is the ability to follow other interests, other professions or activities after the children are grown up, something worthwhile to do for the rest of one's life."

I was not invited to the funeral because it was only for close family, but I organized a memorial service in Wilmington where those who loved or respected her could express their sadness over the loss of such a great woman and great American.

29

After hearing about my success in Sweden, Birger Nordholm asked if he and I could arrange a special festive observance of the 325th anniversary of the landing of the Swedes in Delaware. The Swedish Colonial Society of Delaware usually observed the anniversary with speeches and visits to the historic landing place in Fort Christina Park in Wilmington followed by punch and cookies at the Community Center, but Birger felt that a more festive program might be in order.

A few weeks later my home was the scene of an elaborate dinner party for the Nordholms as well as local dignitaries including Mr. Babiarz, the mayor of Wilmington, and his wife. That evening Birger and I presented the idea of the establishing a sister city relationship between Wilmington and Kalmar, home port of the Kalmar Nyckel – the ship that brought the first Swedes to Delaware in 1638. Sister Cities was a relatively new concept, so it took considerable persuasion to make the Polish mayor of Wilmington, John Babiarz, enthusiastic about a Swedish Sister City. Birger discussed plans for a celebration commemorating the landing of the Swedes. It would be held in March of 1963 and would include Swedish food, singers and dancers, dignitaries from Kalmar, and Prince Regent Bertil of Sweden.

It took many meetings, political juggling and months of public relations efforts to get the various agencies – municipal, state, private and foreign – to agree on procedures. I was in the middle of the whirlwind, again working for the love of it rather than for financial rewards. While I was asked to contribute time and talent that brought me appreciation – never did anyone think to offer me even expense money for my efforts.

When the great day approached, those in power gently attempted to ease me out. Only Birger Nordholm remembered all I had done. At his insistence Chrissy presented a bouquet of flowers to Prince Bertil. While the mayor and the local Swedish Society crowded the scene, Birger Nordholm introduced me as the lady "in whose home the whole idea was born."

Not too long after that I was invited to Kalmar as a guest of the city to celebrate America Day. When I asked if I could bring Chrissy, the generous Swedes welcomed her as well. I immediately wrote our friends in Stockholm, Grandma #2, Virginia and Peter, asking if Chrissy could stay with them while I traveled. By return mail came the reply, "We are looking forward to having her as long as possible." In fact, Grandma #2 met us at the airport and took Chrissy home with her while I continued my journey to Kalmar.

What a charming city, Kalmar! From here the Kalmar Nyckel set forth in 1638 taking immigrants to the new world. The newspapers carried long articles about me and my work, my picture appeared on the front pages, and I was treated as a most honored guest of the city. I toured glass factories, museums, and churches, fortresses and Swedish folk craft shops. Everywhere I found a rich supply of material for my radio programs, and everywhere too I made friends with the supposedly cool and aloof Swedes.

I got along with everyone because I respected their desire to be treated with formality. They click their heels and bow and kiss a lady's hand and remain on formal terms even with close friends. I never met a Swede, male or female, who would have dreamed of calling me by my first name. It just isn't done.

****

Now that I was treated as a celebrity, I realized that I would simply ignore those who envied me, saying of course I have to get my name in the paper if I want to play a role in public life. The important question was what kind of a role. I resolved that there would never be a scandal connected with my name. I did not subscribe to the motto "any publicity, even bad publicity, is better than no publicity." My publicity should stem from my honorable achievements. No skeletons in my closets. I have kept it thus to this day. I also wanted to be a good example for my daughter. I could only influence her life if she could look up to me with respect, which would be strengthened when she saw others' respect for me. The kind of respect I desired had to be earned, not bought. It meant sacrifices – for instance, sacrifices in my relationship with men.

There was Jan in Sweden, a charming professor I met at a party. It was sympathy at first sight. We danced and talked and walked through the silent streets at night. Every time we met, we felt closer, drawn to each other. He never mentioned that he was married. And when I asked him, he gave the usual explanation: marriage because a child had been on the way. And then two more children had come and then thirty years of average married life. He was ready to leave his family and follow me.

"No," I said, "I don't break up marriages." And so we parted. He wrote to me for many years, sent me Christmas gifts, and once came to visit me in America. But I insisted that there could be no future for us. An episode, that was all.

On this same trip I was a guest of the City of Berlin. That was a grim experience in more than one way. The divided city with its guarded wall where hundreds of desperate refugees were shot made me grateful for my American passport. From my vantage at Checkpoint Charlie, I gazed at the bleak, empty streets of East Berlin. I wondered what the East German guards thought. Surely, they could see the difference between East and West. Perhaps their regime succeeded in killing their thoughts. Maybe they had become robots who act on command and without human emotions.

To me it was painful. The temptation to say to myself "after all they brought it on themselves" was dispelled by the remembrance that Berlin was never for Hitler, it was perhaps the only island of opposition in Germany.

The other unpleasant aspect of my visit was my reunion with Professor G. who expected me to come ready to tie the marriage knot and stay in Berlin. He came eagerly to my hotel but was startled to find another woman there – a representative of the Visitors Bureau – who had been delegated to be my guide. She wouldn't budge, curious to see whom I was meeting. Thus, our first meeting after so many months was stilted and uncomfortable. When she finally left, she reminded me of the schedule for the next several days filled from morning till evening with appointments for interviews and visits to points of interest.

"I thought you were coming to see me," said Hans G. "But I see you don't need me. Your days are fully occupied."

"Don't you understand this is the only way I could come to Berlin? I don't have money for pleasure trips, they always have to be combined with my profession."

"Ah, so you still insist on your profession. Can't you live

without it and be just a woman?"

"No! I will always have to be someone on my own. I will never want to be dependent on a man for support and take orders and give up my individuality. If I ever get married again, it will have to be to someone who respects my right to be myself and not as an appendix of another."

He was furious. We spent the evening attending a theater performance to which the lady guide had given me tickets. He did not invite me to dinner. Afterwards he took me back to my hotel, bid me good night. That was the last I ever saw of him.

During the four days in Berlin I marveled at the enthusiasm of the Berliners for President Kennedy who was visiting at the same time. I stood squeezed among a million screaming Berliners shouting "Kennedy, Kennedy," just as the Germans had shouted only a few years back "Sieg Heil" and "Juda verrecke." How times change. Now it was Kennedy they shouted for.

****

I returned to Sweden on a steamboat via the Gota Canal, courtesy of the Government Tourist Office. When the boat docked in Stockholm, I couldn't find Chrissy or Grandma #2. Puzzled, I hailed a cab and went to their apartment. I climbed the stairs and rang the bell. There was no answer. I rang again and again and finally Peter, eight years old, opened the door just wide enough to show his face.

"Peter" I said, "let me in. Where is Chrissy?"

He didn't answer. He just looked at me.

"Peter, can't you talk, where is Chrissy, what's happened?"

He shook his head and ran out of the apartment. I put down my luggage and ran from room to room. Silence. I looked about for a note, a message – nothing. Peter had disappeared. What could I do? where to get information? I was ice cold and wept with despair. I didn't know whom to ask for help. The phone did not ring. I cried and prayed and ran from room to room. Where was Chrissy? Where was everybody? Finally I rang the bell for the next apartment. A lady opened the door.

"Excuse me, do you speak English?"

She did. Oh what a relief.

"Please help me, Peter ran away I don't know where he is, and I have come here to meet my child and she has disappeared. No one is home. They didn't leave any message."

The lady was sympathetic but knew nothing. However she found Peter in the superintendent's apartment and asked him if anything had happened to Chrissy. He just looked at her. He had lost the ability to speak.

The agony lasted until ten o'clock that night. From three till ten. At ten the elevator rose to our floor and Chrissy, her arm in a plaster cast, pale and wan appeared with Grandma #2.

"Chrissy, darling, what happened, I was half crazed with worry. Why didn't you call?"

"We thought Peter would tell you."

It turned out that Peter and Chrissy had been playing near the street when a bicyclist slipped and pushed her to the ground, breaking her arm. Grandma took her to the hospital. Swedish socialized medicine had kept them waiting for hours before a doctor could see them, take X-rays, and set Chrissy's arm. But he set it wrong. So they had put her under complete anesthesia, to break it again, and reset it. Chrissy and Grandma #2 were at the hospital ten hours. They had nothing to eat, and there was no telephone. There was no charge at the hospital, but the doctor who examined her arm before we left for Vienna charged a "private" fee which was twice as much as I would have paid in the United States.

Several days later, we were supposed to drive to Vienna in a Saab put at my disposal, with the stipulation that I bring it back to Sweden. I didn't want to drive all the way back to Stockholm when it would be easier to fly out of Copenhagen. I remembered Cliff's advice: you want it? Do it! I went to a car rental agency, showed the manager my credentials and asked for a car to drive to Vienna in exchange for publicity in Delaware. It worked! I got a Mercedes. Perhaps it helped that I had Chrissy with me, that cute little girl with her arm in a cast.

On our way to Vienna we took the car ferry that crosses the North Sea between Denmark and Germany. It was a big comfortable ship with a huge dining room. After lunch Chrissy and I were on deck, when Chrissy called out, "Mommy look, there is a man in the water."

He was bobbing up and down in a small rubber raft waving his arms. Rescuers brought the man, pale and shivering, aboard our ship. He and two others had fled East Germany on rubber rafts, drifting all night hoping to cross the path of our ferry. The other two had been spotted by East German police and had been shot. I wanted to find out more details, but I was told not to report the event because that would make it more difficult for others wanting to use the same escape route. Much as I wanted to use my eyewitness account, I could not put my desire for a "scoop" above the safety of many who might make it to the West. But it brought home to me again the blessings of freedom and to what length the human being will go to be free.

I wondered if it would ever end, this misery of refugees. We thought we had ended such anguish when we defeated Hitler. But no, this time the refugees were victims of communist oppression. The rescue at sea cast a dark shadow upon a trip which had started out so happily.

When we arrived in Germany it was late afternoon and I was too tired to drive on. We found a lovely room in a small hotel outside Hamburg. The next morning we left for Vienna. It is a lovely drive from north to south, and so fascinating to behold the changes in architecture and landscape. As the landscape, flat in northern Germany, changed to the first subtle hills and dark green forests, so did the houses change from heavy gray squat shapes to lighter and lighter forms. They seemed to become slender and graceful, the colors of the walls suddenly were yellow, white and pastel and the window boxes overflowing with flowers.

Chrissy was a wonderful traveling companion, even though her broken arm in its hard cast must have been uncomfortable and itchy. She never complained, was never in a bad mood, and her readiness to try new foods and to explore and admire sights was a great source of joy. I have never traveled with anyone I enjoyed more.

The changes that had taken place in Germany were amazing. Only a few years back, it had been one vast heap of rubble. There was not a trace of that to be found by 1963. The cities were rebuilt, the fields were producing crops, the stores were loaded with merchandise, the people were well dressed. In other words the Wirtschaftswunder – economic miracle – was going full blast.

Wherever we went, I contacted the tourist office and introduced myself as an American radio broadcaster, so I was given a personal guide who took us around to places and told stories that brought the houses, courtyards, market places, and statues to life. I am amazed today how much Chrissy remembers after so many years. She learned much more of the history and geography of Europe during our trips than she ever learned in school, particularly since in twelve years at Friends School in Wilmington she never once was taught European history.

When we arrived at my mother's house in Klosterneuburg, it was late at night. The house was dark and the gate locked. I had telephoned ahead that we would arrive late, but my mother had fallen asleep. It took forever while ringing the bell, shaking the iron gate, and throwing stones against the window for her to hear us. Time had stood still! It was exactly as it had been when I was a child. How many times had I climbed over the wickedly pointed spikes of the fence, even when all dressed up in my best clothes. As I stood there in the dark, Chrissy asleep in the car, waiting once again for my mother to find the key, I marveled after twenty-five years, a World War, the Nazi and Russian occupations, and the final return to normalcy that the old habits and customs were still in force.

My mother reacted strangely to my annual visits. On the one hand, she was happy that I came to see her; on the other, she resented that my visits were tied to professional purposes. She refused to understand that I could never have afforded to visit her at all had it not been for work. She was hurt and angry when I had to leave her to interview guests for my radio program.

Mothers and daughters, I have come to find out, can either be great friends or bitter enemies. I loved my mother, and I know she loved me and was very proud of me but never to my face. I remember how she always tried to give me the impression that I was not pretty and that my talents left a lot to be desired. Yet in the few letters I had received from her during our separation, particularly after Cliff died, she cautioned me not to take on more than I could handle, to take care of my health, and not to work too hard.

But just like when I was a child, she was unable to show affection. At the drop of a hat, she would pick a fight over some unimportant issue. I suppose some mothers see their offspring always as children, in need of guidance and correction. I am afraid I was not always able to take her quarreling graciously or even wisely. I had too much respect for her to talk back, but her behavior spoiled my visits. What could have been a wonderful time of tender companionship ended, more often than not, in my earlier-than-planned departure.

Yet in all its disheartening dissonance, our relationship brought forth some positive results. I was so hurt by the absence of friendship between us that I resolved there would never be such aggravation between Chrissy and me. We had already established a wonderful accord through our travels together, and I found to my joy that Chrissy responded easily and naturally to my approach. I never raised my voice, I never commanded, and I never beat her as I had been beaten. I knew that reason and a great deal of demonstrative affection would build in her the wish to be close to me, to please me, and to earn my approval.

30

The subjects of my radio programs slowly veered away from small talk and community interests to national, international, and controversial issues. I got into hot water when, on the occasion of the great East coast blackout, I said that I did not buy the story of an accidental interruption; I suspected sabotage. I predicted more of the same (as indeed happened a few weeks later in the Southwest) and urged my audience to supply themselves with kerosene lamps and charcoal burners.

This produced a moderate number of telephone calls from listeners who called me an alarmist. "Sabotage in America? Don't be ridiculous," they said. Such things happened in other countries, not here! The station management demanded that I submit a copy of my programs two weeks in advance.

"How can I do that?," I replied in great agitation, "I have to be up to date, and sometimes I don't know until ten o'clock in the morning what I am going to talk about at eleven-thirty."

It was touch and go. Then the turmoil subsided, and I returned to my usual routine but I did submit a copy of my script to management. Never before had local broadcasters touched the subjects that I discussed. I felt that I had a moral obligation to use that microphone to relate what I knew from experience. I wanted to tell my audience what they could not hear from anyone else. I particularly wanted to make them aware of the privilege of being an American. I was frustrated by the casual way people took freedom for granted. I knew it could be lost so easily and sometimes simply by default.

Therefore with the memory of the dramatic North Sea escape incident still fresh in my memory, I wrote the following program for the Fourth of July.

"Again and again, people ask me why I left Austria to come to the United States. Again and again they ask they ask why I would not prefer to return to my homeland now that it is free and prosperous. Americans in general cannot imagine how one can do such a thing, pack up and leave the place where you were born and raised in comfort and sometimes even luxury; the place where everyone speaks your language, where everyone has the same national background, and where – most important of all – you leave behind your family, your home, and your traditions. If you have to leave to save your life, that's one thing, but to go voluntarily – why?

"Well, because there are people who are not able to be silent, people who feel, when they see a wrong, they must do something to change it or at least must speak up and say, 'this is wrong'; people who have an inner compulsion to participate in the formation of life, people who want to be active – who want to lead within the scope of their talents, who crave the right to speak up, to discuss, to dispute, to disagree if necessary, and put forth their convictions.

"Some people don't need this. They are satisfied to follow the general trend; they do what they are told to do. They follow instructions and are glad someone else takes the trouble and the responsibility to issue these instructions. They avoid the spotlight, they avoid criticism, they play it safe all the time. They smile and bow. They don't get excited over anything because, according to their philosophy, 'it isn't worth it. It doesn't pay enough money. It doesn't get you anywhere except into trouble.'

"If you can do that, fine. I almost envy you. If I could have done that twenty-five years ago, I would have stayed in Austria. I would not have set out alone with twenty dollars in my pocket and a heart as heavy as the Rock of Gibraltar. But I knew where I was going.

"I was going to the land where, I was told, a man or a woman could speak up freely; where you could live in your own way, no matter how you wished to live as long it did not hurt your neighbor or the nation; a land where – to be sure not all was perfect – most of the things which make for life were good things; where one could ask for and get a chance; where people try to live according to the Golden Rule; where there is respect for each other's convictions – sometimes obscured by noises of one sort or another, as during election time, but basically it is there; where one need not be afraid of voicing an opinion; where one could choose one's friends without interference; where one could find peace.

"These things I searched for and these things I found. And for these things I love America and all it stands for. And that is why I speak up rather strongly on this program now and then. I feel I must when my conscience urges me on; when I see things you may not see because you have been either too close or too far away."

Unbeknownst to me one of my listeners requested a copy of the script and submitted it to the Freedom Foundation at Valley Forge. A few weeks later I read an article in the morning paper describing the Freedom Foundation Awards. Listed among the recipients of the George Washington Medal of Honor was Radio Station WDEL in Wilmington "For a radio program 'Why I Prefer America.'" I was not listed as author or speaker.

Suspecting that something was not quite on the up and up, I sauntered in the manager's office. "Harvey, what do you know about this Freedom Award for the station?"

He looked up from his desk, "What award? I know nothing about it."

"Really," I said. "Don't you read the paper? You won an award. Who won it? You are the manager, don't you think you should know?"

"Oh, I suppose someone here, probably someone among the newspeople."

I was furious. "No, my dear Harvey," I said, "Not someone among the newspeople. I won the award for my editorial on America. Why do you suppose my name is not mentioned?"

"I don't know."

That day a festive luncheon was held at the Hotel du Pont Gold Ballroom for the Freedom Foundation Awards. I had not been invited. Harvey Smith was. And so was the head of the Delaware Blue Cross, my sponsor. But not I.

I called Harold Maybee, director of Blue Cross and told him I had been excluded. Mr. Maybee graciously invited me to accompany him. When the awards were handed out, he told the several hundred assembled guests that it was I who had actually won the award, not WDEL and not Blue Cross, both of whom accepted a beautiful bronze medal. There was none for me. But to the surprise of both recipients, my name was etched on the medal. In the end I also got my medal, but no explanation from WDEL nor any word of appreciation for my achievement.

This was an important milestone in my life because the George Washington Medal is "awarded only when the jury feels there has been an outstanding contribution made by an individual over a period of years. For the most outstanding individual contribution supporting human dignity and the fundamentals of a free society."

I recount this story only because it was another one of the milestones at which one stops to evaluate the hurdles that must be overcome. A much more critical hurdle was my continued lack of funds. It was impossible to pay all the bills, no matter how carefully we lived. While WDEL took 50% of my shows' revenues, they also paid me when a sponsor didn't pay on time or, as sometimes happened, defaulted. I was never asked to come up with the balance. On the down side, I did not qualify for Social Security payments, health insurance, the pension fund, or bonuses. I was freelance, and that was the deal. I was on my own, one-hundred percent.

I was fortunate to have a neighbor who was an accountant and who made me realize that I needed to think of the future and to maintain payments into all these funds in order to be protected once I retired. But to do this, I had to have an income. Mine was negligible.

There were times when I was desperate. One night I could not sleep for the worries and my pillow was wet with tears. At such times I pray. I had blind faith. I was sure that my prayer for a solution would somehow be solved. And it was. I decided to ask for help from Emma Hale, who was not a blood relative but was my cousin's mother-in-law. She had lost her husband within one week of my own loss. But her financial situation was of a totally different nature than mine, so I knew that I could ask her for a loan.

I went down to my office at four o'clock that morning and wrote a letter describing my situation and asking for help.

The answer came by return mail: a check with the words "thank you for letting me help you." That cry for help and thoughtful response established a deep bond of a friendship and respect, a sharing of experiences and trust such as I had never before and never since had the privilege of receiving. Emma was a true Viennese lady. She is the last in the long line of women who have played important roles in my life, and she above all others helped me to survive. With uncanny sensitivity she always knew when I was low in spirit, when I was near the end of my wits. It was almost as if my troubles were transmitted to her by invisible ether waves. The phone would ring and Emma would say, "Is something wrong? Can I help?"

She always helped with so much tact and delicacy – as if she wanted me to think I was doing her a favor, not the other way around. For many years we traveled to Europe – Chrissy, Emma and I – wonderful trips. We stayed in luxurious hotels, saw museums, mountains, and lakes. At the Blue Grotto on Capri, we swam in the blue waters and sunned ourselves on the beach and watched women come with their children and unpack huge baskets from which emerged mountains of spaghetti and big loaves of white bread. They sat and ate and didn't see the beauty of the landscape or the clear waters.

We toured Rome, where one of the tourists asked if Moses sat as model for Michelangelo. When we had dinner in restaurants in Italy Emma studied the menu and then always – always – ordered melanzani. It was her favorite. Chrissy was not very experimental either; she only wanted rare roast beef or spaghetti and Coca-Cola.

Once we spent a glorious two weeks in Sirmione, a charming island on the shores of Lake Garda accessible only over a drawbridge and that only after checking with a guard at the gate to make sure that the one way traffic permitted it. The medieval streets were so narrow that pedestrians had to flatten themselves against house walls if a car passed.

By now I had a small portable tape recorder much easier to handle than the large, awkward, heavy, 40-pound machine I used in the past. I took my tape recorder along where ever I went and recorded interviews, music and impressions which previously had required elaborate preparatory set-ups and negotiations.

Since these trips were also business trips, I had official guides who arranged for me to meet prominent and interesting people I probably never would have met on my own. Usually the private guides, particularly in Italy and Switzerland, were highly educated scholars who gave me unusual background stories and showed me treasures I would, on my own, have quite possibly overlooked.

The small three-inch tapes filled with interviews and commentaries I collected on my journeys got back to Wilmington quickly and easily. They were played on WDEL for my ever growing audience. My listeners were used to hearing artists, scientists, diplomats, merchants, politicians, and fashion designers tell about their lives and their work. Their French, Italian, and German accents brought European life into the living rooms of my American audience.

Travel had become an integral part of my profession. There was no one, except for one person in Philadelphia, besides me who traveled to foreign countries. The fact that I was a freelancer able to pick up and go any time I chose put me in this favorable position. Every new excursion was a stepping stone to the next venture.

Looking back now over my long career in broadcasting, I believe that careers cannot be built up over night. In fact, those much publicized overnight successes usually take decades to accomplish.

****

I can see now that life is made up of stepping stones, each with its own importance as we step from one to another, all contributing the mosaic of our experiences. An invitation to meet with President Johnson at the White House in Washington was one of those stepping stones. I had broadcast an approving commentary on the landing of the marines in the Dominican Republic to insure the safety of American citizens in that country. As was frequently the case, there was a strong Communist involvement. I was gratified that the President had not simply sat, as the Eisenhower administration did in the case of Hungary, but had acted forcefully to prevent the establishment of yet another Cuba on our doorstep.

A few days later I received a telephone call at 11:30 a.m. from Congressman Harris B. McDowell telling me that the President wished to see me that very day at 3:30. At first I thought this was a hoax, but knowing McDowell I realized quickly that this was indeed a command performance. I was thrown into a turmoil.

It's funny to remember how one reacts sometimes to extraordinary events. My first thought was my appearance: how did my hair look, what could I wear, did I have matching accessories, were my gloves clean, and what about Chrissy? The hem on her dress had to be raised, so I called my dressmaker, Lena Walden, to see if she could put aside whatever she was doing.

"We have to go and see the President."

"What President?"

"The President of the United States."

"You're kidding!"

"No, I'm not kidding. May I bring the dress now?"

I took the dress to her and then called Friends School.

"Hello, this is Charlotte Shedd, will you permit Chrissy to leave at 12 noon? We have to go to Washington to meet the President."

Silence. Then, "Who did you say is calling?"

"Chrissy Shedd's mother."

"All right, she'll be out front at noon."

It was a strange feeling to drive up to the White House. I had been there so many times during the Roosevelt presidency. Now instead of being ushered upstairs to the family quarters, we went to a side entrance of the White House. We waited only five minutes in an anteroom before a White House attendant opened the door and beckoned us to enter. The President stood waiting for us, and warmly shook hands with me and Chrissy as well as Representative McDowell, who had joined us.

"I read your remarks," the President said. "I thought they were very much to the point and I am glad you approve and that you are on my side. We always like to hear what the people think. We do what we can."

The White House photographer took pictures, and we thanked him for the invitation.

"I'm glad you could come on such short notice," he smiled. "I'd like to spend more time with you but I have several other obligations. So take care and keep up the good work and let other people know how you feel."

We shook hands once more and then were ushered out. We had been in his office not more than fifteen minutes, but those minutes contributed mightily to my prestige as a broadcast journalist. Some of my journalist colleagues had not believed me when I said I was going to see the President. They had gone so far as to call the White House to verify the appointment. For reasons I can't explain, they were told the President had no further scheduled appointments. I was doubly glad to have the photos as proof of my visit with the President.

****

During these encouraging career developments, my private life, unfortunately was not inspiring. I was still the widow, the fifth wheel, the outsider in the couple-oriented society. Men asked me out, but as soon as we were at the dinner table I knew I would have preferred to be alone. Perhaps I was too particular. But why should I spend time with people who irritated me?

While I enjoy my own company, I enjoy the stimulation of friendships, so I began to think of ways in which I could gather friends around me without having them think I wanted to intrude in their lives. I decided to form my own group of kindred spirits, particularly with those of Austrian background who shared a similarity of taste, tradition, and culture.

I knew several families of Austrian background who longed for an exchange of memories, so I invited them to gather one Sunday afternoon for a "Jause," as the afternoon coffee and cake interlude is called in Austria. Six couples appeared. We talked about founding a club to familiarize the community with Austrian festivals, food, and music. Thus was formed the Austrian-American Society of Wilmington, Delaware. The American husband of my Viennese friend Adele Weaver, Bob, drew up by-laws. We decided that our first public event would be a Viennese dinner prepared by us for the community of Arden held in the Gild Hall. The menu consisted of Viennese breaded chicken (Backhendl), cucumber salad, Viennese parsley potatoes, and Sachertorte.

I had no idea what I let myself in for because almost all of it rested on my own shoulders. I fried breaded chicken in two huge frying pans on the restaurant-sized stove of the Gild Hall, finishing up just before the first guest arrived. Meanwhile Chrissy, eager to help, scrubbed the potatoes with SOS pot cleaner pads! I baked the famous Sachertorte from scratch. Since each torte only served ten people, I baked seventeen cakes, so I was ready to drop in my tracks. The party, not surprisingly, was a huge success. Several more Austrians joined our society. My experiment was working.

With more and more members, we decided to earn money for expenses by having a Viennese pastry sale – in my home – with pastries contributed by the fabulous pastry makers in our group. The number of club members grew with each affair. We had now grown from thirteen members to ninety, half of them from Austria or the former Austro-Hungarian empire. It was time to launch a gala event, a Viennese ball, after the model of the famous Vienna Opera Ball, which I remembered so fondly from my youth when I danced the polonaise with a Count Ezterhazy as my partner.

But how to arrange a ball when I had no experience and most importantly no money? Fortunately there was a similar ball – the Blue Danube Ball – in Washington, D.C., which three of us attended. I watched everything. There were tables for ten arranged with seating by name. A corps de ballet danced the Blue Danube Waltz at the beginning of the ball. There was a midnight buffet serving goulash soup and apple strudel and coffee with whipped cream. Without exception, all guests wore evening attire, men in tux, tails or uniform. I made notes about everything.

Returning home, I called together several members and announced that I knew how to put on our own Blue Danube Ball. We located a private club – the Wilcastle Center – with a charming small, but elegant, ballroom and negotiated to get the facility rent free if we guaranteed at least 90 dinner guests. We were not sure we could fulfill that term, but we had high hopes. We sent out 400 invitations. When we had enough patrons, we invited the Austrian Ambassador, Dr. Karl Gruber, and the Governor of Delaware, Dr. Russell Peterson. Both accepted.

The ball was a glittering affair with a ballet danced by the corps de ballet of the Wilmington Academy of the Dance supervised by its director, James Jamieson, an associate of Agnes de Mille.

This event changed my status from a socially abandoned widow to the busily involved chairman of a cosmopolitan society. I was continuously involved with friends who were no longer concerned that I might intrude on their privacy but instead sought out my companionship. My life became vibrant and stimulating. It was a lesson learned by doing rather than waiting.

As the years went by the Blue Danube Ball became not only the outstanding event of the social season but in 1970 began to serve a very special purpose. The profits from the Blue Danube Ball were designated to pay for a six-week scholarship at the world renowned International Summer Academy Mozarteum in Salzburg.

I corraled some of the finest musicians in Wilmington to act as jurors and sent out invitations to music schools and private teachers to register their students aged 18 to 25 for the competition. Fourteen students applied the first year. Katherine Ciesinski, a contralto, won the scholarship. She has credited her first chance at international attention to the scholarship.

Since then dozens of young artists have enjoyed not only superb training at the Mozarteum but have enthusiastically experienced the unique artistic atmosphere in Salzburg where, as all of them have proclaimed to me, "the mere fact that we are musicians earns us the respect of everyone we meet." It is very different, they say, from this country where only monetary rewards count as success. Many of our scholarship winners – such as Kathleen Casello, who is among other successes one of "The Three Sopranos " – have indeed achieved great financial as well as artistic success, several on a wide international front.

The news of my efforts on behalf of Austrian American friendship and cooperation eventually reached the ears of the Austrian Embassy in Washington and was relayed to the Austrian State Department which in turn proposed my name to the President of Austria as deserving a medal of appreciation for my endeavors. Thus, one day the Austrian Ambassador, Dr. Ernst Lemberger, pinned the Silver Medal of Merit on my dress. The ceremony took place in my home in Arden. I invited 75 friends as well as the Governor of Delaware, the mayor of Wilmington, the president of the University of Delaware, the publisher of the local newspaper, and others. It was a great emotional experience, another stepping stone.

But perhaps the greatest fulfillment of my dreams was the manner in which my daughter, Christobel, lived up to every expectation I had ever dared to hope for. She attended Friends School in Wilmington on a full scholarship for twelve years and graduated as a straight A student. She followed that by graduating from the University of Delaware with High Honors on the Dean's List. The crowning glory was a master's degree from Syracuse University, accomplished in one year instead of the usual two. Thus, I had provided her with the only security I have come to recognize as a reliable guarantee for success: education. I have seen property, money, and personal possessions lost overnight. I have seen refugees driven from their homes, wandering into strange lands with nothing but the clothes on their backs and what they carried as indestructible property in their brains. That was the deciding factor. Knowledge made it possible for them, as it did for me, to make a new and successful start. It is more valuable than the most perfect diamond.

Yet with all the honors and decorations, the income from my professional activities remained at an embarrassingly low level. I could not have covered the everyday expenses without the constant and generously offered help of my dear friend, Emma. Whenever she came to visit me for a few days, she asked, "What needs to be done, What is it you need?" Then she left a check on my desk upon departure. And always she gave the impression that helping me was an emotional satisfaction to her. During those years of great professional success, my dire circumstances were always carefully camouflaged because I knew the value of my activities would plummet if people knew how little I earned.

The day came when I heard through my sister that my mother had passed away in Vienna. I could not attend her funeral because I lacked the money for airfare, I could not interrupt my broadcasts, nor could I leave thirteen-year-old Chrissy alone. I knew that no one would understand my precarious situation, least of all my sister, who could not believe that I would not leave everything and come to Vienna to share the responsibility and the sorrow. And I must confess that even though those terrible days of inner conflict and financial pressure have receded far into the shadows, sometimes I still cannot forgive myself for not somehow having managed to go. Yet I know that at that time there simply was no possibility to do so.

Later that year when Emma invited both Chris and me to accompany her on another trip abroad, I drove to Vienna and visited my mother's and father's burial place. Another phase of my life had ended.

****

There was a sizable inheritance from my parents. For the first time I felt relief from the constant threat of bills that stood like dark specters. I paid off my mortgage. I paid off every bill. And after having traveled to Europe almost every year, I fulfilled a longtime dream – to see the USA.

I did not want to spend my money frivolously. So I traveled as a journalist, just as I had in Europe. I wrote the President of Amtrak proposing a promotional trip around the USA. I was issued a ticket valid for 4 weeks train travel in a private roomette. All other expenses were my own. What a wonderful opportunity!

My first stop was Chicago. It was September, the weather was perfect, sunny, cool. I had a fascinating two days of sightseeing in this most American of all American cities.

Then it was off on the Empire Builder to Seattle, Washington. Service on the train was impeccable in those days. The steward in charge of my roomette acted with pride, not servility. The roomette had a comfortable armchair which at night folded down into an equally comfortable bed covered with sparkling clean linen and blankets. I also had my own bathroom facilities. The privacy of the roomette proved to be invaluable when the club car got raucous. I have never been able to cope with drunks and particularly with intoxicated women. Their uncontrolled behavior embarrasses me. I would have liked to remain in the club car after dinner and during the afternoon, but the noise drove me back to my compartment.

The dining car of the Empire Builder was still in the old style of the Pullman service in those days of 1973. The table was properly set with snowy white linens and fresh flowers in silver vases. The knives and forks were not plastic, and we drank from sparkling glassware, not foam cups. The menu offered several choices of freshly prepared food – no packaged airplane style trays. The prices were reasonable. In other words, the meals were events one looked forward to.

Riding in the bubbletop of the club car, I appreciated the grandeur of the landscape, the wide open spaces of Montana, the mountains and flatlands, and to make the spectacle even more remarkable, a thunderstorm with lightning.

Seattle offered the twin delights of sea and mountain tops. Mt. Rainier with its snowcapped peak and wildflower meadows reminded me of my native Austria, while the discovery of underground catacombs, remnants of the original city destroyed in the great fire of 1818 reminded me of Pompeii.

Next on my list was San Francisco. I spent a week visiting the Napa Valley vineyards, taking bus trips to the Muir Woods, sauntering along Fisherman's Wharf, and climbing the many stairs of Ghirardelli Square. I fell in love with this charming city.

While I remembered being told that Los Angeles is nothing but a sprawling assembly of concrete housing, I found the city fascinating precisely because it is such a giant megalopolis. I discovered its many facets in the huge Farmers Market, Hollywood, and Santa Monica, where I found myself comparing the long, palm lined boulevards with those of Nice.

Los Angeles forever remains in my memory for my walking tour. I thought I could walk from my hotel on Wilshire Boulevard to the La Brea Tar Pits where the skeletons of prehistoric animals had been recovered. It was a sunny Sunday in September, So I set out. I walked and walked and walked for two hours. Finally I asked a policeman how far it was to La Brea.

"Where is your car?" he asked.

"I am walking," I answered.

"You what?" he asked unbelieving.

"I walked," I said. "How far is it?"

"How far have you walked?" he asked.

"Two hours so far," I said.

"Well, you may as well keep going," he said. "Another half hour. But take a taxi back to your hotel."

****

The most profound impression of the trip came from the Grand Canyon. Nothing can be compared to sunrise there. I stood by the rim and listened to the music of the wind as it whistled its melodies up and down the chasms and played the accompaniment to the multicolored spectacle unfolding in the sky: first lightly gray, then a fine purple turning to orange, then yellow, then the blazing glory of all these colors combined as the sun rose over the canyon. It is an unforgettable sight, a touch of the eternity which lives in the canyon and reminds us that we are just an infinitesimal speck in the universe. I stood there, barely breathing, and happy to be alone, for at that moment I was talking with God.

The journey ended in New Orleans. I had heard so much about the unique French-Spanish flavor of the city that perhaps my expectations were geared a little too high for the reality. The old part of the city with its lacy balconies and old houses was quaint enough, but the streets were filthy, and I was warned not to go out alone after dusk because of the many drunks and unsavory characters that populated the area. So I found myself restricted to the hotel lobby unable to find out about the much publicized nightlife of New Orleans.

I decided to fly home from there because all of a sudden I wanted to go home. I had had enough of traveling all alone. Yet, the four-week trip had left a deep imprint and filled a vacuum that had existed not only in my knowledge of the country but also of myself. Getting acquainted with a large part of it, coupled with some financial security all contributed to a relative peace of mind which I had never known.

I felt a deep belonging, belonging to America, to my home in Arden, to my child, and very important, to myself. My daughter had left home at eighteen to attend the University of Delaware and while we talked on the telephone almost daily, I was now alone in my house. I was as happy as a lark being able to do what I wanted to do when I wanted to do it. I felt, in fact for the first time, totally free.

In other words, the terrible struggles of the previous years some-how slowly, imperceptibly began to subside and a soothing tranquility descended upon my soul. This is the blessing of aging – if one has a purpose in living – the freedom to do as much or as little as one wants to do, the physical and mental ability to do it, and the utmost reward: the ability to communicate one's experiences and thoughts to others.

America had allowed me to come here when life had become unbearable in my homeland. It was not easy. But unlike so many of the immigrants, I never expected the streets to be paved in gold. I did not expect it to be as hard as it was, and there were times when I did not think I could make it. But I did. Happiness does not lie in being a millionaire. It lies in freedom. And freedom I found. And much more. A wonderful home, enough income to do what I want to do, the respect and admiration of the community in which I have lived for almost six decades, a profession I love, and most of all a child who is everything I ever hoped for. America has given me all of it.

31

In my life full of miracles there was another I was not prepared for. I had reached an age where I did not expect to find a great love. I did not want to fall under what in German is called *Torschluss Panik*, or closing door panic – a state of mind that encourages foolish mistakes because one thinks the door is closing on life; therefore, any man is better than none. Then came the miracle – his name was Gregory.

The telephone rang and a heavily accented voice said, "Hello, I would like to meet you!"

I was intrigued, but I was also on my guard. You never know what the implications will be, so it's best to meet on neutral ground. I had planned a garage sale, so I suggested he visit it.

"That way," I said, " you don't have to identify yourself. Just look around, and if you don't feel like talking to me, simply depart."

"I will do that."

"Oh, what's your name?"

"I am the Gregory," was his reply.

On the day of the garage sale, I was on the lookout for my caller. Early in the afternoon, a tall, elderly, white-haired, handsome gentleman slowly made his way toward the garage. He never said a word, looked around, and began to inspect the records I was selling. I wondered if he was the one. I waited. Nothing happened. He did not leave. I approached him.

"May I help you?"

"Oh, it is you!" he said. "Yes, I am the Gregory. I recognized your voice from the radio. I love your voice."

My heart skipped a beat. Could it really be? I thought love would never cross my way again, that it was time to give up hope of ever feeling the way I felt now.

He sat in a chair and would not leave. As he talked and talked, I observed his hands, beautiful, long-fingered, intellectual hands. He had a generous mouth, straight narrow nose, a most distinguished face – he was my type.

"What do you do?" I asked. "I know it's not polite to ask, but since you mentioned you always listen to my program, are you at home?"

"I am retired. I'm a chemical engineer, and I love to garden. I grow my own vegetables, not flowers; you can't eat flowers."

"The accent?" I asked.

"I'm Armenian."

It later became a joke when people asked how we met. Gregory always explained that he found me at a garage sale.

With the appearance of Gregory Mchitarian, my life changed. There was a relationship to fill my life with the expectancies I had forgotten existed. One waits for telephone calls, has a companion to meet, to talk to – to slowly fall in love with.

Gregory was not like the ordinary men I had met in the fifteen years since Cliff's death. He was extraordinary. One day he invited me to have dinner with him. I couldn't believe it when we drove up to one of the local fast-food restaurants. I had never been to one, and didn't know what to make of his choice. Who was this man? Was he so poor that he could not afford a nicer place for his first dinner with me? I did not want to embarrass him, so I quietly picked up a tray, ordered a steak, and sat down at one of the tables that first had to be cleared of dirty dishes. "Never again," I promised myself.

The next day, I called to thank him. However, I did not see him for the next two months. We talked on the phone, but I pretended to be busy. Meanwhile, I lost twenty-five pounds. After that, I accepted an invitation to swimming with him at a nice lake, a former quarry which was part of a private club he belonged to.

Gregory came with a picnic hamper containing sardines, bread, cheese, and his own homegrown tomatoes and peppers. It was a wonderful day. I fell in love with him. But he was a puzzle to me. He wore expensive clothes, was immaculately groomed, loved classical music. We attended concerts and operas, but not plays because he could not follow the rapid English spoken on stage. My press standing supplied me with a steady stream of tickets, so he was my guest. His first remark was always about the cost. He said he lived only on Social Security and a ridiculously small pension. So I never made him pay for anything. But he was a dear, kind, and gentle man, and I loved him. It was only much later that I learned he had money invested in U.S. Treasury Bonds.

Gregory cried easily, and that too puzzled me until slowly, ever so slowly, his life's story emerged. He was the son of a wealthy industrialist who lived in the Russian Caucasus city of Krasnodar. They had fled there from Turkey at the time of the Armenian massacres. He had graduated from Krasnodar University with an engineering degree. When the Bolsheviks took over Russia, he and his father were arrested by Stalin's NKVD (later the KGB). For two years they were imprisoned and tortured. In the end his father was shot before Gregory's eyes. Gregory was finally released after proving to his captors that he could keep a specialized food factory running that made bread for the Russian soldiers. Near the end of World War II he fled to the West, was interned in a Displaced Persons Camp, and eventually immigrated to the United States.

He wept when he told me the details of his life in Russia and Germany, particularly about how the British forced the repatriation of Russian refugees to the Soviet Union where certain death awaited them. Like me, his gratitude for his freedom in America knew no limits. Many of my radio shows were inspired by his suggestions. I would call him at 6 a.m. asking for suggestions for the day's program. He always came up with an interesting idea.

When I received the prestigious Americanism Medal from the Daughters of the American Revolution, given only to naturalized citizens who have "displayed Trustworthiness, Service, Leadership, and Patriotism," Gregory was at my side.

****

On one of my trips to Vienna I was awakened at my sister's home by a phone call. "Oh my God! What's happened now?" I thought. But it wasn't a disaster, it was an honor. I was to be awarded the Eisenhower Award from the International People to People Organization. How wonderful it is to be recognized while still alive. So two weeks later, at a gala dinner at the Hotel DuPont, I was awarded a beautiful Peace Dove crafted by artists at Steuben Glass.

****

I often dreamed of returning to Karlsbad, now known as Karlovi Vari, its Czech name. My father and grandfather had been born there, and I had spent many wonderful summers there with my beloved

Tante Lotte, who, along with most Jews from that area, was gassed in Auschwitz.

So my sister and I, in September 1993, decided we would like to visit Karlsbad again to see what was left of this lovely city and its once glamorous life after seven years of Nazi occupation followed by the Communist takeover. We took the train because we had been warned that the driving conditions were precarious, particularly for two women driving alone. The Grand Hotel Pupp was basking in its old glory, complete with elegant service from its multilingual personnel. But that was where it all ended! In the old days stores with elegant fashions and delicate china and exquisite jewelry lined the Alte Wiese, the street where visitors from around the world promenaded.

Now it was dull and empty. No one walked along the streets, no shops, no outdoor cafes. I wanted to see the house, Haus Billroth, where I had spent so many summers – alas I could not even identify it. I stood on the bridge over the Tepl River and remembered that just before Tante Lotte and I left for Prague the Nazis had taken the Jewish residents from the Old People's Home and had driven them into the river, then pelted them with bottles until they fell and drowned.

Finally I thought I had found the house. The name, Haus Billroth, was no longer visible. I entered it and climbed the stairs, stood in front of the apartment door. Everything was in disrepair, everything drab and neglected, and I thought how true, in this case, "You can't go home again."

I remembered those cities in Austria in the Russian occupation zone. They too had looked like this until the Russian troops left in 1955. But then the Marshall Plan funds were put into action and within a short time, the towns that had been in ruins were reborn, and today they are more beautiful than ever. But there was no Marshall Plan in Karlsbad! And no one cared, and I assume no one had the money.

So we left, my sister and I, and were grateful that we did not have to live under such drab conditions. But it remains a sad picture in my memories.

****

Gradually my Gregory showed signs of aging. He had become an inextricable part of my life. I loved him deeply and as the years went by, the thought of losing him someday was unbearable. It was such an unexpected blessing to find him in the evening of my life; a second great love with a man so similar to myself in background, interests, and goals.

The years he spent in the clutches of the KGB had damaged his health. He had several fainting spells. Finally it was time for a good nursing home. Even though I spent several hours every day with him, I knew he had a lonely life. The worst was that he realized it was the end of the journey. One day he said, "Don't you dare die before me."

Not long thereafter, in the middle of the night, I received a call that Gregory had passed away. In minutes I was dressed and in my car, driving through the night to be with my beloved Gregory one more time.

He was lying in his bed, eyes closed peacefully, as if sleeping. I kissed his ice cold cheek, knowing it would be for the last time. Twenty years of wonderful friendship, love, and devotion had come to an end. A consolation was the wonderful way in which so many of my friends gathered around me and stood by to help me carry the emotional burden. My friends, the gentle friends from the Austrian-American Society – how grateful I was to them. They had all known and loved my Gregory, and I knew they missed him too.

Just how wonderful my friends are was most eloquently illustrated by my eightieth birthday celebration. My birthdays were usually celebrated in the home of my dear friend Karl Franz, who like myself, was born in the orbit of the old Habsburg empire, though he in Prague and I in Vienna. He loved opera, symphonies, the ballet, and he loved to cook and eat well.

So months before my eightieth birthday, when Gregory was already in the nursing home, Karli advised me to reserve the 13th of January, my birthday. Then sometime later he told he was going to wear his tuxedo, indicating that I too should dress accordingly. I chose a long black velvet skirt with a sequined jacket and wondered what he had in mind.

On the 13th of January several friends called extending their good wishes. And Ady called to say she had to work and couldn't celebrate with me. Then my daughter called to wish me happy birthday and say that her job kept her in California, but that she hoped I'd gotten her flowers. And so it went all day.

At six o'clock Karli picked me up. I thought we were going to his house, but no, we drove all over town. When I asked where we were going, he refused to tell me. At one point we drove into the DuPont Country Club. But then we drove right out.

Finally, we entered the driveway of Brantwyn, a former DuPont mansion, now an adjunct of the Country Club. After he gently guided me into the building, we opened a door, and "Surprise and Happy Birthday" came from fifty voices in the festively decorated room. I was overwhelmed. As I learned later, every person invited came to the party. This was love, this was friendship, this was loyalty.

As I was greeting my guests, a voice next to me said, "Mrs. Shedd?" I turned. It was Chrissy with her husband John. They had come all the way from California to share this event with me. I broke down in tears. It was the high point of the evening. All of my friends and my loving children – how generous the Lord and fate had treated me.

****

I no longer have my daily radio program of interviews and commentary. How it ended after forty years of uninterrupted broadcasting was another one of my unexpected life's experiences. I had just been on a two-week sojourn in Bern, Switzerland where, at the invitation of the Swiss Tourist Office, I had collected a fascinating series of interviews and also attended an International People to People conference. My tape recorder was bulging with interesting program material for the next two weeks or more.

My friend Karl met me at the airport and told me that my daily program was no longer on the air! Without letting me know beforehand, the Charlotte Shedd Vignette was canceled. I was told "format changes." There was not one recognition of my forty years of service to WDEL, not one "thank you," not one "good-bye," no mention of the many awards I had received. Nothing! That too is America.

So varied were the subjects of my programs that the University of Delaware recently asked me to donate my thousands of taped programs and notes to their archives. The letter of thanks says, ". . . they constitute a of mirror of the past."

There was another collection from the past that I was happy to donate – an assortment of works from the now famous Austrian artist, Hans Essinger. He had been my art professor at the Bundes Real Obergymnasium in Klosterneuburg. As the years passed, he stayed in touch with my family and the walls of their house were hung with his very beautiful oil paintings and engravings, many of which were included in the three containers shipped to me so many years ago.

Recently I saw a book by Professor Gerlinda Wolfram about Essinger. One of the illustrations was "Lotte," a picture of me as a young girl, which he had kept in his private collection. Professor Essinger died in his hometown of Mödling in 1977. Now his home is being turned into a museum and a permanent showplace for his works. I decided to donate my collection of his works but with one stipulation: I wanted the portrait he painted of me. It took a lot of discussion, but now on one of my walls hangs a painting of a nineteen-year-old girl in a large picture hat, her white gloved hand touching a thoughtful face. It tells the story of another age – the days of my youth.

Christobel!

My autobiography would be incomplete were I not to mention what I regard as the greatest joy of my life: my daughter Christobel. She was left without a father when she was only five, so it was my obligation to raise her alone. Often, when visiting a church, I would ask for the Lord's help to do the right thing, so that she would grow up to be a decent, honorable, healthy and happy human being. Like all parents, I prayed for her safety as well as her success, and that she would have a fulfilling life!

My prayers have been answered, and she is today a wonderful, compassionate, and tremendously successful person. Not long ago she was chosen Corporate Woman of the Year by the Woman's Referral Service in California. This is what she said in her acceptance speech:

> I had some very strong female role models in my own family – one of whom came all the way from the East Coast to be here tonight. My mother, Charlotte Shedd, was a single mother with a successful career as a radio personality. As I grew up, I watched her be self-sufficient and self-determined and able to balance the demands of a career with a happy home life. She encouraged me to pursue my education and career, and I thank her for all her support.
>
> She also provided me with another strong role model in my godmother, Eleanor Roosevelt, who braved significant criticism from the press and political establishment to champion her agenda of social justice.

How could I not be supremely happy!

Epilogue

Why do I write an autobiography? I kept a diary for years. I began when I arrived in this country on January 11, 1939. I felt that so many of the events in my life were simply miraculous. One coincidence after another. First it was arriving with twenty dollars in my pocket, a huge trunk with a fine wardrobe, but otherwise, only my voice.

What we in Europe always called "das Land der unbegrenzten Moglichkeiten" – the land of unlimited opportunities, proved to be just that for me. Never, even under the most favorable conditions in peaceful times would I have achieved in Europe what I did in America.

"Just do it," Cliff said to me. And I did! It was indeed my voice which helped me to gain success! That, and the freedom from bureaucratic restrictions that I would have encountered in Europe. Countless limitations existed there in the form of licenses, innumerable stamps, and official approvals for everything, not to mention jealousies and envy that would never have enabled me to freelance in journalism as I was able to do here.

It was a fascinating life even though I didn't pursue my original ambition on the stage. My voice got me in front of a microphone, which provided me with a wide audience for over forty years. It ultimately also produced the applause I had wanted so badly and taught me one does not have to go to Hollywood or New York to be a success. To be a big frog in a smaller pond can also bring tremendous satisfaction.

A career in journalism is what I would recommend to all who dream of stardom on the international scene. I had the opportunity to interview kings, presidents, prime ministers, ambassadors, scientists, artists. You don't have to be Barbara Walters to achieve that! As a member of the press corps I was welcomed everywhere.

But there is one ingredient which I found essential to the success I call my own: I was never overbearing. It was a wonderful life, and I now know why the good Lord sent me here!